DEVELOPMENT OF
MORAL REASONING

DEVELOPMENT OF MORAL REASONING

Practical Approaches

edited by
Donald B. Cochrane
Michael Manley-Casimir

PRAEGER SPECIAL STUDIES • PRAEGER SCIENTIFIC

Library of Congress Cataloging in Publication Data
Main entry under title:

Development of moral reasoning.

    Bibliography: p.
    Includes index.
    1. Moral education--Addresses, essays, lectures.
I. Cochrane, Donald B., 1940-   II. Manley-Casimir,
Michael E.
LC283.D43   370.11'4   80-17141
ISBN 0-03-056209-0

Published in 1980 by Praeger Publishers
CBS Educational and Professional Publishing
A Division of CBS, Inc.
521 Fifth Avenue, New York, New York 10017 U.S.A.

© 1980 by Praeger Publishers

0123456789 145   987654321

Printed in the United States of America

258567

To

Eric and Jenna

Naomi, Sean, Rachel, and Kirsten

whose moral growth has been a source of
joy and instruction

ACKNOWLEDGMENTS

A book is in many ways like a work of art. It starts with an idea at first dimly perceived and loosely structured. The direction and pace of movement seem inexorable, yet unpredictable. Minds and hands, together and singly, work on the ideas and shape and refine them until the volume appears in the forum of critical debate. This volume is no exception. We wish to record our sincere appreciation to the many people who have helped to give it form and content.

At the outset, Marvin Wideen, Director of Undergraduate Programs in the Faculty of Education at Simon Fraser University, actively supported both the idea of organizing a Summer Institute on the "Practical Dimensions of Moral Education" and subsequently of publishing a collection of its papers. George Ivany, Dean of the Faculty of Education, furthered the project by making available a wide variety of resources to bring it to completion.

Eileen Mallory has typed and retyped manuscripts over the past 18 months with commendable skill, initiative, and patience. Without her special kind of diligence and commitment, the task would have been very much more difficult. In a real sense this is her book, too.

In the last months before submission of the manuscript, Nancy Carlman has very ably acted as Editorial Assistant. Her work in securing permissions, technical editing, and other aspects of manuscript preparation has been invaluable.

Finally, we wish to thank our wives, Nancy and Elsie, for their support and encouragement. We shall now be able to return to them.

INTRODUCTION

It is perhaps not surprising that in the aftermath of Watergate, social commentators, educators, and parents alike have become deeply disenchanted with the "ethical nihilism" of public life and increasingly concerned with the moral education of the young. The evident lack of moral "marrow" exhibited by the players in that sorry piece dramatized the need to focus attention systematically on the task of moral education—that is, the process by which young people develop into morally capable adults. The burgeoning literature of moral education, mostly theoretical and empirical studies, attests to the interest in the field among scholars and educators. All too often, however, the practice of moral education in the school and—particularly—in the home, is left unexamined. This book is explicitly designed to speak to these concerns: What strategies can the classroom teacher or parent adopt to foster the development of principled thinking and moral action in students or children?

This volume grew out of the summer institute on the "Practical Dimensions of Moral Education" held at Simon Fraser University in British Columbia in 1978. Five scholars whose work in the philosophy and psychology of moral education is internationally recognized—Jerrold Coombs and Jean-Marc Samson from Canada, Thomas Lickona and Peter Scharf from the United States, and John Wilson from England—participated in the institute. Each presented papers that served as the starting points for this collection. In addition, we invited other scholar-practitioners to contribute chapters to enlarge upon the original themes of the institute and form an integrated collection.

The chapters are organized into four parts. Part I makes the fundamental connection between moral education and rational judgments. In the opening chapter, "Practical Moves in Moral Education: An Introduction," John Wilson argues for the need to establish the aims of moral education first, because clarity about aims leads to clarity about the practical steps to achieve these aims. Jerrold Coombs, accepting the task set by Wilson, then clarifies the nature of moral judgment and specifies the attainments required by the fully capable moral agent. The central aims of moral education are thus established: It should promote the development of better moral judgment and nurture the various capacities needed to sustain this reasoning and its translation into moral action. In his second chapter, Coombs expands on the skills required to give substance to these attainments: the tests needed to ascertain the validity of any moral judgment. There are, he claims, four different kinds of tests that may be used to assess the extent to which a moral judgment might meet the standards of moral rationality. (In the Appendix, Barry Walker offers some specific exercises for "Thinking about Thinking," designed to expose the irrationality of various substitutes for thinking.)

In Part II, the setting shifts from this important theoretical backdrop to center stage and to the practical task of effecting moral education in the school and classroom. Don Cochrane opens the scene with his discussion of "Moral Education and the Curriculum: An Introduction," where he identifies and examines the implications of a commitment to moral education for curriculum development. In the following chapter, Michael Manley-Casimir argues that the traditional organization of the school actively mitigates against the development of personal and moral autonomy for students; he proposes instead a model of the school as a constitutional bureaucracy on the grounds that this would provide a more supportive context for fostering moral development among students. Ralph Mosher next relates an impressionistic account in his chapter, "Funny Things Happen on the Way to School Democracy," and documents the very real difficulties and persisting struggle to implement democratic governance in a small alternative high school in Massachusetts. Finally, Thomas Lickona focuses on the character of relationships in the classroom as a source of moral development. He moves "Beyond Justice"—and beyond simply reasoning—and proposes a curriculum of cooperative moral education, which includes 12 classroom-tested strategies for fostering important moral dispositions and for providing opportunities for students to acquire critical social skills.

In Part III, the scene shifts yet again, this time to the family as the cradle of moral development and to the role of parents in promoting moral capacities in children. Gail Peterson and her colleagues, Larry Peterson and Richard Hey, focus on Lawrence Kohlberg's stages of moral development in conjunction with family development concepts to help explain how families function and how they can facilitate moral development in children. John Hower looks more specifically at the influence of parents and identifies parental behaviors shown to be relevant and salient in fostering the development of good moral character in children. Thomas Lickona's chapter discusses the strategies parents may employ if they wish to be more systematic and deliberate about the moral education of their children: these strategies include the moral example of parents, a fairness approach to rules and discipline, democratic family meetings, the development of positive affective relationships with children, and the use of moral perspectives.

Spotlighted in Part IV are a set of special concerns in moral education. Lois Erickson confronts the sex role stereotyping of daughters in the family as an issue of justice. She traces the limiting growth patterns of such stereotyping, argues the need for the redefinition of our conceptions of maleness and femaleness in the interest of a more complete view of humanness, and concludes with several suggestions for transcending sex role stereotypes. Peter Scharf examines the problem of juvenile delinquency through recent findings in developmental psychology and education, considers the implications of the moral and legal reasoning observed in juvenile delinquents as a basis for intervention strategies, and speculates on the implications of developmental theory for the reshaping of the legal institutions of juvenile justice. Jean-Marc Samson analyzes the question of sex education and indoctrination in the context of moral education. He examines four general approaches to the question of sexual values—scientific, moralities, clarification, and cognitive developmental. Preferring the last approach because it provides a defensible theory for the moral educator, he discusses in detail the consequences of adopting this approach for instruction in sexual matters. Don Locke and Yvonne Hardaway examine the problem of moral education in the interracial classroom. Starting from the premise that racism is morally wrong, they discuss the conditions under which moral education can be more effective in interracial classrooms and make practical suggestions for facilitating classroom discussions of race relations.

The Epilogue consists of an edited transcript of a round-table discussion among the participants in the 1978 Summer Institute on Teacher Education mentioned above. Some contradictions in points of view, particularly in relation to interpretations of Kohlberg's stages of moral development, surface; and it is here, in the "cut and thrust" of debate, that the differing positions of the participants stand out most clearly, where these positions are explained and viewpoints reconciled or rejected. The Epilogue with its direct juxtaposition of views, is an appropriate conclusion for a book on practical approaches to moral education—appropriate because it reflects the ferment of debate surrounding moral education: the unanswered questions, the competing ideas and approaches.

CONTENTS

LIST OF TABLES AND FIGURES

1
FUNDAMENTAL ISSUES

1
PRACTICAL MOVES IN
MORAL EDUCATION:
AN INTRODUCTION

John Wilson

I have entitled this chapter "Practical Moves in Moral Education" because I want to avoid the phrase practical methods. Not all the important things we do are methods or teaching methods. Hugging a child when he is upset or making sure that he obeys when he wants to be naughty cannot naturally be described as methods.*
Method is far too close for comfort to technique and, more disastrously, skill. I address here the wider question, What can we do about moral education in practice? The "we" I refer to are those who have the major responsibility for educating: teachers, parents, educational administrators, and society generally. Such people—and I count myself as one—are often justifiably fed up with much of the theory of moral education with its seemingly endless disputes and sectarian warfare among philosophers, psychologists, and other self-styled experts. Educators want to know what should be done. I will try here, so far as possible, to confine my suggestions to points that can either be demonstrated as logically necessary or seen as obvious from a commonsense point of view.

DETERMINING THE AIMS

We are not likely to do much that is useful unless we are first clear about what we are tying to do; that is, unless we have a clear

---

*I note this error having fallen into it myself in entitling a book of mine Practical Methods of Moral Education.

idea of what counts as "morally educated." I have tried to make clear just what the relevant items or components are (see Wilson 1973; and Chapter 2), but the important thing is that teachers or other practical workers should, themselves, be clear; otherwise they may be very active and efficient but in quite wrong directions. Some of us, perhaps, are so naturally clearheaded and well disposed that we have a sort of instinctive and intuitive grasp of the proper objectives (as a loving and sensible parent might, for instance). But morality is peculiarly liable to fantasy and various forms of autism, and I am inclined to distrust most people's instincts in the matter, including my own. The most practical thing to do first, then, is determine the aims of moral education.

I ought to say that insofar as this is not just a matter of common sense and keeping one's head, it is a philosophical matter. By this I do not mean, of course, that we need some philosophy or ideology to give us the aims. The business of expanding the phrase morally educated (or any similar phrase) and so of identifying the pieces of equipment that we aim to give the child is the usual conceptual task of philosophy. It is very definitely not an empirical matter to be handed over to psychologists or social scientists: We are not asking how things in fact are with children or adults but how they must or ought to be if a person is to count as educated in this department of life. This point is equally applicable to phrases such as good at science, a competent mathematician, and educated in history.

OBSESSIONS AND ANTIDOTES

I believe that if teachers and others were really clear about the aims, they would also be tolerably clear about, and able to make, the right practical moves. For many or most of these follow, either by logic or common sense, from the aims. I will try, however, to spell out some of these moves. They emerge perhaps most clearly if we contrast them with some idées fixes that are widely current and interrelated.

Democracy

One detects in our society a compulsive attraction to what may loosely be called a democratic, liberal, or antiauthoritarian style in moral education. This emerges not only in the enormous weight put on moral dilemmas, discussion methods, values clarification, cooperative activities, problems of society, and liberal methods in general but also, I suspect, in the lack of any really solid belief in the

authority of the subject. If, as in other subjects, there are principles of reason governing moral thought and action, then we all accept their discipline and authority—and, in practice, the discipline
and authority of those people, including the teachers, who have a
better grip on them than we have. Naturally, we will not believe in
the authority of the teacher if we do not believe in that of the subject.
In such circumstances we would, at least semiconsciously, regard
moral decision making as a free-for-all or a matter of democratic
consensus, something to be settled by popular opinion rather than by
reason.

Nobody, of course, wants to say that some other style—for
instance, a dictatorial style where teachers just lecture and students
take notes—is to be preferred. What style is required will be a function of what is to be learned, and, on any account, there are many
different things to be learned under the heading of moral education.
If you glance at my list of moral components, it is possible to see
that some may lend themselves naturally to simple explanation on the
teacher's part; others to role play or simulations; others to discussion,
with more or less intervention by the teacher; and still others to practical moves that could not be called "teaching" at all:

Having a proper concept of a person;
Claiming to use that concept, and people's interests, as the over-
    riding criterion for moral decisions;
Having some feelings that support that rule or principle;
The ability to identify, in oneself and other people, emotions, moods,
    and states of mind, both conscious and unconscious;
Knowing facts relevant to moral decisions;
Knowing sources of facts (experts, and so forth) so relevant;
Know-how or skill in verbal communication;
Know-how or skill in nonverbal communication;
Relevant alertness—that is, alertness to moral situations and the
    willingness to bring other components to bear;
Thinking thoroughly about the situation: making full use of components;
Actually making a decision that is overriding and prescriptive and of
    universal force; and
Actually carrying the decision out.

In general, the more cognitive the component, the more it lends itself to instruction. But all this needs more careful thought. What I
am saying here is that to adopt some preferred style, whether democratic or any other, would be a mark of feeblemindedness, just as it
would be feebleminded for a science teacher to teach only by practical experiment or only from a textbook.

One of the worst spin-offs from this obsession in terms of practical moral education is a failure in discipline. Discipline, as I have tried to make clear elsewhere (Wilson 1977), involves the acceptance of and obedience to properly empowered authorities. It is to be contrasted with cases where a pupil does what the teacher says because the teacher is nice or stimulating or has succeeded in conning the pupil into acceptance of the rules. Discipline in school is like discipline in the army: it involves doing what you are told (see Chapter 5 for a rather different view on discipline). <u>Obedience</u> is a word not much found in educational textbooks these days. But any sane person knows without the benefit of philosophy that whatever sort of person one ultimately aims to produce, a prime requisite for educating children is that they obey.

Only educational theorists, perhaps, could lose a grasp of this point. Yet I (and no doubt the reader) have seen schools, supposedly keen on moral education, crammed with the latest visual aids, sets of materials, discussion pamphlets, and so on, where it was virtually impossible for the teacher to make the pupils even sit down in a reasonably orderly manner and start learning something. We have retreated to the idea that the best we can do is to coax, bribe, bully, cajole, or in some other way persuade the pupils to do what they ought to do. It is rather as if one were to try to run an army by saying, "I say, chaps, don't you think it might be a good idea to dig some trenches?" or "Let's have a democratic discussion about whether we ought to keep our rifles in working order."

Of course, schools are not armies. It is entirely clear, however, that there must be, for moral education as for any other kind of education, firm and clear ground rules. These do not have to be moral rules, just whatever rules are needed for learning to go on effectively. Thus, it seems reasonable to say that pupils and university students must not disrupt learning by sit-ins and other such disturbances. If, by contrast, anyone wanted to say that education demanded a certain hairstyle or type of sexual behavior, he would have to make a good case to that effect. Often, we know what is required for serious learning; and discipline, backed up by whatever sanctions are sufficient to ensure obedience, is surely required. This is not to say that there might not be borderline cases such as whether to require the wearing of school uniforms, which, it would have to be shown, was conducive to learning.

The scope of teachers' authority is similarly determined: pupils are to obey them as people empowered to ensure that serious learning goes on. This is perhaps the most important practical requirement for moral education, and it is notoriously lacking in a great many schools. It will continue to be eroded so long as we fail to believe in that authority that derives from the authority of what is to be learned.

The Classroom

The second obsession of many theorists is the idea that the classroom is necessarily the only, or the only important, arena in the school for moral education. It arises, I suppose, because this is where, under our present system, teachers find themselves for most of the day. Thus, there will be emphasis on classroom methods, textbooks, kits, packs, visual aids, materials, curriculum development, and so forth.

I do believe, of course, that the classroom has a crucially important part to play in moral education.* But, again, another glance at the components will show how obviously absurd it is to suppose that the classroom is the only, or even necessarily the most important, arena. We have suffered a good deal in the United Kingdom from having political, social, or ideological battles fought out over what should transpire in the classroom. Originally, it was designed for fairly formal or structured learning on the assumption—perhaps true at the time—that the home and the local community could cope adequately with the less formal learning required to keep pupils morally educated or, at least, out of trouble. That assumption no longer holds, if it ever did.

It seems clear that children require from schools what too few families give them and what no family can entirely give them. Children need a potent community that can build up and retain a moral tradition in which they are surrounded by people committed to using the right kinds of reasons and the right pieces of equipment in their daily lives. Without such a community, all the talk about moral reasons and action will seem largely unreal to all but the most sophisticated students; students will simply have no real-life experience of making moral decisions; there will not be that closeness of relations between teachers and pupils that is demonstrably required for many moral components (particularly the "affective" ones); and, in general, students will simply not invest enough emotion or loyalty in the institution to give it anything like adequate powers for educating.

Arenas in school life other than the classroom must also be potent. I have argued at length elsewhere (Wilson 1971) for something along the lines of "house" systems in private schools. Whatever the details of the institutional structure, not just one to which

---

*My new books, probably titled First Steps to Morality and First Steps in the Emotions, should be published within the next year.

we pay lip service. It seems that only those societies dominated by some fairly clear-cut and partisan ideology have enough nerve to maintain potent schools. Nowadays one thinks perhaps of Chinese communes or reports of schools in the Soviet Union. In England one recalls Thomas Arnold's Rubgy, which was sustained by a firm and common belief in Christianity. Weak-kneed liberals tend to become alarmed by any such notion, tying it unnecessarily to some vague idea of indoctrination or to the perils of a "total community." This betrays, I think, a lack of belief in education, not just moral education, for education involves a good deal of learning in which the student's personality and character are very much involved. Therefore, there must be an institutional structure that gives him the maximum support, encouragement, and discipline for his job as a learner.

Autonomy of the School

I use autonomy here in its normal and, to my mind, its only clear sense to mean something like "political independence." Governed, perhaps, by the extremely curious idea that education exists solely to serve society, we come to accept the way in which it has been institutionalized. Disbelieving or only half believing in education as an enterprise in its own right (Wilson 1977; 1979, chap. 1) with its own experts and authorities, we allow society—politicians, bureaucrats, administrators, and various pressure groups—to more or less dictate what schools shall look like, how whatever money we can afford to spend on education should be spent, what it is socially acceptable to teach, what, if any, disciplinary methods should be used, and so forth. Teachers are an oppressed class, functioning partly at least as mere hired ushers, pipelines between society and the child.

Of course, society, and perhaps particularly parents, has some legitimate demands: whatever else education does, children must become socially viable. By this I mean, very roughly, that they should be literate, employable, able to adjust to (though not necessarily to agree with) social norms, able to defend their society, and so forth. This is not in dispute (Wilson 1977, chaps. 5 and 6). But anyone who thinks that education begins and ends there does not know what education means. Education involves the serious and sustained learning by people as persons, not as role fillers or social pawns. The system, as we accept it, does not represent a serious view of education at all: it reflects merely a disbelief in or misunderstanding of the enterprise and, consequently, a distrust of empowering anybody with the necessary authority to conduct it adequately.

In the area of moral education, surely it is entirely clear that those in charge of the enterprise need far more powers than they now have. They need powers encapsulated in a phrase that used to be common in British educational practice: in loco parentis, in the place of a parent. Such powers, as with actual parents, need to be circumscribed. But teachers need the authority to decide how to spend money, how to structure the school day, what disciplinary measures to use, what sort of curricula to organize for what sort of children, and many other such matters. The kind of potent community required for moral education cannot, in principle, be run by external bureaucrats any more than a family can: it must be run by educators, those who are primarily concerned with the children and what they learn. A bureaucratic regime looks less implausible if we are talking only of children going into timetabled periods to learn particular skills or bits of knowledge; but as soon as we start talking of moral education, or the education of character or anything of that kind—as soon, that is, as we take the children seriously as people— the bureaucratic model becomes patently absurd. Administrators are useful and can be hired (and fired) by educators, but the power must rest with those who conduct the enterprise.

WHAT OUGHT TO BE DONE

I have spent most of my time discussing the kind of practical structure required for moral education, because it seems to me that unless and until we dispense with these obsessions and embrace their antidotes, we shall be unlikely to do much more than scratch the surface of moral education. In what follows, I try to make what I say as practical as possible. To do this, I will say very briefly what ought to be done in practice if—and when—everyone were clear about the basic requirements and follow this with an even briefer account of what needs to be done politically to obtain the basic requirements.

Practical Moves in the School

I remain convinced that since morality is subject to reason, we must anchor our practical moves in some attempt to explain to children just how and why this is so. To put it briefly, we need to teach them what counts as a good moral reason and provide them with the other pieces of equipment they need to be competent moral thinkers and agents (see Chapter 3 for how to test the soundness of moral reasoning). In my view, this requires timetabled classroom

periods just as we have for other school subjects, in which what one
might grandly call the methodology of morality is made clear (Wilson 1971).

I describe this as an anchor because all the other techniques,
methods, and moves we make should be designed to reinforce this
teaching, so as to make it sink sufficiently into their psyches and to
extend their awareness and knowledge in the desired directions.
Most areas in education are relevant to the task. One thinks most
naturally of subjects like literature and social studies, but the kind
of accuracy and tough-mindedness required to solve scientific or
mathematical problems will be just as important for moral agents
as the kind of sensitivity and caring they may hope to get from less
exact studies. The important thing is that these items should be
geared and organized with a close eye on the moral components. It
is, in fact, best to start by taking the components one by one and
simply asking, What, in practice, is likely to improve this particular
piece of equipment? (Wilson 1971; 1973, pt. 4).

Quite a lot of time might reasonably be devoted to educating
or training students out of false or inappropriate modes of thinking.
Students may characteristically justify their thinking and acting with
reasons such as, "Because it's just my thing" or "Because it's to my
advantage." Or they may have some preferred style of action that is
unreasonable such as abiding by an honor ethic (proving to be tough
guys), or following the gang like sheep, or just being "good children."
After at least trying to secure their purely intellectual assent to the
irrationality of pseudoreasons of this kind, we should need forms of
training—perhaps fairly tough-minded forms to habituate them to a
more rational style. How much we can rely on ground covered by
training, habituation, and even conditioning is an open question. No
doubt discussion, psychotherapy, counseling, and other more tender-
minded methods have important parts to play, for after the intellectual
work has been done, most of practical moral education will involve
the education of the emotions. Here again, it would be doctrinaire
to rely on some one method or one type of method.

I can add little more here than a list of methods with which
teachers and others are, or rapidly could become, familiar:

Role play;
Simulation games;
Real-life experiences in the school community;
A real part played by children in making up school and other rules;
The use of literature; various kinds of group work;
Psychotherapy;
The use of "binding rituals" to hold the community together (sharing
    food and drink);

Making children responsible for the repair and maintenance of their school;

A proper study of emotions at both an academic and a personal level;

The moral effects of serious study of other subjects;

The use of prefects or older children in positions of authority to help the younger;

The significance of a strong and adequately charismatic head teacher or principal who acts primarily as a parent-figure rather than as a bureaucrat;

The importance of a nonacademic base or home from where the pupils feel secure;

The transmission of some understanding that performance (being good at things) is not all important and that the children are loved and valued because they belong, not because of their feats and failures;

The overall importance of language (because language is the prime tool of reason) and of various games or other rule-governed systems in which children learn to share and participate under rules;

The total screening out of pieces of irrelevant lunacy that the children may have picked up from elsewhere (not only racial and other such prejudice but also an undue attachment to social or financial success—these should be firmly stamped on); and

The general cultivation and attachment to persons as such.

These are perhaps only the most obvious moves. I want to insist again that they are obvious, if we start our thinking on the right foot. I cannot argue in detail for each here, but I am inclined to say that if some people were to deny at least their prima facie importance, they would not understand what it meant to be morally educated.

Political Moves

I use political here in a wide sense to include not just governmental politics but also something like "public relations." This is important, because it would be very foolish to wait until governments and politicians see the point about moral education and have the nerve and intelligence to decentralize the educational system sufficiently to allow effective moral education to occur. I am tempted to say that there is something, perhaps many things, built into all existing political systems that makes both of these virtually impossible. That is why the future of practical moral education, as I see it, will necessarily be one in which progress is slow. It is only by steadily increasing the number of people who do, in fact, see the point that we are likely to be able to influence the higher levels of government.

Nevertheless, there are things that can be done. In some cases at least, the position may be one that my sociologist friends delightfully entitle "pluralistic ignorance." It may be the case that parents, teachers, and even pupils themselves see the need for adequate discipline and would support a move to secure it. If that is so, we need to make the fact visible in some political form or other and then simply to put enough pressure on bureaucrats or local authorities to enforce change. I suspect that if—a big "if"—teachers in schools came together with parents and pupils in a sufficiently clearheaded manner, they would rapidly come to see what demands must be made in order that schools can be adequately autonomous and teachers adequately empowered. There have been cases where this has happened, and it is always worth trying.

Clearheaded people in positions of power or influence can, with sufficient cunning, generate considerable change. I am thinking of school principals and those in semiadministrative positions. The skillful school principal can often flatter people to live up to their better or saner selves: "We all believe, don't we, in not indoctrinating children. Character is very important, and so teachers must have the power to make sure your children have strong characters, think for themselves, and so on." This may not be a completely accurate picture, for not all parents really believe this or have thought it through, but such an approach may shame them into improvement. Politics has its own standards of success, which are different from those of an academic philosophy seminar. The important thing, as Plato saw, is that the politician be governed by rational ends.

Finally, one thinks naturally of the teachers' unions. I cannot offer an international generalization, but there are certainly some countries, of which the United Kingdom is one, in which the unions seem to have little or no interest in the professional aspects of the enterprise of education. I mean, while they may have the teachers' economic and financial interests at heart, they do not seem to be much interested in what is required to empower them adequately as educators. If I were teaching in any state system of which I have any knowledge, I would press vigorously at the outset not for more money or shorter hours or even smaller classes but for the necessary powers to do the job and—an important point, since we will not attract good teachers without tenure or adequate security—the security to do it without interference.

I am bound to say that the position here, too, seems a depressing one, for the chances are that teachers will not in fact strike for this sort of thing but, if they can, leave the system for less frustrating, more rewarding work. Those who stay, either because they have a genuine love of teaching or because they cannot escape, are unlikely to want to cause political trouble. Because their jobs are likely to be at stake, who shall blame them? As public confidence in the system continues to decline, those who still believe in education will be forced to undertake the enterprise privately. If I may generalize the point, this is what happens when you have non-Platonic politicians in charge of a society. Politicians should have at least this much of Plato's philosopher-king about them: They should be able to recognize what enterprises such as education and moral education involve and willing to trust people with the power to get on with them.

2
ATTAINMENTS OF THE
MORALLY EDUCATED PERSON

Jerrold R. Coombs

Anyone attempting to make sense of the field of moral education confronts a variety of views concerning the legitimate aims or
goals or moral education, for there is within the educational pro-
fession very little agreement on this matter. The practically minded
educator quite rightly wants to avoid protracted debate on this issue
and to proceed with the business of devising moral education programs
and materials. Unfortunately, issues regarding the nature and aims
of moral education are unavoidable, even for the most practice-
oriented educator. Arriving at a clear and defensible conception of
the aims of moral education is necessarily the first step in designing
a practical program of moral education. We can neither design useful learning experiences in moral education nor assess the success
of our endeavors in this area without a clear idea of the objectives
we are seeking to attain.

The clarification, inculcation, and rational deliberation views
represent the three most prominent conceptions of the general nature
and aims of moral education. Since I am primarily concerned with
explicating more particular objectives of moral education, I will not
discuss these general views at any length in this chapter (for a thorough treatment of these issues, see Superka et al. [1976]). A few
remarks concerning their respective merits and shortcomings are,
however, in order. The clarification view holds that the only thing
one can legitimately do in the name of moral education is to help
students clarify the moral values they hold. Any attempt to influence
students to adopt certain moral beliefs is, in this view, an attempt
to indoctrinate. The inculcation view, on the other hand, sees moral
education as a matter of socializing the young into the moral beliefs
and ways of behaving deemed desirable or true in our society. The
rational deliberation view avows that the primary goal of moral

education is to teach students to make, and to act on, rational or well-grounded decisions about moral issues.

How shall we determine which conception of moral education to accept? We cannot, I think, resolve the issue by appealing to the standard meaning of the phrase <u>moral education</u>, for that phrase has no established usage that would permit us to rule out any of the conceptions as not what is meant by <u>moral education</u>. Rather, we will have to judge the adequacy of these conceptions on the basis of whether they are educationally worthwhile and morally permissible.

The clarification approach appears to fulfill the moral permissibility standard; that is to say, it does not seem to involve one in treating students immorally. Rather, its deficiency is in the area of educational worth. Clarifying the moral values one holds is no doubt a good thing, but it does not have sufficient educational significance to count as moral education. Consider the cases of mathematics education and science education. We are not likely to think we have done anything of significance in these areas if all we have done is to help a student become clear about what he really believes concerning the combination of certain numbers or the behavior of gases. After all, a child's capacity to add might be quite deficient, and his beliefs about the effects of temperature and pressure on a volume of gas might be erratic and verge for explanation on the superstitious. In education we must <u>increase</u> the student's knowledge or understanding. Similarly, we must increase the student's knowledge and understanding of moral matters if what we do is to count as moral education.

What is it that leads persons to this rather pallid view of moral education? Basically, it is that they believe that moral judgments are merely expressions of tastes, emotions, or preferences that cannot be justified or supported by argument. Given this conception, the only alternative to clarification is indoctrination, which is to be avoided as immoral. But this preference view of moral judgment is clearly mistaken. Such a view can be maintained only at the expense of ignoring or denying some very obvious facts about our moral life and language: we do not ask for and give reasons for moral claims, we do accept some reasons as relevant and reject others as irrelevant, we do challenge moral claims by offering counterexamples, and we do ask for and give moral advice. None of this would make sense if moral commitments were merely matters of taste or feeling and moral argument merely nonrational persuasion. Since the preference conception of moral judgment is mistaken, there is no reason to restrict moral education to the relatively insignificant business of clarifying students' moral views.

The inculcation approach to moral education is equally indefensible because it is morally irresponsible. To initiate children into

certain moral beliefs and their associated modes of conduct merely
because they are dominant beliefs in one's society is clearly to court
moral indoctrination, for moral indoctrination is fundamentally the
business of bringing about moral beliefs in a person in such a way
that the belief is fixed and not amenable to change on the basis of
relevant evidence or grounds. Indoctrination is morally indefensible
because it involves treating persons as things to be manipulated by
others and not as rational beings having the right to construct their
beliefs on the basis of their own experience.

Why would anyone adopt this seemingly immoral approach?
Proponents of this view tend to believe that it is essential to the welfare of the child and the society for the child to adopt the society's
moral views. Consequently, they regard indoctrination as a necessary evil. Notice that there is little to recommend this approach to
moral education unless one believes that moral views cannot be taught
rationally.

Those who adopt what I have called the rational deliberation
view of moral education believe that moral judgments can and do
differ in the degree to which they are rational or well grounded; that
moral decision making is a complex task that can be done well or
poorly. Consequently, they hold that the primary goal of moral education is to teach students to make and to act on rational, well-
grounded decisions about moral issues. The rational decision conception of moral education provides the most defensible starting
point for our thinking about objectives in moral education. In contrast to the other conceptions, this is the only one that gives moral
education genuine significance and at the same time regards students
as persons and not merely as organisms to be shaped or conditioned.

For one who sees moral education primarily as a matter of
teaching students to make and to act on rational decisions about moral
issues, the development of a practical program of moral education
has several clearly differentiated phases. The first and perhaps
most crucial phase is that of describing and justifying a conception
of what it means to be rational in making moral decisions. The second involves describing and justifying the knowledge, abilities, dispositions, sensitivities, and so on, that students must acquire if
they are to learn to make such decisions. It involves, as well, justifying these attainments as necessary to being rational in making
moral decisions. The third is the development of effective and
morally acceptable educational means for producing the relevant
abilities, dispositions, and the like. In this chapter, I want to focus
mainly on the second phase, namely, the attainments one must acquire to be rational about moral matters. First, however, it will be
necessary to explain briefly what counts as being rational in moral
reasoning, that is, the standards for judging such reasoning. In

describing these standards, I am not proposing any substantive moral view; I am, rather, attempting to make clear the logical standards underlying our use of moral language.

THE FEATURES OF RATIONAL MORAL JUDGMENT

Moral reasoning is a species of practical reasoning, that is, reasoning about what to do. Practical reasoning involves two distinct kinds of reasons: (1) motivational reasons such as wants, purposes, or rules of conduct and (2) beliefs about what actions will fulfill the wants, purposes, or rules of conduct. The conclusion of an instance of practical reasoning is a decision to take a certain action. In moral reasoning, as distinguished from other kinds of practical reasoning, the motivational reason is some moral ideal or principle. A simple case of moral reasoning might go like this. A friend of yours, Doright, believes that it is wrong to endanger the lives of others. Since he is drinking this evening, he thinks he will endanger the lives of others if he drives home. Therefore, Doright decides that it would be wrong for him to drive home. Moral reasoning can become much more complex than this, but this simple example will serve for now. Notice that this reasoning is deductive in nature. Put in the form of an argument, it looks like this:

Major premise: It is wrong to endanger the lives of others.
Minor premise: Since I (Doright) have been drinking, I will endanger the lives of others if I drive home.
Conclusion: It would be wrong for me (Doright) to drive home.

Doright's moral rule serves as the major premise, and his belief about what fulfills the rule serves as the minor premise in this deductive argument. A person making a moral decision does not necessarily rehearse such reasons to himself when deciding, though in more complex cases he may have to do so. Typically, the reasons become articulated only when one is asked to explain or justify a decision.

The important point to remember here is that having a reason for a moral judgment logically implies two things. It implies that one has certain beliefs about the facts of the case. Typically, these factual beliefs are about the characteristics or consequences of the action. In some cases, they also include beliefs about the meanings of terms.* In the preceding example, part of the reason for Doright's

---

*As used here the term <u>factual belief</u> does not imply that the belief is true. It implies only that the belief can be verified by

judgment is his belief that the action of driving home would endanger the lives of others. Having a reason also implies that one has a moral rule for deciding such issues. Doright, for example, holds the principle that it is wrong to endanger the lives of others.

Moral reasoning is sound or rational only when both parts of one's reasons are defensible and when they fit together to form an argument from which one can deduce a moral judgment. To put the matter another way, sound moral reasoning is not merely logically valid reasoning. It is reasoning that begins with value principles and factual beliefs that are themselves true or defensible. To be defensible the factual beliefs involved in one's reasoning must meet two conditions: they must be true or at least well supported by the bulk of available evidence; and they must be comprehensive enough to encompass all of the morally relevant features of the situation.

In many cases, people make poor moral judgments simply because they have false beliefs about the actions they are judging or are ignorant of important facts of the case. Suppose a teacher were to judge that it is unfair to allow Sigafoos to skip calisthenics because Sigafoos is in good health and every other student in good health has to do calisthenics. If the teacher's belief that Sigafoos is in good health is false, he has made a poor moral judgment. Similarly, if he has failed to take into account some other relevant fact—for example, that Sigafoos's religion forbids him to do calisthenics—he has made a poor moral judgment.

A person must rely, in some cases, on the opinions of experts to arrive at true or well-founded factual beliefs. The teacher in the previous example likely would have to rely on the opinion of Sigafoos's doctor to determine the truth of his conjecture that Sigafoos is in good health. In other cases, the judger may form his beliefs about the facts of the case by examining the available evidence. Suppose that a mother is trying to decide whether she ought to forbid her children to eat junk food. She holds the principle that parents ought to keep their children from eating foods that increase the likelihood of their becoming ill. There are two factual questions she needs to answer: Does eating junk food increase the likelihood of illness? and Does forbidding children to eat junk food keep them from eating it? To arrive at a well-founded answer to the first question, the mother must be able to examine critically the work of persons who have studied the effects of eating junk food. The second question may not have been the focus of any systematic study. To answer it

---

empirical investigation or by examination of the meanings of the terms in which it is stated.

intelligently, the mother may have to be able to gather and interpret relevant evidence. Teaching students how to arrive at well-founded factual beliefs has long been one of the primary concerns of education. This is what we are doing when we teach inquiry skills and critical thinking.

In contrast, educators have not given much attention to teaching students how to arrive at defensible moral principles. They tend to be unclear about the standards and procedures determining the adequacy of a moral principle. At least, a moral principle must meet the following standards if it is to be defensible:

1. It must be the case that the person making the moral judgment can accept the moral decisions that follow from the principle in all cases to which it logically applies. To accept a principle is to agree that it is a valid guide to decision and action. It follows logically that if a person cannot accept a judgment following from a principle, he cannot accept the principle.

2. It must be the case that if everyone acted on the principle, the consequences would not be disastrous. To accept a principle is to regard it as an acceptable guide for <u>anyone</u> and <u>everyone</u> to use. Consequently, its use by everyone must not lead to unacceptable consequences if it is to be a defensible principle.

3. It must be the case that the principle can be publicly advocated without defeating the point of adopting the principle. Consider the principle, "It is all right to lie when there is no possibility the lie will be detected." This cannot be an acceptable moral principle because holding this principle is pointless once others find out that you hold it. They would be alerted to the likelihood of your lying. (For discussion and illustration of the use of these standards, see Chapter 3.)

I am not entirely persuaded that these standards are the only ones that moral principles must meet. However, I do think that they are the only standards that can be derived from an analysis of the logical structure of moral language or from a consideration of the presuppositions that are necessary if our moral language is to have any point. (The best attempt to show that additional moral principles can be derived from a consideration of the presuppositions of moral language can be found in Peters [1966].) If further standards are to be derived, it would be necessary to argue for them from considerations other than the logic of moral discourse.

By way of summary, I have argued that it is necessary to have a clear idea of the attainments that qualify a person as morally educated in order to develop sound moral education programs. Any specification of attainments should be based on a clear and defensible conception of moral education. The most defensible conception of

moral education views it as a matter of teaching students to make
and to act on moral judgments that are rational. The reasons supporting a moral judgment include both the judger's moral principle
and his factual beliefs about the case being judged. Finally, a moral
judgment is rational only when the factual beliefs are well supported
by evidence and when the moral principle meets the three standards
discussed earlier.

ATTAINMENTS REQUIRED OF MORALLY
EDUCATED PERSONS

This brief look at the nature of moral reasoning and the standards of rationality that it must meet should make it possible for us
to consider what attainments people must have if they are to be morally educated. There are, of course, different ways of conceptualizing
these attainments. (The clearest and best-known description of the
attainments required of a morally educated person is that provided
in Wilson [1973].) That is to say, we may use different sorts of
language to talk about these attainments. What is needed is a conceptualization that is specific enough so that educators can use it to
plan teaching and testing activities. This does not mean that the attainments must be specified in "behavioral" terms, but it does mean
that the knowledge, abilities, dispositions, and inclinations characterizing the morally educated person must be conceptualized with a
fair degree of concreteness. Serious concern with moral education
implies concrete understanding of the attainments associated with
moral competence and commitment to fostering these attainments in
students. Without such understanding and commitment, moral education tends to degenerate into the interesting but pointless playing
of games and airing of opinions.

Since the attainments characterizing a morally educated person interconnect in a variety of ways, it is difficult to know where
best to begin describing them. The following description starts with
what I take to be the most fundamental attainment.

Attainment 1

Knowing that moral reasoning is guided by two principles:
(1) It cannot be right for me to do X unless it is right for
any person in the same sort of circumstance to do X and
(2) If the consequence of everyone's doing X in a given

circumstance would be unacceptable, then it is not right
for anyone to do X in that circumstance.*

A child who knows principle (1) knows that it is not right to
take her brother's candy without asking unless it is right for anyone
to do likewise in the same circumstances. A student who knows
principle (2) knows that it is not right for anyone to run in the school
hallways, just for the fun of it, if everyone's doing so would be disastrous. Because this knowledge forms the foundation of one's understanding of moral reasoning, it is a basic ingredient of being morally
educated. These two principles of moral reasoning derive from the
standard, mentioned earlier, that a moral principle is acceptable if
and only if one can accept all the judgments that logically follow from
it. Principle (1) is akin to the principles of impartiality, justice, and
equality. All are, in essence, principles enjoining consistency of moral
judgment across all similar persons in similar cases. All rule out any
sort of favoritism for any individual. Of course, merely having this
knowledge is not sufficient. In addition, one must have both the
ability to put this knowledge to use in moral reasoning and the disposition to do so.

Attainment 2

Being sensitive to morally hazardous actions, that is,
actions that require assessment from the moral point
of view.

Basically, this requires people to have the sensitivity that
alerts them to (1) actions that may nave consequences for others that
they could not accept if they were to befall them and (2) actions that
may have unacceptable consequences were everyone to engage in them.
Clearly, people would not be morally competent if they failed
to be aware of situations calling for moral deliberations and assessment. Without sensitivity to such situations, moral reasoning would
not start. Moral sensitivity is not an all-or-nothing affair; rather,
it can be present in varying degrees. Some people see a great many
actions as morally hazardous; others see very few actions as being
of this sort. Nor should it be thought that moral sensitivity is a
unitary psychological trait or mechanism. It is more likely that such

---

*This statement of the principles of moral reasoning is a
modified version of that appearing in Singer (1963).

sensitivity is aided by a variety of more specific attainments including the following.

Knowledge of Moral Rules

Don't kill.	Don't break promises.
Don't cause pain.	Don't cheat.
Don't dislike.	Don't deceive.
Don't disable.	Don't break the law.[*]
Don't deprive of freedom.	

Knowing moral rules is part of being morally sensitive because they are reliable guides to morally hazardous actions. If an action contravenes one of these rules, there is a very strong possibility that it will have consequences for another that the moral agent could not accept were it to befall him. Most people could not accept that it is morally acceptable for them to be killed, hurt, disabled, deprived of freedom, and the like, by the actions of others. I want to emphasize the point that these moral rules should be taught as rules for detecting morally hazardous actions. They should not be taught as exceptionless guides to conduct that obviate the need for moral reasoning. In some cases, one can avoid breaking one moral rule only by breaking another.

Suppose, for example, that Marsha holds both the rule that she should not hurt others and the rule that she should not lie. An insecure classmate asks Marsha if she likes her. Since Marsha does not like her classmate, she will be lying if she says yes. But if she says no or refuses to answer, she will hurt her classmate's feelings. Deciding what to do in such cases requires moral reasoning. Moreover, not all morally hazardous actions are cases in which these moral rules are likely to be broken. For example, a child's carving initials in a school desk does not (unless it happens to be illegal) violate any one of these moral rules. But since the consequences of everyone's doing this would cause others considerable inconvenience, such behavior is morally hazardous.

---

[*]This statement of moral rules is adapted from that found in Gert (1966).

Knowledge of What Generally Harms Human Beings
Either Physically or Emotionally

Knowledge of what generally harms human beings either physically or emotionally is part of moral sensitivity because it enables a person to detect actions falling under the moral rule that one should not hurt others. Children who know that other children are hurt when you take their bicycles, poke fun at them, exclude them from games, pull their hair, and the like, are more morally sensitive than those who do not know such things because they are better able to detect when someone is being hurt.

Possession of a Wide Range of Moral Concepts

The possession of a wide range of moral concepts includes such concepts as cheating, stealing, lying, bullying, demeaning, indoctrinating, and belittling. The greater the number of moral concepts people have, the more likely they are to see an action or situation in moral terms. Our concepts are very important in determining how we see a situation or what we see in a situation. The fact is that we tend not to be aware of certain features in a situation unless we have concepts that pick them out. A child who has the concept of bullying and one who does not will see different things when confronted with a bigger boy pushing and threatening a smaller boy on the playground. A child without the concept of bullying may see the incident as merely a case of the bigger boy having fun and not something about which moral judgments need be made. In contrast, the child having the concept is likely to see the bigger boy's action as morally suspect, because he recognizes this pattern of activity as bullying.

Persons who tend to think of moral sensitivity as involving such traits as altruism and love of one's fellow man may find my characterization of moral sensitivity disconcerting, for I have characterized it basically as sensitivity to actions that might harm others and not as sensitivity to actions that might do good for persons or further their interests. Altruism and love of one's fellow man are, no doubt, admirable traits, but morality does not require us to act so as to further the good of others except when that is a duty accruing to a particular role we have in society or arising from an agreement we have made. As parents or husbands or wives, people have the duty to promote the good of their children and spouses. As teachers people have the duty to promote the good of their students. What morality does require is that we neither do harm to our fellows nor permit harm to be done to them. <u>Harm</u>, as I am using the term, includes not only physical and emotional injury but also things like denying people equal access to the resources they need to promote their own good. Of course, there are many borderline cases where it is not clear whether we should regard the case as one of promoting good or preventing harm. Still, the basic distinction is clear. A person may be faulted on moral grounds for not contributing money to build a much needed hospital. That same person could not be so faulted for failing to contribute money to establish a symphony orchestra, for no issue of causing or preventing harm is raised by this case.

It is somewhat misleading to suggest, as some moral educators have done, that moral sensitivity entails having the attitude of regarding other persons' interests as being of equal weight with one's own in deciding what to do. Most of the time, people quite rightly pursue their own interests. They could take no action at all if every action had to further the interests of everyone equally. It is enough that in pursuing their own interests they do not significant harm to the interests of others. Interests must be treated as of equal weight only in the sense that they must be willing to be treated according to the same principle they have adopted as the guide to their own actions.

Attainment 3

Ability and disposition to seek out all of the morally relevant facts about actions that are morally hazardous.

Such attainments are necessary for the morally educated person because, as I mentioned earlier, the more relevant facts one takes into account in making a moral judgment, the better one's judgment will be, other things being equal. Currently, an approach to moral education that focuses on the discussion of moral dilemmas is very popular. One of the limitations of this approach is that it inhibits rather than encourages the inclination to seek out all the relevant facts about the action being judged. This inhibition is a product of the fact that the dilemmas are fictional and that students are specifically requested to work within the facts presented.

Attainment 4

Ability and inclination to imagine, when contemplating a morally hazardous action, the consequences that would ensue if everyone in your circumstance were to engage in the action.

These attainments are necessary to be able to determine whether a moral judgment is consistent with the second principle of moral reasoning (principle [2]). Commitment to the second principle manifests itself as an inclination to reject the action as wrong if the imagined consequences are unacceptable. Consider the following example. Franklin has a strong urge to go exploring on his own when his teacher takes the class on a field trip to a saw mill. He also, however, has the abilities and inclinations we are discussing. Consequently, he tries to imagine what would happen if everyone were to do what he wants to do. Having a good imagination, he foresees the teacher frantically running around but being unable to keep track of all the children and warn them of dangers. He anticipates that some children might get lost for hours or caught in the machinery and injured. Since he judges these consequences unacceptable, he decides that it would be wrong to set off on his own.

Attainment 5

> Ability and inclination to put oneself imaginatively into
> the circumstances of another person and thus come to
> know and appreciate the consequences of a proposed
> morally hazardous action for the other person.

The disposition to reject the action as wrong if the consequences would be unacceptable is in the same category. This set of attainments is desirable for the morally educated person, because the technique of "putting oneself in the other person's shoes" is one of the best means of determining whether an action fulfills the first principle of moral reasoning (principle [1]).

In the following example, Sara exhibits the abilities and dispositions in this category. Sara's class has ten girls. She would like to invite nine of them to her birthday party. The girl she wants to exclude idolizes Sara, but she is so shy that she is not enjoyable company. When making decisions like this, Sara is disposed to imagine herself in the circumstance of the person who may be adversely affected by her action. She imagines she is in the circumstance of the girl who is excluded and is very hurt by the exclusion. She decides that it would be wrong for someone to hurt her this way, when she had done nothing to deserve the hurt. She concludes that it would be wrong to exclude the shy girl from her party.

Attainment 6

> Ability and disposition to seek advice and counsel from
> others about moral decisions one is making.

Too often we picture moral decision making as a solitary pursuit. But there is much to be gained by discussing moral issues with others. Such discussion may help people to grasp more of the morally relevant facts in a situation. It may also help them determine whether their reasoning conforms to the two principles of moral reasoning. It can do this by helping them imagine themselves in the shoes of others or by helping them imagine the consequences of everyone's doing what they are thinking of doing. Morally educated people will make use of all of the best resources available to them—in this case, the reflections of other persons. This does not mean, of course, that they will or should substitute the advice of others for their own moral reasoning in determining how to act.

Attainment 7

Ability and disposition to check the validity of moral arguments and to reject invalid arguments.

These attainments are necessary for morally educated people if they are to weigh intelligently the arguments of others and provide others with sensible advice.

Attainment 8

Disposition to require justifying argument from others who propose morally hazardous actions.

Moral agents do not live in isolation; they live in a moral community. This attainment is necessary for morally educated people if they are to be responsible members of their moral community.

One important step in promoting justice in a community is to establish the expectation among its members that they will be required to justify their morally hazardous actions. A teenager who has this disposition will ask for justification when members of a gang propose such things as harassing elderly people and plugging up school toilets. A younger child will ask for reasons when observing someone bullying or making fun of someone else. Notice that exercising this disposition requires moral courage.

Attainment 9

> Resolution to do what one has decided is right and to
> refrain from doing what one has decided is wrong.

Obviously, the payoff of moral education is evident in how
people act. It is not enough that they be experts in making rational
moral judgments. To count as morally educated, they must have
learned to act on these decisions.

Attainment 10

> A sense of self-worth, including the belief that achiev-
> ing one's plans, pursuing one's interests, and so on,
> is important.

What is required here is not the sense of self-esteem that
comes from achieving excellence at something. It is, rather, the
sense of worth that is associated with seeing oneself as an autonomous agent rather than as a creature to be used or manipulated
by others. Those who have this sense of self-worth believe that
they and their interests <u>count</u> just because they are human beings.
This attainment is necessary for morally educated people, because
it provides the basis for their appreciating that people and their
interests are significant. Without this belief, the whole institution
of morality is pointless. Morality is, after all, fundamentally a
way of settling conflicts of interest among people.
      Some educators have claimed that the most basic attribute of
morally educated people is that they have respect for others. If
respecting others merely means believing that people and their
interests are significant, then this claim is true. The claim is
much more suspect when it is taken to imply that morally educated
people must have warm, positive feelings toward others. People
are morally educated when their conduct is governed by rational
moral decisions. Neither making nor acting on such decisions requires that people have warm, positive feelings toward others.
What they <u>must</u> feel is that others are entitled to be treated according to the same principles as themselves. This they must feel
passionately, for they must insist that others be treated justly even
when they are angry with them or dislike them. This is not to
denigrate the desirability of having warm feelings toward others.

Just as acting morally is not a matter of treating people well because of warm feelings for them, neither is it necessarily a matter
of grimly doing one's duty to others toward whom one is indifferent.

One more remark is necessary before leaving the topic of
respect for persons. We must not explicate the term person exclusively in biological terms. If other animals or beings are found to
have plans, purposes, hopes, and the like, we will have to allow
that for the purposes of morality, they are persons. Even now many
people have qualms about treating animals as mere instruments to
be disposed of as man sees fit.

Attainment 11

>Knowledge of any way in which peoples' pepceptions of
>things harmful to themselves differ radically from those
>of people in general.

Masochists, for example, must know that people in general do
not derive pleasure from being hurt. This attainment is necessary
if they are to be accurate in their appreciation of the consequences of
actions for other persons.

Some moral educators such as Peters (1966) take the view that
involving persons in worthwhile activities is a part of moral education. In the case of Peters, this follows from his belief that any
decision about what one ought to do is a moral decision. Consequently, decisions concerning what studies I ought to take up, what
games I ought to play, what music I ought to listen to, and so on,
are moral decisions. I take the view that moral judgments are
basically judgments about what I ought to do when the significant
interests of others may be affected by what I do or when what I do
may amount to treating myself as less than an autonomous person.
Resolving this issue is really a matter of deciding the bounds of
moral education. I have opted for the narrower conception of moral
education, recognizing this conception will face us with a very complex and demanding enterprise.

SUMMARY

The various attainments to be fostered by moral education
suggest the complexity of the enterprise. Knowledge must be
acquired; abilities, inclinations, sensitivities, and commitments
formed; and emotions and imagination developed. Several of these
attainments will have to be analyzed into more specific subcomponents

if they are to be taught effectively. Given this complexity, we must expect that moral education will be a long, gradual process requiring a variety of teaching and learning activities to be effective. We must avoid simplistic approaches that foster only a few of the necessary attainments. Keeping the whole range of attainments clearly in mind is a prerequisite for developing defensible moral education programs.

3

VALIDATING MORAL JUDGMENTS BY PRINCIPLE TESTING

Jerrold R. Coombs

Much of what is currently being written about moral education gives the impression that by learning a few relatively simple techniques or by using certain learning materials, a teacher can make a significant contribution to the moral education of students. As I argued in my first chapter, this impression is seriously mistaken. If they are to be effective, teachers in the area of moral education must be well versed in the concepts and modes of reasoning peculiar to this field.

Oakeshott (1966) makes the point that judgment in any field cannot be taught by didactic methods alone. It is imparted obliquely by those who have it and exemplify it in their lives and in their work. The good teacher of rational morality, whether in the classroom or the home, is not the one who merely teaches us moral rules or standards of moral reasoning. Rather, he is the one who engages us in moral thinking with him, attuning us to the fruitful question, the important distinction, and the weighting of a bit of evidence. Having students attempt problem solving under the guidance of a teacher who knows little about scientific reasoning has not proved to be a fruitful approach to teaching science. It seems unlikely that having students discuss moral problems under the guidance of teachers who know little about moral reasoning will prove to be any more fruitful. More generally, it is unlikely that any moral education material will be very useful to a teacher unless she has a firm grasp of the nature of moral reasoning. Thus, although this chapter is primarily concerned with the teaching of certain aspects of moral reasoning, a considerable portion of it will be devoted to explaining these aspects.

In Chapter 2, I pointed out that being rational about moral decisions involves, at the minimum, the following:

Being in possession of the morally relevant facts about the action being judged and

Basing one's judgment on moral rules or principles that conform to the following standards: (1) the judger can accept the moral decisions that follow from the principle in all cases to which it logically applies, (2) the consequences of the principle's being acted upon by everyone entitled to act on it would not be disastrous, and (3) the principle can be publicly advocated without defeating the point of adopting the principle.

This chapter will focus on the ways in which one can test the principle used in making a moral judgment to determine whether it conforms to the three standards. After explaining the nature of these tests, I will offer some suggestions about teaching students to use such tests in checking their own moral reasoning. Basically, there are four kinds of principle tests:

1. New Cases Test. This test consists of determining whether the principle yields acceptable judgments when applied to other relevantly similar cases.

2. Role Exchange Test. This test consists of determining whether the principle yields an acceptable judgment when viewed from the perspective of the person likely to be most adversely affected by the action being judged.

3. Universal Consequences Test. This test consists of determining whether the consequences of everyone's acting on the principle would be acceptable.

4. Subsumption Test. This test consists of determining whether the principle can be deduced from a more general principle already regarded as acceptable. Its function, as will be explained later, is somewhat different from that of the other three tests.

Using these tests is more an art than a science. After we have examined them in some detail, I will offer some very general guidelines for using them appropriately. Proficiency tends to develop gradually as one attempts to use the tests in a variety of cases.

NEW CASES TEST

Since an acceptable principle yields only acceptable judgments, we can test this principle by taking a new case, real or imagined, to which the principle is relevant and consider whether we can accept the moral judgment that ensues from applying the principle to this new case. The principle can be accepted only if the judgment of this new case can be accepted. Let me offer the following example to illustrate what this means. Macho decides that it is all right to hit Wimpy, who is two years younger than he is, because Wimpy bumped into him in the hallway. Macho's moral judgment in this case is based on a principle to the effect that it is all right to hit a younger kid when he bumps into you in the hallway. This moral principle of Macho's we will call principle R. Now, to apply the New Cases Test, Macho might ask himself something like this: "Suppose my kid brother bumped into some guy a couple of years older than him—would it be all right for the guy to hit him?" This new case Macho is considering falls under his principle H. Thus, he must accept the judgment that it would be all right for the older boy to hit his brother, or he must reject moral principle R. If Macho abandons moral principle R, this means that his reason for thinking it all right to hit Wimpy is not a good reason, for a reason is only as good as the principle behind it. Of course, Macho may, upon reflection, find some other reason for thinking it all right to hit Wimpy. For example, Macho may decide it is all right to hit Wimpy because Wimpy bumps him every time they pass in the hall- way and will not stop even though Macho has frequently asked him to stop. Finding a new reason entails finding new facts about the case being judged and calling into play a new principle to be tested.

This example illustrates several important features of the New Cases Test. Notice that this test comes into play after one has considered the relevant facts about a morally hazardous action and has tentatively decided that these facts provide sufficient reason for making a particular moral judgment about the action. In our example, Macho considers the facts that Wimpy bumped into him in the hallway and that Wimpy is several years younger than he is; he then decides that these are sufficient reasons to hit Wimpy.

The first step in applying the New Cases Test is to call to mind some real or imagined case that logically falls under the moral principle underlying our moral judgment. The simplest way to identify a relevant new case is to call to mind a situation in which someone else engages in the same kind of morally hazardous action with the same sort of reason. Thus, Macho needs to call to mind a case in which someone hits a person younger than himself for the reason that the younger person has bumped into him in the hallway. (Notice that in identifying the kind of case one needs to call to mind, one is, in effect, identifying the moral principle on which one is operating.)

Having identified a relevant new case, we are ready to take the second step in the New Cases Test. This step consists of considering whether we can accept the same judgment about this new case as we made about the original morally hazardous action. With regard to our example, Macho has to consider whether he can accept the judgment that it is all right for the older boy to hit his brother, since his original judgment was that it was all right for him to hit Wimpy. If we cannot accept the same judgment of the new case that we made of the original morally hazardous action, the moral principle has failed the New Cases Test and must be rejected. Rejecting the moral principle means rejecting our reason as a poor reason. Since our moral judgment is based on our reason, the moral judgment, too, must be rejected, unless we have some further reason to support it.

The fact that a principle passes a New Cases Test does not guarantee that the principle is acceptable. It has merely survived one of many possible challenges. This points up an important feature of all the principle tests we will examine. These tests can show a moral principle to be unacceptable but not that a moral principle is acceptable. What we do when we use these tests is to try as hard as we can to find out if the principle is unacceptable. If the severest tests we can contrive do not show it to be unacceptable, we gain confidence that it is acceptable. This means that in using the New Cases Test we want to select cases such that there is a real chance we may not be able to accept the same moral judgment about them as we made about the original morally hazardous action. For ease of reference, we will call such cases "vulnerable cases." The new case Macho considered was a vulnerable case because there was a real chance that Macho would not think it was all right for his brother to be hit. Suppose Macho had called to mind a new case in which one of his friends hits a boy Macho dislikes. This new case probably would not be vulnerable, since Macho likely would not care if his friend hit this boy.

In using the New Cases Test, then, we want to use the most vulnerable cases we can find, for these provide the severest test of our moral principle. The more severe the test we use, the more confidence we have in our principle when it passes the test.

It may be useful to summarize the important features of the New Cases Test. The test is employed after we have made a tentative moral judgment about an action or practice and are clear about the reasons for the judgment. The first part of the test involves calling to mind a new case that is both relevant in that it involves a similar action or practice supported by the same sorts of reasons and vulnerable in that there is a real chance we may be unwilling to judge this case in the same way we judged the original action or practice. The second part of the test involves deciding whether we can accept the same moral judgment about the new case as was made about the original action or practice. If we can accept the same moral judgment of the new case, the moral principle underlying our tentative moral judgment has passed this particular New Cases Test. We may then proceed to apply another New Cases Test or one of the other kinds of principle tests. When satisfied that the principle has been submitted to the most severe tests possible, we may conclude that the principle is acceptable and thus that the reason supporting this tentative moral judgment is a good reason. If we cannot accept the same judgment of the new case as we have made of the original action or practice, we must conclude that the moral principle used is unacceptable and that the reason that supports this tentative moral judgment is not a good reason. Consequently, we must either change the tentative moral judgment or find a new reason to support it and begin the principle-testing process anew. The steps in the New Cases Test are set out in schematic form in Figure 3.1.

ROLE EXCHANGE TEST

A rough version of the Role Exchange Test is used by most of us in trying to convince a child that a certain action is wrong. We say to the child who has taken a friend's toy: "How would you like it if he did that to you?" In its most responsible versions, this test involves imagining oneself in the situation of another person who may be adversely affected by a proposed morally hazardous action. The point of doing this is to gain a full appreciation of the consequences the action would have for the other person as the result of imaginatively experiencing those consequences oneself. If we cannot accept the judgment that it is morally right for others to engage in an action or practice that has such consequences for use, then we cannot accept that it is morally right to engage in the same action and so bring the same consequences to others. The <u>cannot</u> here is a logical "cannot." If we are basing our judgment on a moral principle, then the same actions taken in the same circumstances have to be judged the same way, regardless of who is engaging in the action and who is experiencing the consequences. Thus, we can test the principle underlying our proposed morally hazardous action by considering whether we would still regard the action as right if we were suffering the untoward consequences.

Consider the case of Dogood who is trying to decide whether it would be right for him to borrow his brother Pigeon's best jacket without having his permission. In applying the Role Exchange Test, Dogood would ask himself something like this: "Suppose I were in Pigeon's place and I had a good jacket that I liked very much; how would I feel if Pigeon borrowed it without asking me just because he liked my jacket better than his own? Knowing that I would be angry and upset were he to do this, could I still think that it would be right for me to do this?"

FIGURE 3.1

New Cases Test

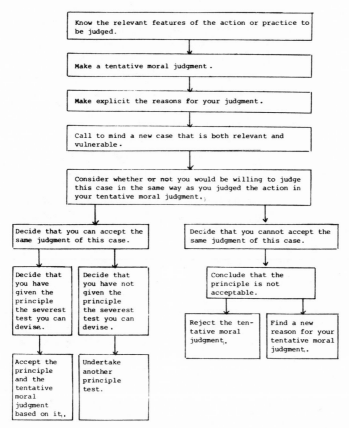

Source: Constructed by the author.

If Dogood cannot accept that it would be right for Pigeon to take his best jacket without his permission, the moral principle underlying his judgment is not acceptable. Consequently, he must reconsider the judgment that it is right to take Pigeon's jacket without his permission.

Keeping this example in mind, we will now consider the important features of the Role Exchange Test. It is applied after we are clear about the nature of the morally hazardous action to be judged, including the reasons we have for engaging in the action. Dogood's reasoning begins with a fairly full account of the relevant features of the action to be judged; the action involves borrowing Pigeon's best jacket without permission and doing so for the reason that he likes that

jacket better than his own. Having a full account of the relevant features of the action is very important. Suppose, for example, that Dogood's reason for wanting to borrow the jacket were different. Suppose
he wants to borrow it because it is the only thing available to warm
an accident victim suffering from shock. Having a different reason for
the action makes it, at least in moral terms, a very different action.
The action taken for this reason could very well pass Dogood's Role
Exchange Test, even though the action taken for the earlier reason
failed it. That is to say, Dogood could accept that it would be right for
Pigeon to take his jacket to help an accident victim but not for Pigeon
to take his jacket just because Pigeon likes it better than his own.

The first step in applying the Role Exchange Test is to imagine what it would be like to be in the situation of the other person
and experience the consequences the other person would experience
as a result of the morally hazardous action being judged. Thus,
Dogood tries to imagine what it would be like to be in Pigeon's
situation and how he would feel if Pigeon were to borrow his jacket
without his permission. Since the point of principle testing is to
give our moral principle the severest test possible, we must imagine
ourselves in the situation of the person likely to be most adversely
affected by the action under consideration. Dogood imagines himself
in the situation of Pigeon, because Pigeon is the person most likely
to be hurt by the action he is considering. In some instances, more
than one person is likely to be adversely affected by a proposed
action. Cases of this sort may require us to perform a separate
Role Exchange Test for each of the adversely affected persons.

The second thing we must do is to decide whether it would be
right for the other person to engage in the action that would have
the imaginatively experienced consequences. In carrying out this
step, Dogood considers whether it would be right for Pigeon to
borrow his best jacket without his permission and, thus, produce the
hurt and anger he imagines he would suffer. If we judgers cannot
accept that it is all right for the other person to treat us this way,
then the moral principle on which we are operating is unacceptable,
and we have no good reason for thinking the action is right. Unless
we can find some previously overlooked feature of the action that
may lead to a different outcome when we apply the Role Exchange
Test, we must conclude that it would not be right to take the action
we are considering. If we think that it would be right for the other
person to engage in the action in question, then we may either submit the principle underlying our judgment to other tests or accept
the judgment as following from a principle that has passed the
severest test we can devise.

Since some form of the Role Exchange Test is used in the
moral reasoning of most people, it might be thought that we do not

need to waste our time teaching it. Unfortunately, few people are inclined to apply this sort of test consistently or accurately. It might be instructive to digress briefly to discuss some of the mistakes made in applying this test. Often the test is put in the form, "How would you like it if he did that to you?" The implication is that if you would not like to have something done to you, then it is wrong to do that thing to someone else. What causes the difficulty is the word like. The important thing to know is not whether we would like having something done to us but whether we would think it right for someone to do that thing to us. These are two very different matters. Suppose I am trying to find out if it would be right to require restaurant owners to refurbish their restaurants to meet health standards. I may decide that if I were a restaurant owner, I would not like to have someone force me to do this. But I may still agree that it would be right for someone to force me to do it.

A second mistake made in the use of this test arises in the context of judging the action after we have imagined ourselves in the situation of the other person. Since this sort of mistake is easier to exemplify than to describe, let us consider an example. Suppose a mother is trying to decide whether to make her child take his medicine. Since the medicine is foul tasting, the child does not want to take it. The mother, however, knows the medicine will make him feel better and help him recover more quickly. Although the mother tells the child about these benefits, the child does not really pay attention because he so violently dislikes the medicine. As the first step in applying the Role Exchange Test, the mother asks herself what it would be like to be in the child's situation and to be forced to take the vile-tasting medicine. So far so good. It is in taking the next step that mistakes are often made. Suppose the mother were to ask herself, "If I were the child in this situation, would I still think it right for my mother to force me to take the medicine?" The mother then decides that if she were the child, she would not think it right, because taking the medicine would be very unpleasant and she would not really appreciate the benefits of taking it. The mother might then conclude that it would not be right to make her child take the medicine.

What has gone wrong is that the mother has asked herself the wrong question. She has asked how she would judge the action were she the child. Thus, her judgment is based only on the knowledge and sensitivity the child has. But the point of imagining oneself in the situation of the other is not to judge the action as the other person would judge it. Rather, the point is to come to a fuller appreciation of the consequences the action has for the other person and thus to be in a better position to judge the action oneself, using all of one's own knowledge and understanding as well as one's own moral sensitivities. What the mother should have asked herself is something like this: "Knowing what it would be like to be a child forced to take foul-tasting medicine without really understanding why, can I (as an adult knowing all the facts and having my present moral sensitivities) still accept that it would be right for someone to take this action if I were the child suffering the consequences?" The mother is required both to imagine that she is the child experiencing the consequences of the action and to step back from this imagined role and judge the action as herself, using whatever knowledge and moral sensitivities she possesses. What the mother must not do is judge the action as she supposes the child would judge the action.

A third mistake made in using this test is to assume that the person in whose situation one is imagining oneself is the same sort of person as oneself. When this mistake is made, one is unlikely to be accurate in imagining and thus appreciating the consequences the action would have for the other person. If Hardy accepts disparaging remarks made in jest as just harmless fun and Patsy is stung by such remarks, Hardy will not be able to imagine himself in Patsy's situation accurately, unless he is aware of this difference. To do a good job of imagining oneself in the situation of another, one must know something of the other person's interests, likes, and sensitivities, for all of these count as part of the other person's situation. The steps in the Role Exchange Test are diagrammed in Figure 3.2.

UNIVERSAL CONSEQUENCES TEST

A moral principle cannot be acceptable unless the consequences of acting on it are acceptable. Some moral principles are such that the consequences of any one person's acting on them would be quite acceptable but the consequences of their being acted upon by everyone having a reason to do so would be unacceptable. If everyone's acting on the principle would be wrong, justice demands that we regard it as wrong for anyone to act on the principle. The Universal Consequences Test asks the person who is contemplating a morally hazardous action to imagine the consequences of everyone's acting in that way and to consider whether these consequences are acceptable. This test, too, is often used in a rough form to persuade someone of the wrongness of an act. For example, when a child throws a candy wrapper on the ground, we ask him, "How would this place look if everyone were to do that?"

FIGURE 3.2

Role Exchange Test

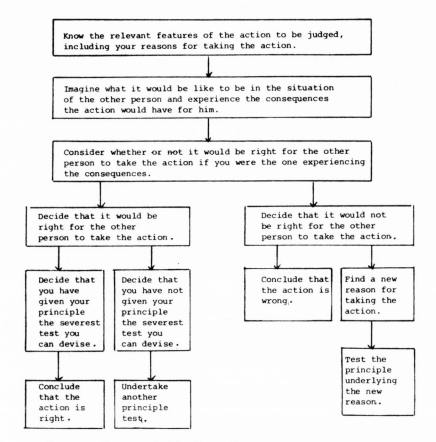

Source: Constructed by the author.

The Universal Consequences Test is applied after one is clear about the features of the action or practice to be judged, including the reasons for engaging in the action. Consideration of the following example should help make clear the essential features of this test. Mary is thinking of parking her bicycle in the school hallway while she is in class. Her reason for doing this is to keep it dry and clean. Since the school hallways are fairly wide, the consequences of Mary's doing this would not be serious. No one would be likely to run into it and get hurt, nor would the halls be made noticeably more dirty. Wanting to be certain that it would be all right to bring the bicycle in, Mary asks herself, "What would the consequences be if all students who wanted to keep their bicycles dry while at school were to park them in the hallway?" Mary calculates that on any given day more than a 100 children ride to school. She imagines, too, that most, if not all, of them would like to keep their bicycles dry and clean. Mary decides that having all of these bicycles in the hallway would result in injuries to people and a dirty, unpleasant hallway. Since she regards the result as unacceptable, Mary decides that it would not be right for her to park her bicycle in the hall.

After Mary is clear about the action she is judging and her reason for wanting to take the action, she begins the Universal Consequences Test. The first step in this test is the most complicated. It involves imagining what the consequences would be if everyone, who is likely to want to engage in the same action for the same reason, were to do so. Several features of this part of the test are worth more careful consideration. Notice, first, that a certain amount of factual information is required by the judger. Mary must know, at least roughly, how many children would want to park their bicycles in the hallway. The consequences of this being done by a few would differ, of course, from the consequences of its being done by a great many. Notice, too, that Mary is concerned only with those students who share her reason for taking the action.

In describing this aspect of the Universal Consequences Test, I have talked of the judger imagining the consequences. It can be seen now that this is actually a complex business involving several predictions. First, we must predict how many people are likely to want to undertake the same action for the same reason. Then, we must predict the consequences that would follow were this number of people to take the action. Finally, we must imagine what it would be like to have these consequences realized. This last is a necessary preliminary to our taking the second step in the Universal Consequences Test—that of deciding whether the imagined consequences would be acceptable to us. Mary decided that the imagined consequences would not be acceptable. If we decide these consequences would not be acceptable, we must conclude that taking the action in question, for the reason we want to take it, would not be right. This leaves open the possibility that it might be all right to take the same action for some other reason. It might, for example, be all right for Mary to park her bicycle in the hallway because she wants to have it handy to use as a prop in the school play. Since few people are likely to want to park bicycles in the hallway for this reason, the consequences of their doing so would likely be acceptable. Keep in mind, however, that in the context of moral deliberation, an action undertaken for a different reason counts as a different action. This new action also needs to be tested by the Universal Consequences Test.

Suppose we can accept the consequences that would result from the action's being taken by everyone who is likely to want to take it for the same reason we want to take it. In this case, the moral principle underlying the action has passed the Universal Consequences Test. We should continue to apply other principle tests until we are satisfied that the moral principle on which we are planning to act has passed the severest tests we can devise. Figure 3.3 portrays the steps in the Universal Consequences Test.

SUBSUMPTION TEST

The point of the Subsumption Test is somewhat different from that of the other tests we have considered. The Subsumption Test attempts to determine whether the moral principle on which we are planning to act follows logically from a more general or inclusive principle that we believe to be acceptable. If the principle underlying our moral judgment can be derived from a more inclusive principle already established as acceptable, then it, too, must be acceptable. In a sense, this test attempts to determine whether the principle underlying our moral judgment is consistent with our other, more considered moral principles.

To make the essential characteristics of this test clear, I will begin, as usual, with an example. Suppose that Patsy is being urged by several of her friends to play a game of tag while the teacher is out of the classroom. Although Patsy is tempted, she tentatively decides that it would not be right to play the game. Taunted by her friends for refusing to play, Patsy starts to reflect on her decision to make sure it was the right one. She begins by asking herself why she thinks it would be wrong to play tag. Her answer is that if they play tag, they might break one of the exhibits the teacher has set up in the classroom, and it is wrong to run the risk of breaking classroom exhibits for a few minutes of fun. Being still unsatisfied, Patsy asks herself why it is wrong to risk breaking classroom exhibits in the course of having a little fun. Patsy's answer to this is that breaking classroom exhibits amounts to destroying things that belong to other people, and it is wrong to risk destroying other people's property in order to have a few minutes of fun.

This schema shows the two stages in Patsy's completed argument:

1. Major Premise   It is wrong to risk destroying
   (Patsy's more inclusive   other people's property in order
   moral principle)   to have a few minutes of fun.

FIGURE 3.3

Universal Consequences Test

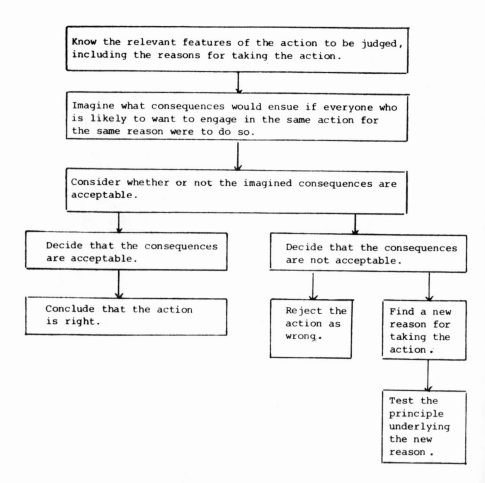

Know the relevant features of the action to be judged, including the reasons for taking the action.

Imagine what consequences would ensue if everyone who is likely to want to engage in the same action for the same reason were to do so.

Consider whether or not the imagined consequences are acceptable.

Decide that the consequences are acceptable.

Decide that the consequences are not acceptable.

Conclude that the action is right.

Reject the action as wrong.

Find a new reason for taking the action.

Test the principle underlying the new reason.

Source: Constructed by the author.

42

Minor Premise (factual information)	Breaking classroom exhibits amounts to destroying other people's property.
Conclusion (moral principle underlying Patsy's moral judgment)	It is wrong to risk breaking classroom exhibits for a few minutes of fun.

2.

Major Premise (moral principle underlying Patsy's moral judgment)	It is wrong to risk breaking classroom exhibits for a few minutes of fun.
Minor Premise (factual reason)	Playing tag would risk breaking classroom exhibits for a few minutes of fun.
Conclusion (Patsy's moral judgment)	It would be wrong to play tag in the classroom

Read from the bottom up, these two arguments portray the course of Patsy's reasoning in applying the Subsumption Test. The first step, as in several of the other principle tests, is to clarify the reasons one has for a moral judgment. Patsy does this by asking herself why she thinks it would be wrong to play tag. Her reason is that doing so would risk breaking classroom exhibits just to have a few minutes of fun.

The second step is to make explicit, at least to oneself, the moral principle on which the judgment is based. Although this is a fairly simple thing to do, many people seem to have difficulty doing it. After we have clearly in mind the facts about the action that serve as the reasons for the moral judgment, we should ask ourselves this question: "Why do these facts about the action count as reasons for judging the action as I have judged it?" The answer we give to this question reveals the moral principle on which our judgment is based. In the example above, Patsy had no trouble in making her underlying moral principle explicit. Had she had difficulty taking this second step in the Subsumption Test, she could have overcome it by asking herself the question, "Why does the fact that playing tag risks breaking classroom exhibits for a few minutes of fun count as a reason for thinking it is wrong to play tag?" The answer is obvious. This fact counts as a reason for Patsy because she believes that it is wrong to run the risk of breaking classroom exhibits just to have a few minutes of fun. This, then, is the principle underlying her moral judgment.

There are several things we should keep in mind when trying to make an explicit formulation of the principle on which our moral judgment is based. First, this formulation must always contain the same judgmental term as is used to express our moral judgment. If our moral judgment says that some action is wrong, our moral principle must say that a certain kind of action is wrong. If our judgment says that something ought to be done, our principle must say that a certain kind of thing ought to be done. Notice that the formulation of Patsy's underlying principle fulfills this condition. The term wrong, which is used in her moral judgment, also appears as the judgmental term in the formulation of her underlying moral principle.

Second, the kind of action to be mentioned in the principle is any action having the same features as those that were cited as our reason for our original moral judgment. In the example above, the feature of playing tag, which Patsy cites as a reason for judging it wrong, is that it risks breaking classroom exhibits for a few minutes of fun. Thus, the kind of action to which the term wrong must be applied in formulating Patsy's moral principle is any action that risks breaking classroom exhibits for a few minutes of fun. In effect, then, we formulate the moral principle underlying our actions by taking the judgmental terms used in our moral judgments and applying them to the classes of actions having the features identified as the reasons for our moral judgments.

For those who are familiar with deductive argument, it may be useful to keep in mind the logical role that our moral principles play in our reasoning. The moral principle must be such that it and the reason for our judgment form premises from which our moral judgement can be validly deduced. Although several different principles representing different levels of generality can fulfill this logical requirement, we need to be committed only to the least general such principle.

To come to a better sense of how our underlying moral principles relate to our moral judgment and the reasons that support them, consider these three examples:

Example 1.   Judgment: It is wrong to hit Hanky.
              Reason: Because hitting Hanky hurts him.
         Principle: It is wrong to hurt anyone.

Example 2.   Judgment: You ought to give Tom $5.
              Reason: Because you promised you would give him $5.
         Principle: You ought to do what you promise.

Example 3.   Judgment: Paying John a quarter to post a letter is unjust.
              Reason: Because you paid Frank more than that to do the same thing yesterday.
         Principle: It is unjust to pay one person less than another for the same job.

If we understand the relationships amohg judgment, reason, and principle exemplified above, we should have no difficulty formulating the principles on which our moral judgments are based.

In the second phase of the Subsumption Test, we subject our moral principles to the same inquiry that our moral judgments were subjected to in the first phase. We begin by considering our reasons for holding the moral principle. Since a moral principle is, in effect, a judgment about a class of possible actions, the reasons for holding it will pick out certain features of this class of possible actions. A procedure similar to that used in formulating our moral principle can be used to formulate the more general moral principle on which they are based: Take the judgmental term used in a moral principle and apply it to the class of actions having the features picked out by our reasons for holding the moral principle.

The first argument in the outline of Patsy's reasoning illustrates this phase of the Subsumption Test. Patsy's moral principle concerns that class of actions that involves the risk of breaking classroom exhibits for a few minutes of fun. Her principle holds that all actions of this sort are wrong. To discover her reason for holding this principle, Patsy asks herself why she thinks such actions are wrong. The feature of these actions that she picks out as the reason for thinking them wrong is that they involve the risk of destroying other people's property for a few minutes of fun. Thus, the more general principle, on which her moral principle is based, is that actions with these features are wrong.

When concluding the Subsumption Test, we must determine whether the more general moral principle is acceptable to us. If it is acceptable, then our original moral principle—i.e., the principle on which our moral judgment is based—has passed the test. If we are in doubt about the acceptability of our more general principle, we may test it by using the New Cases Test or by applying the Subsumption Test to it in the same way as we applied it to our original moral principle.

Our moral principle fails the Subsumption Test when the more general principle from which it derives is not acceptable to us. In this case, we have three possible courses of action. We may find different or additional reasons for holding the original moral principle. Then we could perhaps derive it from a more general moral principle that is acceptable. Our second option is to reject the moral principle and the moral judgment based on it. Finally, we may find new reasons for our value judgment. This would call into play a new moral principle and thus a new round of principle testing.

In some cases, we can offer no reason for holding our moral principle because we have a no more general moral principle from which it derives. This happens when the moral principle underlying our judgment is itself very general. For example, the moral principle that one should not hurt people is so general that it is unlikely anyone would hold a more general principle from which it could be derived. In such a case, we have neither good grounds for accepting the principle nor good grounds for rejecting it. We must use other sorts of principle tests to decide the issue. (The steps in the Subsumption Test are diagramed in Figure 3.4.)

TEST SELECTION AND EXEMPLIFYING PRINCIPLE TESTING

No one of these tests takes precedence over any other. If a principle fails any one of them, the moral judgment that it warrants must be reconsidered. How then do we decide which test to use in any given situation? Basically, we must choose the test we think the principle is most likely to fail. Some principle tests are inappropriate for some cases. This is not because they are logically inapplicable but because they are extremely unlikely to show that the principle is unacceptable. Using such a test is like testing the strength of a tire by kicking it. The tire must be able to withstand a kick, but its doing so does not significantly increase our confidence in its strength.

The New Cases, Role Exchange, and Subsumption tests are all applicable to cases involving a moral judgment about an action that is likely to have adverse consequences for one or more other persons. The Universal Consequences Test, on the other hand, would not provide a strong test of the principle in a case of this sort. Recall our earlier example in which Macho decides to hit Wimpy for bumping him. Little would be gained from asking Macho to consider what the consequences would be if all children who were bumped in the hallway were to hit the children who bumped them. The Universal Consequences Test is most appropriate for cases in which the moral judgments concern actions that would have adverse consequences for others only if many people were to engage in them. The other principle tests are ill-suited to cases of this sort. Consider the example where Mary is trying to decide whether it is right to bring her bicycle into school. It would be of little use to ask Mary to imagine what it would be like in the situation of the teacher. So long as Mary is the only student to do this, there is no adverse effect on the teacher or on anyone else. Consequently, the Role Exchange Test is powerless here.

The number of principle tests we need to use will vary from case to case. Ideally, we would continue to test the principle until

FIGURE 3.4

Subsumption Test

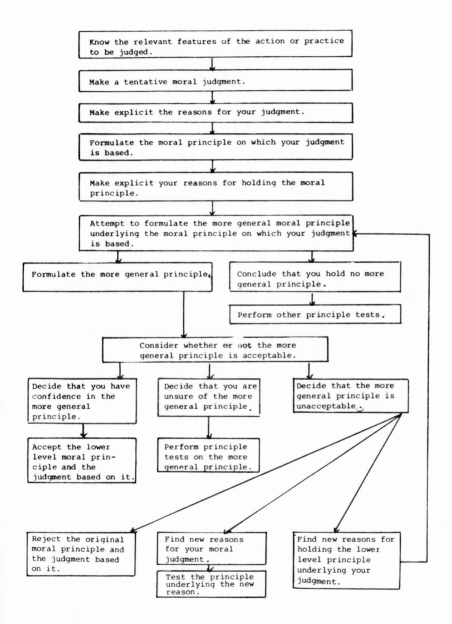

Source: Constructed by the author.

we become convinced that it had withstood the severest tests we could devise. Often, we need not go beyond a single Role Exchange Test or Universal Consequences Test, for that will be the severest test we can devise. Sometimes, we may have to perform a number of different Role Exchange Tests because several people are likely to be adversely affected by the action being judged. In very complex cases, we may need to use a combination of the various tests.

It should be clear by now that there are many abilities and dispositions children need to acquire if they are to do an adequate job of testing the principles underlying their moral judgments. It seems likely, too, that it will take a number of years to acquire these abilities and dispositions. No single unit of study or set of lessons will do the job. There are a number of things parents and teachers can do to help students acquire the necessary abilities and dispositions. I will not attempt to recount them all here. Rather, I want to call attention to the importance of exemplifying principle testing to children and to offer some suggestions as to how this might be done.

Given the sophisticated level of mental performance required to do principle testing, one may be tempted to think that young children can be taught very little that is relevant to this task. Piaget's research suggests that children below the age of seven do not even understand the relevance of reasons. Granted that very young children are incapable of learning principle testing, there are still a number of important things they can learn that will put them on the right path.

The ability to test principles is, to a considerable extent, a matter of knowing what questions to ask, being disposed to ask those questions, and knowing how to adjust one's reasoning in the light of the answers to these questions. A person who is good at using the Role Exchange Test, for example, has learned to ask questions such as these: What are my reasons for doing action X? Who is likely to be most adversely affected by my doing X? What would it be like to be in the situation of the person most adversely affected when X is done? If I were in that person's situation and he were in mine, could I accept that it would be right for him to do X?

Perhaps the best way to start children on the road to competence in principle testing is to ask them the questions that eventually they must learn to ask themselves. The point of this sort of questioning is to make children expect that certain kinds of questions need to be asked about their actions and that certain kinds of questions are legitimate, relevant, and important. They become disposed to raise these questions and consider them even though they do not yet know why. In other words, children learn the form of questioning used in principle testing even when they do not yet see the point of it. As children grow older, teachers can begin to explain the point of the questions they ask. When children are able to understand the point of the questions, the questioning takes on another function. It helps children do a better job of testing the principles on which some of their important moral judgments are based, while it continues to exemplify the relevant questions and reinforce the disposition to consider them.

It should be clear now why it is important for moral educators at home and in school to understand principle testing. Only with such understanding can they do a good job of asking the necessary questions. There is no simple set of rules by which one can determine the right question to ask at any given time. Even to know which sort of principle test to use in any given case requires understanding and experience, for not every test is appropriate for every sort of moral judgment.

When teachers have acquired an understanding of the principle tests, the best way for them to become adept at questioning children is by practicing in situations where children have actually made moral judgments. Here are some points to keep in mind when practicing. When asking principle-testing questions, it is very easy to give children the impression that you disapprove of their judgment and are challenging it. (This is because the principle tests are designed to show that the moral principle is unacceptable.) You must always attempt to ask the questions in such a way as to make clear to children that the questions are to help them reason about their judgments rather than to make them justify the judgments to you.

If you ask a question that seems pointless or lacking in bite, move on to a new question. Remember that for some judgments some of the principle tests are inappropriate. Remember also that there are a number of questions young children may not be able to answer without help. They may be unable to identify the people most likely to be adversely affected by their actions. You may have to do that for them. Children may not appreciate what it would be like to be in another person's situation. You can help by portraying that situation for them in vivid detail. Children may not be able to predict the consequences that would follow if everyone were to take the action they are considering. You may have to describe these consequences to them. Children may not be able to identify new cases that are both logically relevant and vulnerable. You may have to construct such cases for them.

Finally, it should be kept in mind, especially when dealing with older children, that people generally do not like to admit that they are wrong. Thus, it is unwise to try to force children to change their original judgments when their principles have failed one of the tests. If, for example, children cannot judge a relevant new case in the same way they judged the original case, it is sufficient to point out that they are being inconsistent. Do not expect them to agree that their original judgments were wrong.

When children have reached the stage where they are capable of performing abstract mental operations, the teacher may want to be somewhat more explicit in exemplifying principle testing and helping students see the point of it. One useful way to do this is to give students written dialogues that exemplify the questions one asks in applying a principle test and then to discuss the dialogues to help students see the point of the questions.

EXERCISES IN PRINCIPLE TESTING

Exercise A

In Exercise A, May questions Sam, forcing him to apply the New Cases Test. Sam's principle fails the test in this case. The discussion questions are designed to increase the student's understanding of the salient features of the New Cases Test.

Sam: I think students should be able to print what they want in the school newspaper. Teachers shouldn't be able to censor it.

May: Why do you think students should have that power?

Sam: It'd be a good business because students would learn a lot by making their own mistakes.

May: And you think students ought to be given the chance to learn from making their own mistakes?

Sam: Right!

May: Do you think students ought to be allowed to rush out of the building any way they like when there is a fire alarm?

Sam: Of course not. Somebody might get hurt.

May: But wouldn't students be learning from making their own mistakes?

Sam: Yeah, I guess so.

Discussion Questions:

1. Is the reason Sam gives for his judgment true? Why does it matter whether it is true?
2. What is the moral rule Sam is using in making his judgment?
3. Why did May ask the question about rushing out of the building during a fire alarm?
4. Can you think of any other question you would ask Sam to help him test his principle?
5. Did Sam's principle pass the test May proposed?
6. Should Sam accept his reason as a good one or reconsider his judgment? Why?
7. How might Sam change his moral principle to meet the test proposed by May? How would this change the moral judgment Sam has made about censorship?

Exercise B

In Exercise B, Lil asks Fay questions that require her to use the Role Exchange Test.

Fay: I've got a problem. That creepy guy, Sigafoos, told Mary that he is going to ask me to the graduation dance.

Lil: Yuck!

Fay: What am I going to do? I won't go to the dance with him, but I don't want to hurt his feelings either. People are always hurting him. Maybe I should just lie to him and say I already have a date.

Lil: I don't know. Try putting yourself in his position. How would you feel if someone lied to you about something like this to keep from hurting your feelings?

Fay: Well, I don't like the thought of being lied to, but if our places were reversed, if he were me, I guess he would be doing the right thing if he lied to me; especially if there was no chance I would find out it was a lie.

Lil: I'd never tell. I may not like Siggy, but I wouldn't be mean to him.

52

Discussion Questions:

1. Why does Lil ask Fay to put herself in Sigafoos's place?
2. What does Fay have to know about Sigafoos in order to do this?
3. Can you state, at least roughly, the moral principle that lies behind Fay's judgment? Why does she not have to know exactly what the principle is before she can test it this way?
4. Can you think of any other question you could put to Fay to help her test her principle?
5. Did Fay's principle pass the test Lil proposed?
6. Should Fay regard her judgment as a good one or reconsider it?

Exercise C

Exercise C contains a dialogue in which Mary induces Paul to apply the Subsumption Test.

Paul: You shouldn't kick soccer balls against the school. You might break a window.

Mary: How does that make it wrong?

Paul: You're destroying property unnecessarily.

Mary: You think that people shouldn't destroy property unnecessarily?

Paul: Yes.

Mary: What makes you think that?

Paul: People have to work to produce property. If you destroy it, you're making people work unnecessarily.

Mary: You think it's wrong to make people work unnecessarily?

Paul: Definitely.

Discussion Questions:

1. What is the principle underlying Paul's moral judgment?
2. How is Mary able to determine the principle on which Paul's moral judgment is based?
3. Why does Mary ask Paul what makes him think people should not destroy property unnecessarily?

4. Did Paul's principle pass the test Mary proposed?
5. Do you think Paul's principle should be tested further?

Exercise D

Exercises D and E do not exemplify principle testing. Rather, each of these sets the stage and then requires the student to ask the crucial question that would result in the judger's testing the principle underlying his moral judgment.

> Jim: If I were in a war, I'd torture enemy prisoners to get information from them.
>
> Sue: Why do you think it would be right to do that?
>
> Jim: Well, they might have information that would save the lives of the guys on my side.
>
> Sue: Let me get this straight. You think it is right for people to torture enemy captives whenever the prisoners might have information that would save lives of their own soldiers?
>
> Jim: That's right.

Question:

What would you ask Jim to help him test the principle behind his judgment that it is right to torture enemy prisoners?

Exercise E

> Jan: My parents get "up tight" when I stay out past eleven on weekends, but I don't see anything wrong with it so long as I'm not getting into trouble or anything.
>
> Flo: Why do your folks object?
>
> Jan: Aw, Mom thinks it's dangerous and she gets all worried about something happening to me. There's no way I can convince her that I'm not going to be raped or killed in a car accident or something.
>
> Flo: Well, things like that happen all the time.
>
> Jan: Yeah, but not to me.

Question:

What question would you ask Jan to help her test the principle
   underlying her judgment that staying out past eleven is all right?

Exercise F

When the student has a fairly good grasp of principle testing,
dialogues such as these can be used to teach rather subtle, yet
important, points about principle testing. Consider the two dialogues
in this exercise.

Dialogue 1

Sam: I'm going to refuse to pay that part of my
income tax that goes to pay for the military.

Tom: Do you think it is right to do that?

Sam: Yes, because it is immoral for a government
to spend money on military forces.

Tom: Do you think it is right for a person to refuse
to pay his share of taxes any time the government is using the money in an immoral way?

Sam: I sure do.

Tom: What do you suppose would happen if everyone
were to refuse to pay his taxes when the
government is using it in an immoral way?

Sam: The government would have to stop doing
immoral things, wouldn't it?

Tom: Boy, that would be great.

Dialogue 2

Sam: I'm going to refuse to pay that part of my
income tax that goes to pay for the military.

Tom: Do you think it is right to do that?

Sam: Yes, because I think it is immoral for a
government to spend money on military
forces.

Tom: But what would happen if everyone were to refuse to pay his taxes when he thought the government was being immoral in its use of the money?

Sam: Well, I guess people would refuse to pay taxes for all sorts of things.

Tom: What are some of the things that a lot of people would refuse to pay for?

Sam: Probably welfare. A lot of people think it is wrong to pay healthy people for not working.

Tom: What would be the result if a lot of people refuse to pay the part of their taxes that goes for welfare?

Sam: Well, the government would either have to cut back welfare spending or take the money from some other program to spend on welfare.

Tom: Do you think that would be a good thing to have happen?

Sam: Probably not, because either way some people will suffer hardship needlessly.

What we want the student to see in Exercise F is how a subtle difference in the wording of a question can lead one astray in principle testing. In Dialogue 1, Tom induces Sam to apply the Universal Consequences Test by asking him what the consequences would be if everyone were to refuse to pay his taxes when the government is using the money in an immoral way. This does not give Sam's principle a genuine test, for it ignores a crucial feature of Sam's action. Sam is the one who is deciding what is an immoral use of the tax money. There may be a difference between what Sam thinks is immoral and what actually is immoral. Tom has asked his question in such a way as to ignore the possible difference. Tom does a better job in Dialogue 2 when he asks Sam what would happen if everyone were to refuse to pay his taxes when he thought the government was being immoral in its use of tax money.

It is possible to construct a great many different sorts of dialogues to teach different aspects of principle testing. What I have provided here is merely a sample of what can be done. Hopefully, it is enough to start teachers constructing their own dialogues and discussion questions.

2
MORAL EDUCATION IN THE SCHOOL

4
MORAL EDUCATION AND THE CURRICULUM: AN INTRODUCTION

Donald B. Cochrane

DILEMMAS OF MORAL EDUCATION

Public education in North America is replete with official statements of aims for moral education (see Cochrane 1977; Cochrane and Williams 1978; Sanders and Klafter 1975) yet starved for their implementation.* Curriculum development, a field that attempts to translate goals into practice, is caught between the flurry of "paper policy" and the inertia of ministries and boards.

This neglect at the ministry and board levels is politically prudent, if educationally disastrous: promoting moral education is liable to turn citizens (and an electorate!) into hornets, and politicians are sensitive to the prospect of being stung. Most people are content with a process of "values socialization" in which students are molded or shaped to conform to some set of prevailing standards. Adults, it is claimed, know reliably in advance what is or will be right or wrong. This knowledge, usually codified into a set of rules, needs only to be instilled into the minds of children. Occasionally, there is serious disagreement among members of the adult population about what constitutes the details of the moral life. Though several options are

---

*Reports on several other countries (Gou-Zeh 1979; Hakkarainen 1978, Kärrby 1978; Seshadri 1978; Shaw 1979; van Pragg 1979), though not as detailed, suggest that this phenomenon is very widespread.

open in such a case, including moral education, one solution is to institutionalize the differences. In the name of freedom, a sectarian—even public—school system is established.

What results, however, is not an alternative to values socialization but simply multitrack socialization: differing groups of adults inculcate "their" children with their definitive version of The Good. As for the students, no one pleads that they should be free from indoctrination from whatever source. By accident of birth, they find themselves the inheritors of one tradition; they are to reflect it, not appraise it. Freedom in such circumstances is a slogan that makes it legitimate for a variety of adult groups to socialize their children in distinctive ways. It certainly does not guarantee the rational liberation of the minds of the young. And in such circumstances, the role of the teacher would be to reinforce the prevailing norms. On issues where there is likely to be disagreement, the teacher would strive for some kind of neutrality. Such an approach provides an alternative to moral education (for the latter is conceptually connected to the development of rationality) and might rest on one of the following assumptions:

1. There is no such thing as moral reasoning that is in any way independent of cultural groups and their commitments. Hence, there is no methodology to be transmitted. For different sorts of instrumental reasons, inculcation is the best alternative.
2. Moral reasoning does exist, but it is relatively unimportant because there is a higher source of values (the state, a religion, or a class ideology) that ought not to be seriously questioned. Hence, there is no premium on developing a student's capacity to reason morally, and to the extent that it is nurtured, its scope should be carefully confined.
3. Moral reasoning does exist, but it is difficult to transmit. In any case, it is an ineffectual guide to action.
4. Moral reasoning does exist, and it is all too effective. For though it may lead to moral autonomy, it also results in the breakdown of community and the rise of anarchy.

It is impossible here to respond to these positions, though they present serious challenges to moral educators. Each position, if sustained, would undermine either the possibility or desirability of moral education and would buttress the position of those who wish to retain and even reinforce crude forms of inculcation.

But imagine what public outcry there would be if a similar situation existed in science or, possibly, in history. Imagine the reaction if a teacher were discovered doing any of the following:

1. Teaching astrology in place of science;
2. Leading students through a series of exercises designed to help them clarify their views about the empirical world and concluding that the requirements of teaching science had been satisfied;
3. Teaching bright, high school students "facts about the world" so simple that they could be understood by any grade-three student and in a way that avoided "difficult cases" and explanatory theory; or
4. Inculcating a partisan view of history in such a way that students are incapable of reconsidering their views later on.

Parents would be justified in their outrage. In the first case, the methods of inquiry characterizing science would have been misrepresented. In the second, the failure to be concerned with the correctness or falsity of students' view would be rightly deplored. In the third, we would recognize that something about science had been taught but that the students' capacity to do science had been grossly underrated. The students would never have had the opportunity to use the scientific method to test the alleged facts and would never have understood the role of theory in structuring our view of the world; nor would their capacity to handle complicated cases ever have been developed. In the final case, we parents would cry out that our childrens' rational capacity to understand our past— and so our present and future—would have been permanently stunted. All of these protests center around the justified belief that the purpose of education is at least to provide students with those methods and procedures for thinking rationally about the world and their place in it. When these methods and procedures are misrepresented, ignored, undersold, or opposed, there are grounds for protest. Nothing less than the autonomy and dignity of our students are at stake.

It has been mooted that there is nothing so practical as a good theory. In the same vein, I would add that there is nothing so important to the building of sound curriculum as clear and coherent aims. Phrases that encapsulate important but very general goals in education need to be dismantled into their constitutive parts so that these may be inspected and understood and their interconnectedness appreciated (see Chapter 2). Various general goals have been advanced at different times and in different places: the Christian gentleman; the good citizen; the faithful Catholic, Moslem, or Sikh; a loyal Canadian; a solid Marxist; a living example of the free enterprise system; and so on.

By contrast, I have proposed (Cochrane 1975) that a justifiable goal for a program of moral education would be to produce morally autonomous agents (MAA). However, a clearer idea of the MAA is needed before entertaining the serious problem of justifying this candidate against others or facing the challenge of implementation. Could the MAA ever be regarded by the authorities of the time as a bad citizen, and, if so, how is this to be explained? Bertrand Russell, Mohandas Gandhi, Martin Luther King, and Alexander Solzhenitsyn provide interesting, internationally known test cases. In Canada one thinks of Louis Joseph Papineau, William Lyon MacKenzie King, and Henri Bourassa. Could a Marxist be a good MAA? If a capitalist were an MAA, would there be times when the pursuit of profits would have to be tempered, and if so, on what grounds? Most difficult of all, we would have to decide whether the MAA would have to be informed and moved by a religious point of view.

For a more precise picture of the MAA to emerge, further questions would need to be pursued. Would it be possible to characterize the stance such a person would take toward authority figures or peer group pressures? Would it be possible for one to be an MAA without the capacity to empathize, the disposition to consider the interests of others, the possession of a range of inter-personal skills (such as the ability to console, share another's joy, express gratitude, "read between the lines," and a host of other possibilities), and the psychological resources needed to sustain moral action? These are only a few of the questions that need to be fully addressed. What emerges from the discussion of such questions is a list of the components that the MAA would need to possess. From such a reckoning, curriculum planners could decide which fall within their jurisdiction and set about designing curriculam to promote these attainments.

SPECULATIONS FOR CURRICULUM SPECIALISTS

Let me offer a series of speculations to open discussion with curriculum specialists. First, as in other fields, students will not learn in abstraction what they do not work with in the concrete. The close study of the United Nation's Universal Declaration of Human Rights is unlikely to have much impact if students have no experience of rights in their own lives in school, family, and society. Admittedly, this concern is predicated upon the belief that moral agents are people who by virtue of seeing themselves and others as persons believe that they have rights and attendant responsibilities (see Chapter 5). Thus, I would recommend that a growing, immediate experience of rights and responsibilites be built into the curriculum. Our present practice seems to rest on the rather fanciful view that the acquisition of the concept of rights, and the development of a deep commitment to it, arrives on a date set by state and provincial legislatures. Thus, belief in social magic substitutes for learning theory.

Second, students will not become skilled in making impartial judgments about issues of justice unless they have practice. We cannot do students' moral thinking for them any more than we can do their mathematical or scientific thinking. Imagine cases in these subject areas where students were presented with problems and immediately referred to the answer sheets so that the correct response could be copied. It is difficult to imagine how independent thinking could ever begin. Looking up the answer is a check on one's thinking, not a substitute for it. Students, then, will have to be given opportunities to succeed and to make mistakes in their moral reasoning. Demonstrating that there have been mistakes in moral thinking need not be a process far removed from what is considered good practice in mathematics and science classes now.

Third, if a curriculum is to contribute to students' moral education, then moral reasoning must have a central place (see Chapter 3). At the moment, most board and ministry curriculum guidelines—where they even hint at it at all—make moral reasoning an incidental, almost accidental matter. Piaget (1965) offers a useful parallel with this aphorism: "Logic is the morality of thought, and morality is the logic of action" (p. 398). Classes in logic may or may not be effective ways to teach students to reason better, but if they are not, it is still valid to demand logical thought in the tasks we set our students in all their other subjects. Just as there is more to scientific and historical thinking than reasoning logically, there is more to deciding what to do (at least on most occasions) than reasoning from the moral point of view. Nevertheless, the canons of logical and moral reasoning ought not to be broken if we are to be rational in thought and action. Logic and moral reasoning may be treated as separate subjects, but because of their special status, they cannot be confined to particular classes. We offer students a distorted picture of "epistemological reality" if we treat them as if they can be hived off from other human pursuits.

Fourth, subjects form the academic curriculum, and the life of the school compromises the social curriculum for the student (see Chapters 5 and 6). Both convey important lessons. The social curriculum has often been referred to as the "hidden curriculum," but to equate the meaning of the two would be a mistake. The social or structural curriculum may be hidden, but it need not be. If we are seriously interested in moral education, we need to examine

carefully the effects on students of different modes of social organization, select those that most foster moral education, and proclaim
openly what we are doing. But whatever the details, there must be
the practice and atmosphere of rational discourse about moral
issues. Sometimes students' views on such issues will be unacceptable, but their right to put them forward in the social context of
rational discussion must always be respected. As a corollary to
this, the decisions of teachers and pronouncements of administrators should be subject in principle to the appraisal of all members
of the school community—and, by definition, this includes the
students. This follows logically from the nature of the enterprise;
what we are trying to teach about rational discourse is that a proposition is true or a moral imperative is justified not by virtue
of who said it but because the reasons given are convincing.
Scheffler's (1965) general remarks are challenging and pointed
when applied to our specific concerns:

> The person engaged in teaching does not merely want
> to bring about belief, but to bring it about through the
> exercise of free rational judgment by the student.
> This is what distinguishes teaching from propaganda
> or debating, for example. In teaching, the teacher
> is revealing his reasons for the beliefs he wants
> to transmit and is thus, in effect, submitting his
> own judgment to the critical scrutiny and evaluation
> of the student; he is fully engaged in the dialogue by
> which he hopes to teach, and thus risking his own
> beliefs, in lesser or greater degrees, as he
> teaches. [Pp. 11-12]

Far from being alarmed, not to say threatened, should students
begin to question life in the school, teachers and administrators
ought to be prepared to encourage such a development and celebrate
it when it happens. Indignation is not by definition insubordination
just because it is directed at authorities. To fail in this respect
is to add confirmation to Kozol's view (1975) that schools exist to
contain youth by domesticating their ethical capacity. He would
claim that the horror of My Lai was not an aberration in our social
system but a perfect flowering of it. We are trained to cast our
ethical gaze on situations remote from us but not to scrutinize
and, where necessary, challenge morally hazardous situations in
our immediate environment. We feel free to criticize Calley for
not objecting to Medina's orders for what took place far away from
us. But would we have acted differently had we been there? We may
have been exhorted in our classrooms to stand up for principles,

but were we given much practice, especially with respect to the authority figures in our schools? Were we trained in our homes and schools to resist the pressures of peer groups and encouraged not to obey blindly the orders of our "superiors?" The social curriculum in most schools needs radical revision.

Fifth, it has been inferred from the work of Peters (1966) that to educate students takes care of their moral education. After all, to educate necessarily is to promote states of mind thought to be intrinsically worthwhile. I think that this is to make too much out of a rather limited conceptual point. However, to educate does require a commitment to the pursuit of truth. To teach within the restrictions of this process in the social studies, arts, sciences, and so on, does require one to exhibit and secure adherence to conceptual consistency, public procedures for testing knowledge claims, and so on. Clearly, these are moral elements. Further, educating is a moral enterprise in that one of its purposes is to liberate students from ignorance and superstition and so make an indispensible contribution to the students' autonomy. Thus, to educate by initiating students into the disciplines does contribute to students' moral education. There is, however, more to the notion of moral education than education simpliciter.

There are further considerations for the curriculum planner. Even if it is granted that history contributes to someone's being educated, the planner must then decide whether Canadian students, for example, should study Canadian or Byzantine history; if the former, whether they should study the French or English versions, or both; and whatever decision is made on these issues, whether, for example, they should be initiated into Marxist or traditional approaches to that history (see Anyon 1979). At each stage, the planner is engaged in decisions that contain value elements. The consequences for the student are considerable; each decision will result in the selection of a special range of facts that will reflect the underlying theory or point of view and will present to the student a picture of reality. This, in turn, will shape what the student is likely to see as relevant from the moral point of view.

Sixth, it is common knowledge that our students are heavily influenced in their thinking by sources outside the curriculum and, indeed, outside the school and family altogether. They are innundated daily with advertisements that convey, among other things, ideals of human relationships, attitudes toward large corporations (invariably we are led to the comforting belief that they are working primarily for us and our interests), and the desirability of certain life-styles (necessarily, it seems, involving a high level of consumption). They are likely to have formed attitudes toward war from watching films like The Green Berets, not

The Battle of Algiers, The Cranes Are Flying, or All Quiet on the
Western Front. They will have seen René Simard and Glenn Campbell
but are less likely to have been exposed to Buffy St. Marie and
Peter Seeger. From the general conduits of Canadian culture they
are likely to have the impression that the record of the Canadian
government, army, and police in defense of the civil liberties of
its citizens are unblemished. (The same was most certainly true
in the United States until the Nixon debacle.) Hence, there is little
need to be vigilant, much less suspicious. Canadian students are
unlikely to be intimately familiar with or, in any case, disturbed
by events in the Winnipeg General Strike of 1919 or the strike at
Asbestos in 1949, the plight of Japanese-Canadians at the outbreak
of World War II, and any of the unofficial versions of the October
Crisis of 1970. They came to school having developed deep and
pervasive attitudes toward native Americans, women, children
(themselves and their peers), and a variety of minority groups. If
recent studies are valid, many will come to school with considerable
prejudice toward such groups. (See, for example, Rosenstock
and Adair 1976.) (And even more distressingly, the school may
reinforce these prejudices [see Pratt and McDiarmid 1971].)
A student is unlikely to be a moral tabula rasa.
   Kaufman (1973) captures the situation succinctly:

> Early processes of socialization tend, in the over-
> whelming majority of cases, to promote unreflective
> identification with the prevailing culture. Pervasive,
> deep, and tenacious, this process of acculturation
> tends to be reinforced by traditional ways of
> practicing a discipline. . . .
>   The best way to educate for autonomy lies, then,
> not in rejecting traditional works but, at least in
> part, by carefully selecting from among them those
> works most likely to help a student win through
> to autonomy; that is, selecting those that pose the
> most thoughtfully radical challenge to prevailing
> modes of thought, feeling and judgment. [Pp. 53-54]

His analysis and cure are not attacks on conservatism, only on
prereflective conservatism: "If the student is autonomously
reconfirmed in his originally conservative viewpoint, so be it.
His conservatism now has a basis in reasoning it previously
lacked" (p. 54). Kaufman's challenge to the curriculum planner
committed to the aim of autonomy in moral education is clear.
He must examine the prevailing culture that will be acquired un-
reflectively by most students and offset the imbalance through the

careful selection of materials. His job is not simply to present the balanced view, much less to confirm the prevailing culture.

MORAL EDUCATION IN THE CURRICULUM

How then should moral education enter the curriculum? Should it appear (1) as a discrete item on the timetable, (2) as the special responsibility of certain subjects such as religious education, literature, and social studies, or (3) as an objective of all courses? To suggest that not all of the evidence is in is to imply that some of it is. I know of no study that makes the comparison needed to help us decide this question. We do not want to know what motions we need to go through to satisfy ourselves that we have taken a "shot" at it; rather, we want to know what is effective in promoting the moral education of our students. A second point needs to be made on this question: debate on the three options ought not to be conducted as if the categories were mutually exclusive. It is quite consistent to maintain that certain objectives—say, developing a strong commitment to pursuing what is true and making students more sensitive to the moral dimensions of a wide array of situations—should be the aim of all subjects. Others—say, developing the capacity to see the other's point of view, empathizing, overcoming racial and other forms of prejudice and acquiring a range of interpersonal skills—should be the special province of subjects like drama, social studies, and counseling. And still others—say, improving a student's ability to reason morally and learning to "see" the moral dimensions of their lives in their classroom, school, and society generally—might be the special responsibility of a class called "Moral Education" (or "Social Living" or whatever) that has its own place in the timetable.

Essentially, this proposal acknowledges that moral education is the responsibility of the whole school but assigns some of the tasks to certain subject areas for specific attention. The first advantage of this approach is that there is a greater likelihood of teachers taking the job seriously; a responsibility that is everyone's is often one that is undertaken by no one. Second, these institutional arrangements highlight the varied components by locating them in areas of the curriculum where they might be best promoted; in particular, it recognizes the distinctiveness of moral reasoning and provides it with the same opportunities for being taught and learned as other forms of reasoning. Finally, a place in the curriculum increases the chances that budget and other resources will be adequately allocated.

This chapter began on a pessimistic note and should end there. There are no strong grounds for believing that in the near future our schools will take moral education seriously. The reasons are many and easily imagined. On this point, John Wilson has counseled patience: we are in moral education where science was in the era of Galileo. We need more time to clarify and gain acceptance of our subject matter and its methodology. But do we have the time?

5
THE SCHOOL AS A CONSTITUTIONAL BUREAUCRACY

Michael Manley-Casimir

In his introduction to Friere's Pedagogy of the Oppressed (1972), Richard Schaull observes that

> there is no such thing as a neutral educational process. Education either functions as an instrument which is used to facilitate the integration of the younger generation into the logic of the present system and bring about conformity to it, or it becomes "the practice of freedom," the means by which men and women deal critically and creatively with reality and discover how to participate in the transformation of their world. [P. 14]

By drawing attention to the essential value commitment underlying any educational process, Schaull correctly identifies a central dilemma facing both educational theorists and practitioners: Should the purpose of education be to socialize the young by inculcating the dominant values of the culture, by developing attitudes supportive of the status quo, and by inducing conformity to traditional authority, or should its purpose be to equip the child with the knowledge and skills necessary for critical assessment of these values, attitudes, and patterns of authority and, subsequently, for creative action in their lives and upon their world? As such, the issue raises fundamental questions about the character of education and the properties of the school charged with educating the youth of the society.

In this chapter, I argue that education must be concerned with liberation rather than socialization. At the very least, to educate a child means to transmit what is seen to be worthwhile in the culture, to empower the child with the knowledge and understanding of self, community and, society, and to develop the child's moral and practical capacities for dealing critically and creatively with the events and context of daily life. Since the school is the agency charged in large part with these tasks, the organizational character of the school becomes materially relevant to the achievement of these ends; accordingly, this chapter focuses on the organizational properties of schools as factors influencing the character of the educational experience of students.

Moving initally from a critique of the traditional organization of the school and its associated effects, the chapter proposes a model of the school as a constitutional rather than an authoritarian bureaucracy on the grounds that such a model is more conducive to the development of autonomous, purposive, and morally capable individuals—individuals capable of "practicing freedom" in their lives.

THE TRADITIONAL SCHOOL: EFFECTS OF THE AUTHORITARIAN BUREAUCRACY

> Our schools have become vast factories for the manu-
> facture of robots. We no longer send our young to them
> primarily to be taught and given the tools of thought, no
> longer primarily to be informed and acquire knowledge;
> but to be "socialized." [Lindner 1956, p. 168]

Lindner's criticism of the public schools is symptomatic of the debate that swirled turbulently about the schools through the later 1950s, the 1960s, and early 1970s. During these decades, the schools stood accused of sapping creativity while inducing conformity, of arresting spontaneity while teaching docility, and of discouraging initiative and independence while instilling passivity and dependence. So, for example, Reimer (1971) and Illich (1971) indicted the schools for preparing young people to conform to a consumer-oriented capitalist society; Henry (1955) documented the process whereby urban middle-class elementary-school children acquire the habit of giving their teachers the answers expected of them; and Silberman (1970) accused the schools of joylessness and mindlessness and of discouraging independent learning:

> More important, schools discourage students from de-
> veloping the capacity to learn by and for themselves;
> they make it impossible for a youngster to take respon-
> sibility for his own education, for they are structured
> in such a way as to make students totally dependent upon
> the teachers. [P. 135]

Why is this the case? Why are the public schools indicted as malevolent and countereducational? A partial answer may lie in the structure of the school viewed as a formal organization. Indeed, I submit that several major preoccupations of traditional, authoritarian, bureaucratic school organizations are inimical to the moral development of schoolchildren. Consider three of these preoccupations: order and control, routine and efficiency, and teacher-centered instruction.

Preoccupation with Order and Control

The preoccupation of the school with maintaining order and control is one of the most commonly cited of these effects and is attributable in part to the structure of the school as a formal organization; and, more particularly, to the distinction between staff members and students and the institutionalized dominance and subordination characterizing the relationship of the teacher to student.

The Staff Role-Student Role Distinction

Fundamental to the traditional definition and operation of the school is the distinction between the staff role and the student role. The staff role is an achievement role—that is, persons enter the role voluntarily, as adults, and on the basis of approved professional qualifications reflecting demonstrated academic and professional achievement. The student role, by contrast, is a recruitment role—that is, children enter the role involuntarily, on the basis of an age-grade placement (Bidwell 1965, pp. 973-74). In effect, this distinction underlies everything else that happens in the traditional school: the adults, be they teachers, administrators, paraprofessionals, or secretaries, hold their positions by virtue of their achievements and are charged with the responsibility of educating students; not surprisingly, the adults have power while students are relatively impotent—what Jackson (1968) calls "the fact of unequal power" that students must learn to cope with from their first day at school (pp. 28-29).

The legal definition of the relationship between teachers and students has traditionally reinforced this basic power inequality. The doctrine of in loco parentis has conferred substantial discretionary power upon school administrators and classroom teachers to regulate student behavior while at school. It was not until the 1968 U.S. Supreme Court decision in Tinker v. Des Moines that the authority of school officials was successfully challenged on the grounds of the students' claim to constitutional protection. Although modified to some considerable extent by this and other more recent decisions, the authority of the school still rests in large part on statutory delegation of authority based on the in loco parentis concept (Manley-Casimir 1978, p. 103).

Institutional Dominance and Subordination

The staff-student distinction, legitimated by in loco parentis, emerges in the traditional school as a pattern of institutionalized dominance and subordination. Waller (1967) characterizes the relationship this way:

> Teacher and pupil confront each other in the school
> with an original conflict of desires, and however much
> that conflict may be reduced in amount, or however
> much it may be hidden, it still remains. The teacher
> represents the adult group, ever the enemy of the spon-
> taneous life of groups of children. The teacher repre-
> sents the formal curriculum, and his interest is in im-
> posing that curriculum upon the children in the form of
> tasks; pupils are much more interested in life in their
> own world than in the dessicated bits of adult life which
> teachers have to offer. The teacher represents the
> established social order in the school, and his interest
> is in maintaining that order, whereas pupils have only
> a negative interest in that feudal superstructure.
> Teacher and pupil confront each other with attitudes
> from which the underlying hostility can never be alto-
> gether removed. Pupils are the material in which
> teachers are supposed to produce results. Pupils are
> human beings striving to realize themselves in their
> own spontaneous manner, striving to produce their own
> results in their own way. Each of these hostile parties
> stands in the way of the other; in so far as the aims of
> either are realized, it is at the sacrifice of the aims of
> the other. [Pp. 195-196]

Waller goes on to point out that because authority is always on the side of teachers, they must win in any confrontation with students. Failure to win effectively means failure as a teacher. So the child or student must of necessity lose; not only because the balance of power is tipped so heavily in favor of the adult world but because for the adults to discharge their professional lives they must be dominant. It is, thus, not surprising that disruptive class behavior and direct challenges to teacher authority pose such critical "discipline" problems for teachers (Duke 1978, p. 124).

Preoccupation with Routine and Efficiency

The preoccupation of the traditional school with routine and efficiency, attributable in large part to the bureaucratic imperative of managing the instruction of large numbers of students by relatively few adults, has caused the school to develop a series of responses that routinize school procedures in the interests of efficiency.

Jackson (1968) characterizes the role of the teacher as a gatekeeper managing the flow of classroom activities, as a supply sergeant allocating space and resources, as a rewarder granting special privileges to deserving students, as an official timekeeper deciding when to switch students from one task to another. He points out that these actions "are all responsive, in one way or another, to the crowded condition of the classroom" (pp. 12-13). So the classroom teacher, faced with the demands of managing the learning of groups of children, institutes routines—standard ways of handling classroom procedures—in the interest of efficiency and, perhaps, sanity.

In primary and intermediate grades, the extent of routinization varies considerably among teachers and among schools, but at the secondary level, routinization becomes pervasive. One viewing of Wiseman's film High School is enough to document the pervasiveness of bureaucratic routine and the impersonality induced thereby. Cusick (1973) characterizes the movement of students through the school as "batch-processing"—a label that well connotes the routine attending the practice. Silberman (1970) argues that the "tyranny of the lesson plan in turn encourages an obsession with routine for the sake of routine" (p. 125) and observes further that

> Administrators tend to be even guiltier of this kind
> of mindlessness and slavish adherence to routine for
> the sake of routine. It is, in a sense, built into their
> job description and into the way in which they view their
> role. Most schools are organized and run to facilitate
> order; the principal or superintendent is considered,

and considers himself, a manager whose job is to keep
the organization running as efficiently as possible.
[P. 126]

The consequence of the preoccupation with routine and efficiency all too often is that the character of the student's educational
experience also becomes routinized and depersonalized. The
student must learn to function in an organizational context that
rewards standardized behavior, that defers gratification and recognition, that organizes learning into discrete and time-limited packages,
and that, most telling of all, fails to acknowledge the student as a
person.

Preoccupation with Teacher-Centered Instruction

The persistence of teacher-centered instruction as the
dominant mode within the public school, commonly understood as
that mode wherein the teacher makes all decisions about instruction and classroom management, adopts a didactic approach to the
process of teaching—essentially viewing students as vessels to be
filled from the fount of the teachers' knowledge—and tends to render
students passive learners, to induce dependence upon the teacher,
and to instill appropriate bureaucratic, but docile, behavior in
students. This mode of instruction emerges logically from the
vesting of authority in the person of the teacher, from the achievement basis of the teacher's role, and from the traditional expectation of what it is to "teach."

> Far from helping students to develop into mature,
> self-reliant, self-motivated individuals, schools seem
> to do everything they can to keep youngsters in a state
> of chronic, almost infantile, dependency. The per-
> vasive atmosphere of distrust, together with rules
> covering the most minute aspects of existence, teach
> students every day that they are not people of worth,
> and certainly not individuals capable of regulating
> their own behavior. [Silberman 1970, p. 134]

This brief analysis has shown that some of these effects may
be attributed to the structural features of the school as an authoritarian bureaucracy. I now turn to the question of an alternative
conceptualization of the school, one that is more compatible with a
view of education as liberation.

THE SCHOOL AS A CONSTITUTIONAL BUREAUCRACY

What other mode of the school as a formal organization might be more conducive to encouraging the development of autonomous, purposive, and morally capable persons? The model proposed here is that of the school as a constitutional bureaucracy. It represents a dramatic shift in perspective: such a view of the school implies a fundamental change in the character of the organization—a change resting on quite different assumptions about the individuals involved in the organization, about the relationships among these persons, and about the governance structure of the school.

Assumptions

About Persons

At the heart of a constitutional bureaucracy is the assumption that all individuals involved with the organization are persons with attendant rights and duties, interests, and obligations. All of the adult members of the school community possess the rights that generally apply to the adults in the wider society; the exercise of these rights in school is necessarily constrained by the educational function of the school, by the roles these persons occupy in the school, and by the responsibilities attached to these roles. What is particularly distinctive of the constitutional bureaucracy, however, is that it is predicated on explicit recognition of the child as a person. To recognize children as persons means to acknowledge both conceptually and operationally that children are human beings with rights and interests normally associated with members of the class of human beings; it implies a view of children as legal entities in their own right. Such a view must, of necessity, recognize children and students not as full adults but as becoming adults and so would not confer upon them at birth rights coextensive with those of adult citizens; it would, however, recognize the essential personhood of children; it would recognize the need to care for children in a manner compatible with their emerging and developing personalities and claims to rights; and it would require the adult members of the community to guard and respect the rights of children and, similarly, school officials to guard and respect the rights of students. In the first instance, then, what defines the constitutional bureaucracy is the conceptual and operational recognition of the "rights" of organizational participants as "persons."

About Relationships between Persons

To recognize organizational participants as persons implies qualitatively different relationships among these individuals and those present between teacher and student in the traditional school. Fundamental to these relationships is respect for persons. As Peters (1966) observes:

"Respect for persons" is therefore a principle which summarizes the attitude which we must adopt towards others with whom we are prepared seriously to discuss what ought to be done. Their point of view must be taken into account as sources of claims and interests; they must be regarded as having a prima facie claim for noninterference in doing what is in their interest; and no arbitrariness must be shown towards them as participants in discussion. To have the concept of a person is to see an individual as an object of respect in a form of life which is conducted on the basis of those principles which are presuppositions of the use of practical reason. [Pp. 136-137]

At first glance, to recognize the adult members of the school—community, teachers, and parents—as persons seems no different from present practice. Schools, some might argue, are organized like this. Some, it is true, may be. By contrast, it can be argued that the staff members of the traditional school are as much trapped by the assumptions and practices of the authoritarian bureaucracy as are students and that far from treating principals, teachers, and parents as persons, the structural features of the school in fact deny this possibility. What Peters draws attention to is that the view people have of themselves as persons is distinctly affected by the way they are treated, by the kind of relationships that obtain between and among them, and by the character of the organization in which they live (p. 133).

From this perspective, then, to argue for a view of the school based on the assumption that organizational members, whether adult or student, are persons is tantamount to viewing the school as a system of rights and corresponding duties and of interests and obligations. Such a view rests on the correlative nature of a right—that is, if A is said to have a right, then B has a correlative duty to respect A's right and an affirmative responsibility to allow A the full exercise of his right. Thus, in the case of the school, if parents have the right to full consultation before school officials make any decision that substantially and materially affects the educational interests of their children, then school teachers and administrators have the correlative duty to ensure that full consulation occurs before making any such decision. Similarly, if teachers or students have rights, other members of the school community have corresponding duties to ensure that no action of theirs negates the rights in question. In effect, then, what characterizes relationships between persons in a constitutional bureaucracy is recognition and understanding of and respect for the rights and interests of the other participants and commitment to a form of organizational governance compatible with these assumptions.

About the Governance Structure of the School

The idea of a constitutional bureaucracy carries with it full participation in the life of the organization. Recognition of individuals as persons enjoying relationships characterized by mutual respect set in a context of a system of rights and obligations forms the cornerstone of such a view. What is imperative, of course, is that the day-to-day governance of the organization reflect these characteristics in structure and operation. Inevitably, therefore, questions of participation in decision making (inter alia) arise. For an organization to be a constitutional bureaucracy implies that those affected by decisions of the organization should participate in the process of decision making—this particularly applies to students and parents who are often most directly affected by school decisions and who often have the least voice. Such a proposal requires that the school operate in a manner analogous to a self-governing democracy (see the account of such an experiment in Chapter 6), recognizing always the essential educational function of the school and the necessary constraints such recognition places upon action. These assumptions are fundamental to the proposed constitutional bureaucracy—they are the linchpins of the argument. Their effect is to radically alter the character of the school as an educational agency. The school is a distinctive social invention charged in large part with preparing young people to enter adult life with the knowledge, skills, and competence they need to function as mature, intelligent, moral people. As such, the educational function of the school must be quintessentially to create learning opportunities for students so that when they leave school, they are capable of dealing critically with, and acting creatively upon, their world. A constitutional bureaucracy seems to offer a powerful means of facilitating this goal and of overcoming some of the effects normally associated with the traditional authoritarian bureaucracy (see Table 5.1).

TABLE 5.1

Features of Authoritarian and Constitutional Bureaucracies

	Authoritarian	Constitutional
Defining character	Authority is hierarchically differentiated and resides with staff members of the organization	Hierarchical differentiation of authority is limited by recognition of the essential personhood and rights of each participant
Relationships	Relationships between organizational participants are characterized by institutionalized dominance and subordination	Relationships are characterized by mutual respect and fairness
Governance	A system of imposed rules and regulations with limited opportunities for participation in decision making	A self-regulating organization characterized by full membership for all participants in decision making

Source: Compiled by the author.

Effect on Traditional Preoccupations

Rendering the school a constitutional bureaucracy will not necessarily directly alter the three major preoccupations of the traditional authoritarian bureaucracy (order and control, routine and efficiency, and teacher-centered instruction) but it will have the cumulative effect of dramatically changing the character of the school and, in some cases, will directly change the conditions giving rise to the preoccupation in question.

Persons and the Preoccupation with Order and Control

The defining characteristic of a constitutional bureaucracy is the recognition of organizational participants as persons with attendant rights and interests. Given this, the dominant emphasis or preoccupation in such an organization becomes mutual respect and fair treatment. This affects both the character of the staff-student relationship and the pattern of institutionalized dominance and subordination.

Affirmation of the rights of children, and derivatively, of students, changes the character of the relationship of staff to students by altering the power distribution in the school. Recognizing students' rights places limits on the power of teachers and administrators by requiring them to ensure that their actions do not negate these rights and the valid educational interests of students. Under the conditions of a constitutional bureaucracy, adults would no longer exercise total power over the student and could no longer act with substantial impunity or decide educational matters unilaterally—their actions would have to be consistent with the established rights and interests of students. School officials would have to recognize parents' rights to participate fully in administrative and educational decisions affecting their children. Under this regime, principals, too, would have to recognize the rights and interests of teachers. All such recognition—of the rights of students, parents, and teachers—would have to occur bearing in mind the particular educational purpose of the school and the growth of the child to adulthood.

Inevitably, even in a constitutional bureaucracy, the distribution of power between adults and students would remain unequal, but at least students would be recognized as persons having rights and so would derive some substantive and procedural protections from the duty placed upon school officials to guard the rights of children. No longer would the pattern of institutionalized dominance and subordination characterize the relationship of adult to child;

such a pattern in a constitutional bureaucracy would be replaced by institutionalized respect for the person, albeit in the case of students a "growing" person, and by institutionalized mechanisms of organizational participation and redress of grievances for all organizational participants.

Mutual Respect and Fairness versus Routine and Efficiency

Clearly, any formal organization has to be concerned about being efficient, and, since routine aids efficiency, it is not surprising to find that routine and efficiency become preoccupations. This may be acceptable in a commercial enterprise manufacturing widgets, where cost efficiency, profits, and fiscal solvency are important ends. Widgets are, after all, inanimate. It is not, however, acceptable in client-serving organizations like schools because schools differ from a widget-manufacturing plant in at least two important respects: the school's purpose is educational, not commercial, and it "produces" educated persons, not widgets. Hence, the preoccupation of the school should flow from its educational task, not from misplaced concerns with routine and efficiency.

Responsible Participation versus Teacher-Centered Instruction

Undergirding the idea of a constitutional bureaucracy is the proposition that those affected by organizational decisions should participate in making them. Clearly, this changes the character of the organization and affects the traditional role definitions operating within schools, including the role of the teacher. Even so, the teacher by virtue of demonstrated knowledge and competence remains a central instructional figure in the school. Shifting the emphasis away from the traditional practice (the student as passive learner, the teacher as didactic instructor) to a relationship where the student actively participates in making decisions about curriculum and classroom and school management creates opportunities for responsible participation in the school by students as well as parents.

The self-governing school, therefore, operates from the presupposition that learning to think and to act in rational ways is quintessentially educational (see Chapter 2). The task of the school is to create opportunities that foster the development of the capacity for rational thought and action among students and among the other adults in the organization. In effect, a self-governing school is designed to engender a sense of constitutionalism in the organization; by this, I mean a legal and moral order characterized by mutual respect and justice, by recognition of the rights and interests of those participating in the organization—a "just community" to use Kohlberg's (1975) phrase.

Students do not, however, arrive at school capable of participating fully in decision making about their lives. What is distinctive of the school, meaning kindergarten through grade 12, is that children enter the school before the full development of their powers of rationality and end their schooling 10 to 12 years later, with, supposedly, better-developed powers of rationality, more knowledge, heightened abilities, and competences. The educational function of the school is to guide and shape the child's development during this time. Hence, the school's responsibility is to create, with deliberation, educational opportunities for students to enhance their development. Undoubtedly, young children will need substantially more guidance in learning about their rights and their duties to others, about right relationships, and about responsible participation than older students. As children mature and become more rational, as they demonstrate the capacity to regulate their behavior, as they become more capable of exercising wise judgment about their education, so the reins of adult guidance should be loosened (see Chapters 10 and 11). These changes occur in the context of the school as well; and the responsibility of the school, the educational responsibility of the school, is to recognize these changes and to create opportunities for the young person to move from dependence to independence, from childhood to young adulthood.

CONCLUSION

An organization that is deliberately designed to educate children and students must examine the character of its organizational structure, the kind and quality of relationships permitted by this structure, and the opportunities for participation existing within it. The argument made in this chapter is that a constitutional bureaucracy is more compatible with the goal of creating autonomous, purposive, and self-regulating adults than the more traditional authoritarian bureaucracy. A school, organized as a constitutional bureaucracy, could make possible learning conditions conducive to helping young people deal critically with their world and become morally capable adults.

6
FUNNY THINGS HAPPEN ON THE WAY TO SCHOOL DEMOCRACY

Ralph L. Mosher

I can think of nothing so important in this country at present as a rethinking of democracy and its implications. Neither the rethinking nor the action it should produce can be brought into being in a day or a year: The democratic idea itself demands that the thinking and the activity proceed cooperatively. My utmost hope will be fulfilled if anything I have said plays any part, however small, in promoting cooperative inquiry and experimentation in this field of the democratic administration of our schools.

John Dewey, "Democracy and
Educational Administration"

INTRODUCTION

For the past two years, I have been involved as a consultant in an experiment in student self-government of a small alternative high school in Brookline, Massachusetts. This chapter is an

This chapter is an edited and revised version of "A Democratic High School: Damn It, Your Feet Are Always in the Water," by Ralph L. Mosher. Reprinted from Norman A. Sprinthall and Ralph L. Mosher, Value Development . . . As the Aim of Education. (Schenectady, N.Y.: Character Research Press, 1978), pp. 69–116, with permission of the publisher.

essentially impressionistic account of the funny things that happen on the way to school democracy. I think, also, that we now have enough experience to say some considered, tempered things about democracy in school: for example, like every constructive, substantial school reform, democratic governance is hard to vitalize and sustain; and translating powerful political, educational, and psychological theory about democracy into human or institutional behavior and commitments is hard, often frustrating work. I suppose the founding fathers might very well reply: Did anyone ever promise it would be otherwise? All of us underestimate the task of mobilizing people on behalf of higher ideals. But that it is important to do so I continue to believe on the grounds of both ideology and evidence.

This account of school democracy is presented in three major sections. The first section deals with the origins of our applied research and the critical issue of defining school democracy. Kohlberg's conception of the "just community" school and, in particular, Dewey's ideas on democracy in education are examined carefully as definitional sources. The next section of the chapter is a detailed case study of the experience of one alternative school in its efforts to become democratic. The purpose is to give a concrete description of what happened in establishing the conditions for and the process of genuine student self-governance and decision making in a school. The last section draws more general conclusions from our experience to date regarding school democracy in terms of both its promises and paradoxes.

SCHOOL DEMOCRACY: ROOTS

Let me begin with some intoxicating and persuasive rhetoric from Hutchins (1976) that has moved us to study ways to have high school students learn about democracy directly by governing themselves:

> The people of the United States are in fact defaulted citizens, with an indifference and even a hostility to government, politics and law that would have astounded . . . the founding fathers. Instead of being a citizen, the American individual is a consumer, an object of propaganda and a statistical unit. In view of the condition of our education, our mass media and our political parties the outlook for democracy, the free society and the political community seems dim. . . . The founding fathers meant us to learn . . . how to form a more perfect union, to establish justice, to insure domestic tranquility, to provide for the common defense, to promote the general

> welfare and to secure the blessings of liberty to our-
> selves and our posterity. They founded a political
> community; a community learning together to discov-
> er and achieve the common good, the elements of
> which they set forth, but did not elucidate, in the
> Preamble. . . . The Constitution is to be interpreted,
> therefore, as a charter of learning. We are to
> learn how to develop the seeds the fathers planted
> under the conditions of our own time.

The gap between the latter vision and my modest effort
to assist one school to become democratic is sobering. Nonetheless, Hutchins's imperatives make the case for learning democracy unequivocal. They cut like a January wind in New England
to the political, constitutional, and moral case for vitalizing in
each generation the "truths in which America was conceived."
Powerful ideas, after all, are the only ones worth holding to.

The Democratic School as a Means to Stimulate Students'
Moral Development

A second impetus to my study of democracy in school has been
Kohlberg's (1978, 1976, 1975), research on moral development and
moral education. Kohlberg is best known for a theory of moral development describing how our thinking concerning right and wrong
evolves, what we ought to do, questions of value, and what our rights
and obligations are. He has found that our moral reasoning becomes
both intellectually more complex and morally more principled. There
are in this developmental process identifiable stages or characteristic ways of thinking morally; experience, not the calendar, causes this
evolution to occur. One whole stage of moral reasoning in Kohlberg's
theory, Stage 5, describes the moral position underlying the Consti-
tution and the democratic process.

Significantly, Kohlberg's data suggest that Stage 5 moral reasoning is used by less than 20 percent of adult Americans and by few
adolescents, although it can be understood, intuitively, by a larger
proportion of people. If true, this may explain why the Equal Rights
Amendment has yet to pass; why equality of opportunity or access to
education, justice, medical care, and jobs is denied to so many
people; why democracy is so hard to establish and sustain; and why
the American Revolution is unfinished. Kohlberg sees the problem
partly in psychological terms; the moral and rational capacity for full
democracy and justice is latent in human thought and must be stimu-
lated by experience, in particular, through living in a community that

is democratic and just. It is clear also that Kohlberg's essential preoccupation (and moral principle) is justice and that constitutional democracy is one procedural means to bring about justice. Kohlberg argues that the central objective of moral education is to promote justice in individuals and in human institutions. To do that requires a community where real moral issues of justice, rights, and obligations are decided by all. His own applied research has involved creating and studying such "just" communities in prisons and schools. The democratic school project reported here is broadly influenced by Kohlberg's psychology. However, it does not conform to the exact modus operandi, organizational structure, or justice ideology of Kohlberg's prison or school studies. Democracy or justice does not have one, Platonic institutional definition or form; it is especially important for people to be democratic according to self-selected general principles rather than specific practices.

John Dewey: The Philosopher of Democracy

The real roots of my efforts at democratizing schooling lie in the philosophy of John Dewey. My discussion of Dewey is organized around two objectives. First, it is intended to help clarify what I mean by school or classroom democracy. My position is that it is very difficult to innovate in schools—in this case, to effect moral education, school democracy, or just community—without clear definitions of what is intended. I do believe that, over time, an alternating cycle of hard thinking and carefully examined practice helps us understand something like school democracy in its full applied complexity. But definitional clarity is critical to me, and I turned to Dewey for help.

Second, the aspects of Dewey's thinking relative to school democracy cited here are selected in part because they speak to problems in the realization of this process at the School-within-a-School. Specifically, in our efforts, we have encountered many hard questions including the following: Is school democracy essentially student self-government? Is that all there is? Can self-government, in fact, be a substantial enough process to affect students? If school democracy is more than self-government, what more? Is it possible for a group of students relatively homogeneous in terms of race, social class, or ethnicity to be democratic? To what extent is the individual in a democratic school free to do his own thing, that is, to ignore his school community, its rules, its governance, or its development? What claims may a democratic school make of its members, and what obligations has a student in a democratic school? What purposes and processes uniquely characterize a democratic alternative school? It was with these very thorny and practical issues in the implementation of school democracy in mind that I read Dewey.

Democracy as Self-Government

In contrast to some of Dewey's other writing, the conceptions of democracy he offered are complex but not obscure. He talked, first, about democracy as a political process. Most people, I suppose, would so construe it: "Democracy is a special political form, a method of conducting government, of making laws and carrying on governmental administration by means of popular suffrage and elected officers" (1968b, p. 57). Dewey described political democracy in familiar terms: as a way to effect the will and the interests of the majority of the people where consent is freely given to the purposes and the rules by which the individual or the institution is to live. Agreement as to the common purposes, rights, and obligations is embodied in a social contract; the political procedures in a democracy ensure the right of the individual to a voice and a vote in its decisions.

The Democratic Way of Life: Many Shared Interests and an Open Door

Dewey was quick to stress that these political procedures were means for realizing democracy as the truly human way of living. Democracy, he argued, is more than a form of government; it is primarily a way of living together. And the democratic community will have two essential characteristics: the interests its members consciously share will be numerous and varied; and it will have a full and free interaction with other forms of social association. Thus, a democratic community (whether it be a classroom, school, New England village, or a nation-state) will share many common interests that require the individual member to consider the views, wishes, and claims of others relative to these common concerns. When the individual identifies and pursues such common interests with others, he will hear, at least, conflicting opinions and claims and may come to consider them against some criterion such as the preferences of his friends, neighborhood interests, the law, or majority interest and will or a principle such as fairness. Taking the perspective of others into account begins to break down the barriers of race, sex, class, or creed, which obviously are antithetical to viewing individuals as equal in either a constitutional or a moral sense. The greater the diversity of people pursuing common interests, the more encompassing in his viewpoint the individual may come to be.

Dewey, too, was interested in the relationship between the society (or the political process in which the individual lived) and what he learned from it. Thus, he recognized that we learn from novelty and that the greater the diversity of people we encounter, not as tourists but around common objectives, the more likely we are to learn. Nothing is so profoundly educative as to live in another culture. Democracy, ideally, would have us live with different people and cultures within our broader community but with whom we had to work out tasks in common.

For reasons such as the opportunities afforded for role taking and the reduction of stereotyping, Dewey (1968a) argued that a democratic group will be characterized by full and free interactions with other social groups in the community at large such as young people, workers, blacks, and women.

> The two points by which to measure the worth of a form of social life are the extent in which the interests of a group are shared by all its members and the fullness and freeness with which it interacts with other groups. An undesirable society . . . is one which internally and externally sets up barriers to free intercourse and communication of experience. A society which makes provision for participation in its good of all its members on equal terms and which secures flexible re-adjustment of its institutions through interaction of the different forms of associated life is in so far democratic. [P. 99]

For Dewey, the individual and society are inextricably related. The process of the individual's development is an enlargement of his social perspective and his social and moral commitments—a fundamental progression empirically validated by the contemporary psychological theories of development advanced by Piaget, Kohlberg, and Loevinger.

Individual Freedom in a Democracy

Dewey was concerned that democracy with its belief in legal and constitutional equality and the maximizing of individual liberty can be understood as unbridled individualism: a hunting license and a 12-month open season for doing one's own thing. Much earlier, de Tocqueville has remarked that democracy fosters individualism and that individualism first saps the virtues of public life and ends in pure selfishness. Americans would be forced, he predicted, by the necessity of cooperating in the management of their free institutions and by their desire to exercise political rights, into the habit of attending to the interests of the public. But Dewey (1968a) was clear that democracy is an interaction between society and selves:

> The democratic idea of freedom is not the right of each
> individual to do as he pleases, even if it be qualified
> by adding "provided he does not interfere with the
> same freedom on the part of others." . . . the basic
> freedom is that of freedom of mind and of whatever
> degree of freedom of action and experience is neces-
> sary to produce freedom of intelligence. The modes
> of freedom guaranteed in the Bill of Rights are all of
> this nature: Freedom of belief and conscience, of
> expression of opinion, of assembly for discussion and
> conference, of the press as an organ of communication.
> They are guaranteed because without them individuals
> are not free to develop and society is deprived of
> what they might contribute. [P. 61]

Democracy as an Acquired Taste

Dewey also knew that democracy, unlike the wheel, must be continually rediscovered in people's understanding and in the institutions they create. It is an idea and a process that, by definition, has to be "reinvented" through the hard thinking, practice, and majority consent of each group of people trying to be democratic.

Dewey (1968a) argued further that the reinvention of democracy in the individual's understanding and in our institutions must go beyond knowledge or information about "the anatomy of the government" (studying the federal and state constitutions, the names and duties of all of the officers, and so forth) to understanding "the things that are done, that need to be done and how to do them" (P. 50). People need an understanding of democracy that permits them to be democratic.

Given his recognition of the profoundly educative effect of the social groups and institutions in which the individual participates, it is not surprising that Dewey argued that democracy cannot be taught or understood in institutions such as schools or families that are nondemocratic. Neither old-fashioned civics classes, newer political science methodologies and theories (I have in mind the use of systems analysis by Gillespie and Patric [1974]), nor student government can do more than caricature democracy in repressive institutions, such as that portrayed in Fredrick Wiseman's documentary, High School. As Dewey (1968a) said, so pointedly:

> Schools in a democracy . . . must be willing to undertake whatever re-organization of studies, of methods of teaching, of administration including that larger organization which concerns the relation of pupils and teachers to each other and to the life of the community. [P. 48]

From this, it seems evident that Dewey was prepared to go whatever distance was necessary to educate people both to understand democracy and to be democratic. If we are serious about educating for democracy, we will have to begin to democratize classroom management, school governance, and the relations among administrators, teachers, and students—a task whose complexity may be exceeded only by its enduring significance. Of the practical complexities of this task, more shortly.

Elements in the Democratic Creed

Dewey (1968a) believed that there are two articles of faith that must be fundamental both for any democrat and any democratic educator. First, democracy requires a basic commitment to the reasonableness of, the potential fairness of, as well as the human frailties of each group trying to be democratic.

> A faith in the capacities of human nature; faith in human intelligence and in the power of pooled and cooperative experience. It is not belief that these things are complete but that if given a show, they will grow and be able to generate progressively the knowledge and wisdom needed to guide collective action. [P. 59]

Second, is a belief in the equality of human beings. Dewey is careful to point out that this is not a belief that all people are psychologically equal (in terms of intelligence, judgment, or character). Rather, they are legally, constitutionally, and morally equal. As individuals, they are, as a matter of fact, markedly different in capacity and achievement, but in terms of their rights/claims, they are equal. Their legal and constitutional rights are foundational and uncompromisable in a democratic society, as is "the opportunity of every individual to develop to his full capacity" (P. 14).

Good Fences Do Not Make Good Democrats

Dewey made at least one other observation about democracy that is important for educators. It is that those of us deprived for whatever reasons of significant interaction with classes or groups of people different from ourselves, such as Blacks, Chicanos, Jews, Evangelical Christians, and homosexuals, are denied significant opportunities for growth in our social understanding. Both the priviledged who live in $150,000 homes in the planned, idyllic, amenity-rich communities of southern California and their Chicago gardeners are deprived of learning that talent, intelligence, character, and strength (as well as frailty) exist in all of us. Stated more pretentiously, it is precisely these experiences of strangers that help us to see our common aspirations, goodness and humanity, and the essential respect that all of us as individuals deserve. In this sense, Dewey was saying that good fences do not make good neighbors—that unfamiliarity, not familiarity, breeds and sustains contempt between people.

Democracy—The Governance, Social, and Educative Conditions to Stimulate All-Around Student Growth

The conclusion that Dewey meant to create in schools, the governance, social and curricular-instructional conditions supportive of children's full development is inescapable. That is the ultimate criterion of a fully democratic school.

Presumably, Dewey recognized that children would be at very different points in their understanding and skill in democracy, just as their schools might be at very different stages of becoming democratic. One of the things we are learning from our present studies of the effects of democracy on children is the converse: how dependent students' understanding of democracy is on the stage of their cognitive, moral, and personal-social development. Students at Kohlberg's Stages 2 or 3 understand and appropriate the experience of democracy in their school very differently from students at Stages 4, 4.5, or 5. Further, it appears that schools or groups of teachers, students, and administrators trying to be democratic will collectively understand and represent democracy in qualitatively different ways and that we should expect this to be so.

The evolution of democratic schools from titular student government (the present norm) to self-governing communities offering equality of access to the social, governance, and educative conditions for every individual to develop to his full capacity presumably will take as long to realize as it will in the larger U.S. community. How long that may take has been documented by Lipset and Schneider (1977)

in an article entitled "America's Schizophrenia on Achieving Equality."
But it is important to recognize as Dewey did (and for which modern
developmental psychology can offer certain plausible explanations)
that this progression will not happen in a day, a year, or a decade;
that it will occur in individuals or institutions in stages; and that
Stage 2 and Stage 3 democratic schools (and students) have integrity,
just as certainly as a caterpillar, a cocoon, and a butterfly are re-
presentations of one evolving organism. Of this, more later.

THE SCHOOL-WITHIN-A-SCHOOL: AN ONGOING CASE STUDY OF
STUDENT SELF-GOVERNMENT

The School-Within-A-School (SWS), an alternative school that
is part of Brookline High School in Brookline, Massachusetts, was
established in 1969. Its roots were in the turbulence and unrest then
affecting the nation's institutions of higher education as well as many
secondary schools. A group of students, teachers, and parents proposed to the school committee an alternative school that would offer
the students a larger voice in their education and a more equal and
personal relationship with teachers. One of the enduring emphases
from that period is what appears genuinely to be a more equal and
personal relationship between the students and teachers. Students are
intimately known to the staff and treated with respect as individuals—
key elements in the earlier definitions of a democratic group. Certainly the present enrichment curriculum gives students the opportunity to learn and do many things. If one understanding of the ultimate
democratic school is as a community offering the social, governance,
and educative conditions supportive of the full development of every
student in it, then the enrichment courses are as important means to
that end, just as the school's process of self-governance is. How
well any means works—in particular, how much it is part of a conscious and coherent effort to be a democratic school—is less clear in
the case of the SWS.

Another legacy of the school's origin may be the remarkable
freedom that students have. One of the critical (and classical) issues
in this school is the extent to which the community—in terms of
shared purposes—can be established/constructed in relation to freedom for the individual student. Dewey (1968b) points out that "the
system of liberties that exists at any time is always the system of
restraints or controls that exists at that time. No one can do anything except in relation to what others can do and cannot do" (p. 113).
His point has yet to be understood in the SWS. Locke's (1956) warn-
ing is apt: "One of our essential freedoms is the freedom to have
obligations and that those who fail to understand this are doomed to
perpetual immaturity."

When I first became involved with the SWS in the spring of 1975, school rules and policy were made largely by the director and staff. Students were encouraged to attend staff meetings at which rules and policies were discussed and to voice their views. Sharp or angry conflicts between students and staff were rare. There was some concern on the part of the staff and some of the students that the SWS had an insufficient sense of purpose and community. The general lack of community, uneasiness about a small unrepresentative governing body, and an interest in the Danforth Moral Education Project, then ongoing in Brookline, influenced the staff and some interested students to pursue the "just community" approach. An initial ballot vote established clear support for developing democratic self-governance procedures.*

A brief description of the SWS is in order. It is a part of Brookline High School—occupying three classrooms (instant Goodwill Enterprises in decor) and an office. It can enroll up to 100 students.† The staff includes two half-time English teachers, one full-time mathematics and science teacher, a half-time social studies teacher, and a full-time coordinator and counselor. Most students take at least two courses in the SWS (a policy voted by the school in its first

---

*This point may be of some small historical interest. Of all the present-generation "just community" school projects in Cambridge, Pittsburgh, California, and elsewhere, the SWS students—not a group of parents, teachers, or consultants—voted for democracy as self-government of their school. In the subsequent, rocky evolution of the project, that fact has made, it seems, little qualitative difference in their degree of commitment to school democracy. It is in the nature of many adolescents (and academics) I have known to be better at talking than doing, to forget commitments, and to be tentative or irresponsible. But as consultants, we did not come to these modern-day Thoreaus with the conscious design of doing them good, nor did they run for their lives. Our position was that we would assist them in their efforts to establish self-governance and would remain as long as that was a central commitment or until asked to leave. The former coordinator, Ryan (1976), put it succinctly: "We didn't buy a moral education package, but we are applying the principles in our decision making."

†This number of students was enrolled at the time the chapter was written. For the first time in the school's history, there was a waiting list for admission.

year of democratic self-governance largely to protect the positions of the teachers) and the rest of their academic load in the regular high school. The SWS classes themselves are traditional in content; the difference is mainly in the classroom atmosphere, which is relaxed, and in the students' relationships with teachers, which are more personal. "SWS is an 'alternative' to a traditional setting in terms of the way the school is run more than in terms of the content of the curriculum" (DiStefano 1976). The enrichment program, as noted, is an added feature of the curriculum. Its classes are usually held in the evening, and students, teachers, parents, and others—such as university professors like me—may offer courses. The goals for students are stated as: (1) taking as much responsibility for their own education as possible; (2) sharing in the governance of the SWS; and (3) contributing to the building of the SWS community (DiStefano 1976). The basic assumptions with which our consultation at the SWS began were several. It is important to stress the word <u>began</u>. These glib declarative sentences from the Danforth proposal have been altered by what we have learned since:

a) Programs in moral education must go beyond the classroom discussion of moral dilemmas to effect, directly, the justice structure of the school (its rules and discipline, the process by which they are decided, the rights and responsibilities of the students and staff).

b) Students, given instruction and support, can govern themselves. In so doing, they experience the complexity of real moral decision and choice and see the consequences of such decisions both for individual students and their school as a community.

c) In the process of governing their own school, students learn important democratic or parliamentary skills (how to chair a meeting, how to establish an agenda, how to speak to the point). They also learn to take into account the perspective and rights of other students and staff and will develop more comprehensive and fairer thinking. In a broader sense, the present studies of the democratic school are concerned not only to teach students essential democratic and citizenship participation knowledge and skills; they further assume that such systematic experience will have significant developmental effect on the students' social growth and moral reasoning. [Mosher 1976].

Fortunately, our study of the relationship between democracy as a process and how people are affected by it also began with the demurrer that we were "in an early phase of educational development and testing" and with a number of questions:

How best to begin democratic governance experiments in different high schools; what are the practical organizational units of the high school (individual classrooms, alternative schools, houses?) in which to introduce student self-government; how to vitalize representative student government; how to develop formal courses (in social studies, law, English) which inform, analyze and support experience in student self-government; how to educate students, teachers, administrators, parents to make school democracy workable; the appropriateness of such experiences for students at junior high school and middle school level are examples of the questions concerning which much further educational development remains to be done.

Again, and in retrospect, it is interesting to note the equation of student self-government and school democracy in the excerpts. This simply reflects the fact that I had not done my homework on democracy in education. Despite the demurrers, I underestimated the degree to which democracy is a very complex ideal, idea, and process either to understand or to make real in a school. At first, I was to learn much more about democracy from the SWS than I would be able to contribute. It remains sobering to realize how many of the questions we have identified remain to be answered.

Two Years before the Mast—Year 1

In the next two sections, I will summarize the main developments of our association with the SWS over the first two years. I will not do so in the detail necessary for the reader to go and do likewise. As noted before, democracy is a process that, by definition, has to be reinvented by people trying to be democratic. Any speculative or descriptive papers of just or democratic schools should be understood against this qualification.* Finally, the general sense we

---

*Impressive participant observation and empirical studies of just high schools or democratic classes are already available. See Wasserman (1977).

make of this experience at the SWS is more pertinent than its concrete
details. Hopefully, what follows will summarize adequately some of
the funny things that have happened on the way to Stage 5.

In September of 1975, there was an air of curiosity and excite-
ment about the impending changes in the governance structure of the
SWS. Initially, the students became quite involved in elaborate discussions about the structure of the weekly community meetings. Much
debate was given to establishing fair procedures, such as developing
rules of order for the community meetings, determining a way to set
agenda, and choosing a chairperson. The students and staff were
ready to discuss whether the Town Meetings, as they came to be called
(perhaps not surprising in New England), should be mandatory. This
issue continued to be raised throughout the first two years of the
participatory democracy. In many respects, it has embodied the
tension in shifting from the school's tradition of autonomy for the individual toward a democratic community. The classic dilemma , of
course, is the individual's freedom "to do his thing" in relation (not
versus) to the need to work together to achieve common purposes.
Changes in the students' thinking and the impact of the new governance
structure may have been reflected in a gradual shift from a position
of maximum freedom for the individual student toward an increasing
recognition that the SWS, as their social community and school, was
the responsibility of every student. Certainly, this recurrent issue
generated heated debate throughout the first year. For example,
motions to make Town Meetings mandatory were defeated on each of
several formal votes, although by increasingly small margins. (It
was not until the end of the following year that students approved
mandatory Town Meetings.)

The consultants (Peter Scharf, Nancy Richardson, Diana
Paolitto, and the author) encouraged the staff to turn over as many
issues as possible to the Town Meeting. Gradually, the staff helped
students to share decision making on such genuinely sensitive issues
as attendance policies (what to do with truants or the chronic absentee-
ism from homerooms), discipline, admissions procedures, and the
curriculum. The discussions that occurred during the Town Meetings
were quite sophisticated, often centering on abstract issues. At first
the students were more comfortable with such issues and were reluctant
to discuss individuals or to make judgments about their peers. In
addition, they found it easier to criticize the administration than themselves. So, for example, the students, in a discussion of "the viola-
tion of another person's rights," were reticent about discussing the
SWS students who were smoking and acting disrespectfully to teachers
in the quadrangle outside the school. However, when a student brought
up an incident involving the restriction, by the school administration,
of a group of the SWS students' right to freedom of speech, the

community became actively engaged. Discussions about the limits of freedom of speech, the meaning of words such as <u>facts</u> and <u>slanderous</u>, and the issue of responsible reporting were the focus of a number of community meetings. These culminated in a well-thought-out letter that was sent to the editor of the school newspaper and to the principal of the larger high school. As a result, the headmaster agreed to form a committee to establish the specific criteria that should be used for determining whether a poster should be displayed in the high school.

A number of other interesting discussions occurred over the criteria for selecting students for the SWS, the question of whether students who were enrolled in the larger high school should be allowed to take courses at the SWS, and the process to be used for selecting new staff members. Again, there was a slowly emerging tendency to create policies that recognized the need to restrict certain individual choices in order to legitimize and maximize the growth of the community. These included a rule that required that a student take at least two courses for credit in the SWS and the creation of an Absent-without-Leave (AWOL) Committee, which placed restrictions on the number of times a person could skip a class. The AWOL Committee met with students who were missing school in order to determine whether there were problems that might be resolvable with the help of the community.

A brief mention of the role of the consultants to the SWS in Year 1 is in order: Nancy Richardson took primary responsibility for the Town Meetings. She met each week with members of the Agenda Committee to establish the topic for Town Meeting and to outline the justice/moral issues in connection with these topics. She also spent time with the students who chaired the meetings to teach them leadership skills and rules of order adapted from parliamentary procedure. She and Peter Scharf met regularly with the staff to discuss the progress of the school and to help them share their authority and power effectively with the students as a whole. She also served during Town Meetings as a friend-of-the-chair (really as a speaker to whom complicated procedural questions were appealed).

Scharf was more directly involved with staff development. The SWS teachers expressed concern about wanting their classes to reflect the just community philosophy. They wanted to learn how to teach their classes more democratically and how to apply developmental psychology to their curriculum planning and presentation. During Town Meetings, he acted as a catalyst for examining the issues being discussed from as many different perspectives as possible. This function often involved introducing a conflicting viewpoint or asking students to be explicit about the assumptions underlying their reasoning. My own role in Year 1 was that of a harried

participant-observer. To learn about democracy requires an invest-
ment of both hard thinking and hard practice: I really did too little
of either.

Overall, it is probably reasonable to characterize

> The first year of the SWS community [as] largely a
> year of establishing, legitimizing and refining a new
> governance structure which allows and requires that
> all major issues affecting the community be debated
> and resolved in the Town Meeting. The community
> is clearly pleased with and committed to the gover-
> nance structure. . . . It voted, without dissent, con-
> tinuation of the new town meeting form of government
> and the Danforth consultants for 1976-77. The inten-
> tion is that the second year will be a year of develop-
> ing more fully the skills which are required to main-
> tain this structure. Also, there is general interest
> in conducting a systematic evaluation study which
> would determine the impact of the just community on
> the individual student's level of moral reasoning and
> on the moral climate of the institution. [Kohlberg
> and Mosher 1976].

Snatching Victory from the Jaws of Defeat—Year 2

A story is told about President Nathan Pusey of Harvard. During the height of the campus turmoil in 1969, he was asked by a
friend, "How are things going?" Pusey's reply was: "Well, some
days you win and some days you lose. My problem is I can't tell the
difference any more." That story is pertinent to an unbiased effort
to summarize Year 2 at the SWS. I think it is safe to say that the
democratic school project went through a period of considerable
crisis yet managed to snatch a victory from the jaws of defeat. There
were at least three sources of uncertainty in the project.

First, a mea culpa. As a new principal consultant to the staff,
I was clear neither about the meaning of democracy in a school nor
how to go about its practical implementation at the SWS. I had bits
and pieces of the necessary understanding, but I spent my year going
back and forth from Robert's Rules of Order (Robert 1973) to
Democracy and Education to Kohlberg and Town Meetings in a cram
course. My honest uncertainty limited by ability to assist the staff
or the community until late in the year (indeed, it must have made
me seem like the Wizard of Oz at the moment of truth with Dorothy,
the Cowardly Lion, the Scarecrow, and the Tin Woodman). I draw

some comfort from the fact that I was learning much of what I needed to know in the process. Significantly, Fenton (1977) reports analogous difficulties in the first operational year at the Civic Education Project in Pittsburgh:

> The heart of the problem came from inexperience of the entire staff. None of us had run a community meeting; none of us had run an advisory group; none of us had organized a program of community building exercises and only one of us had given a course in interpersonal skills. We made many mistakes as we learned new skills and developed new materials and techniques. [P. 4]

The point is obvious. Where we are attempting change as complex and as unfamiliar in real understanding and practice as democracy is to schools, teachers, students, and consultants (even if it is democracy defined as narrowly as "self-government"), we should expect tough sledding at first because there is so much for us to learn.

Second, staff changes in the SWS introduced a further source of uncertainty. The former coordinator took a leave of absence and then resigned. The new coordinator was not confirmed until April. Three part-time teachers were to be staff members during 1977/78. The effect has been to move to a larger and predominantly part-time faculty. Inevitably, commitments must be affected. Further,

> not all of the staff is in total agreement with the moral education project and therefore not wholly committed. . . . There is certainly no hostility or lack of co-operation among the staff nor is there, however, enthusiastic acceptance, which I see as a distinct drawback in the ultimate implementation of the program with any degree of energy and commitment. [Barrett 1977, p. 7]

Again, the point is clear. Without teachers who are committed to it, school democracy will not happen. Staff turnover further complicates any school innovation, especially in a small alternative high school where the individual teacher has great personal influence.

Third, related to the issue of a part-time staff is the problem of a part-time student body. Many students have only two classes at the SWS and, consequently, are not around a great deal. Further, a number of students have active lives and ties in the regular high school, which inevitably dilutes their commitment to the Town Meeting form of self-government, to the SWS, and to its very vitality as an alternative school. It is clear that the students' very different understanding of commitment to democracy, and ability to be democratic, is the most severe challenge facing this project.

The Business before the House

Against the backdrop of these constraints, it is important to describe the impressive range and complexity of the issues that the Town Meeting dealt with throughout the year. These have included a policy for student withdrawal from classes; the reporting to the Town Meeting of what is discussed in the staff meetings; a policy for visitors; the need for active recruitment of new members; SWS policy relative to a new Massachusetts law requiring a moment of silence at the beginning of each school day; a grading policy for the SWS; a probing review of a research proposal from the Harvard Center for Moral Education; the problem of cliques in the SWS; how to improve the Town Meeting with a revision and relaxing of the rules of order; behavioral guidelines for the SWS parties; black history week and the SWS policy toward the racial issues it created; the appointment of two half-time English teachers for 1977/78; the appointment of a new coordinator; how to strengthen the SWS as a community, including the planning of a day-long retreat; the issue of a member's obligations to the SWS; the approval of mandatory Town Meetings in 1977/78; and constituting student advisory groups for the next year. As a regular participant observer, I would characterize discussion of these issues as serious (if sometimes desultory around what were termed mickey mouse—that is, school maintenance issues), protracted (often too much so for the preference of some students), and unquestionably decisive as to official school policy. How well the community remembers or effects commonly decided policy is less clear, but it was certainly enough to get by. Nor, in my judgment, did the community duck or finesse any issue with the exception of the observance of the moment of silence. Students became very competent in chairing Town Meetings even to the point of choosing a student speaker to replace the project consultant in that role. Membership on the Agenda Committee was much sought after; interestingly, in 1977/78 all students are to be eligible to serve on the Agenda Committee through a lottery system.

Three other standing committees—namely, the Hiring, Waiver, and AWOL committees—continued to function in 1977/78. The Hiring Committee, comprised of five students and four staff, was directly involved in the interviewing and appointment of the new part-time English teacher. Decisions regarding the appointment of the other half-time English teacher and the coordinator's position were made,

as noted, by the Town Meeting. The AWOL Committee deals basically with students who have been referred to it for cutting classes.
Teacher notification of cuts comes directly to this committee rather
than to parents. The committee, meeting with the student, determines
the reasons for the student's absences and an appropriate plan: "The
idea behind this is that students can help other students and, as community members, have a responsibility to do so; also, ultimately
students are responsible for their own behavior (the reason why
parents are not notified)" (Barrett 1977, p. 4). In the SWS the AWOL
Committee is the only discipline committee per se.* The Waiver
Committee is made up of one faculty member, the coordinator, and
three students chosen randomly from volunteers and is concerned
primarily with student appeals to drop classes or to schedule classes
or working during Town Meeting time. An individual contract is set
up with each student waived.

So What Is the State of the Union at the End of Year 2?:

The Town Meeting met twice weekly. The standing committees,
too, functioned regularly. In the process, substantial issues were
discussed and important policy decisions made. The problem of the
Town Meeting was not so much the rules of the house, which were
modified in response to student and staff criticism (generally in the
direction of less formal procedures), nor in the ability of the community to debate or decide, which continued at an impressive level.
The problem of the Town Meeting was in the unevenness of the issues
brought before it. When the issue was seen as vital (e. g. , the re-
appointment of a favorite teacher), the Town Meeting was seen as
vital. When the issue was school management, the Town Meeting was
perfunctory. However, as one member put it: "Even if an issue is
mickey mouse, is it not the responsibility of an SWS member to attend
Town Meeting?" (Finegold 1977).

In this regard, it is heartening that the community voted mandatory once weekly Town Meetings for 1977/78. This was a near
unanimous vote of the sophomores and juniors, those who will be
directly affected by the new policy. The SWS is, I believe, the first

---

*This is unlike Cambridge Cluster School, which has a committee
designed to enforce all school rules. Decisions of the discipline committee at the Cluster School are often appealed to the community meeting, which leads to fruitful discussions regarding fairness.

democratic school to do so by majority vote. Other such schools have not made mandatory attendance a matter of student choice or vote. My impression is that this decision reflected a more basic concern and commitment by the students and staff to build the SWS as a community rather than to drift or to end with a whimper.

In summary, at the end of Year 2, the SWS was well launched toward self-government. Most of the ingredients for that to happen were in place. Research was under way to document the effects of all of this on the students' moral and ego development. Buth the community and/or the consultants, for different reasons, may conclude that self-government is not enough. Whether the SWS will, can, or should opt for Dewey's much more profound conception of a democratic school then becomes a moot issue.

Assuming for purposes of discussion that the SWS chose to be a more democratic school, what might that mean in practical terms? Let me hazard some suggestions. A first need would be to identify and develop more shared purposes. These could come in the form of programs and activities (retreats, parties, athletics, drama, enrichment courses, community action, and so on) that cut across existing cliques and involve students in contacts with members they do not know. I think it would be useful for the community to debate and clarify what at present attracts students to the SWS, what the school stands for, in what ways it is an "alternative," and, most important, how its programs and common purposes can be strengthened. In this connection, I think the community should give serious consideration to opening up the SWS to other groups of students (that is, to actively recruit more boys, blacks, and working-class youngsters) so as to introduce more diversity and energy into the school.

Concurrently, I think that an effort to expand the SWS as a caring community—as a group that really cares about it members—would have positive effects. Retreats and the proposed advisory groups offering peer counseling and personal and academic support might be practical ways to accomplish this. The goal would be to make certain that being a member of the SWS means that one is treated as an individual—one who is truly known, cared about, and supported by the faculty and many other students. To care deeply about other people (and to be cared for by them) is not only a developmental need for adolescents; it is a deep, persisting human and social need that is worth learning well.

Related to this, I can report that the staff is already very good at individualizing their relationships in the teaching and counseling of students. Students in the SWS are known and cared about personally and academically by the staff; their personal and scholastic development is monitored closely. The enrichment curriculum offers students the opportunity to pursue many special academic, artistic, and other interests for credit. How much the enrichment curriculum depends on student initiative or how much it is used by the staff and school as an intentional way to individualize learning is less clear. Nonetheless, important elements—a scale of operation, teachers who know and care about students as individuals, and a flexible curriculum structure—are in place to permit genuine individualization of student learning and development, which is at the core of Dewey's conception of the democratic school.

Finally, it also seems critical, as the community had decided, to keep self-governance going and to expand the Town Meeting's focus to the major task of community building.

EVEN IF YOU CAN GET THERE, IT IS NOT ENOUGH

This section will summarize what we have learned from a modest effort during the two years (1975-77) about developing self-governance in one alternative school:

1. These high school students can learn to govern themselves. They can establish their own Robert's rules of order, make reasoned arguments and proposals, and deliberate and legislate school policy on a variety of complex sensitive issues ranging from student grading, moral development research at the SWS, the appointment of new staff members and a school coordinator, and voting on mandatory Town Meetings. Nor do they finesse or avoid difficult issues (although dealing with what they see as arbitrary school authority exercised against them is easier than applying sanctions to irresponsibility by their own members). After two years of observing their weekly Town Meetings, it would be hard for me to say they govern themselves any less responsibly or democractically than do teachers, school committees, Town Meetings, or university faculties I have known. That may sound cynical or like damning with faint praise. It is not intended to be so at all. These students practice self-government with more good humor, forgiveness of their own frailties, and lightheartedness than their elders. That may have something to do with the fact that I observe little covetousness or abuse of authority on their part. Self-government, it must be noted, is not a compelling interest to the majority of these alternative school students; its effects on their development (see point 3 below) are therefore restricted. I will turn shortly to an explanation of this as a function of their stage of development. The fact that many students are defaulted or indifferent citizens makes them no different, of course, than their parents. Hutchins (1976) has

said precisely this—the average American is not a citizen. And, as noted, the SWS has voted mandatory participation in Town Meeting for all its members in 1977/78. But the lack of interest in school democracy displayed by many students over the first two years must be acknowledged and faced.

2. I think it is valid to say that those students who participate in school democracy learn important parliamentary skills—chairing meetings, speaking to the point, taking other students' views into account, and so on—that should generalize to their later lives. In fact, we do not know whether this happens. In the meantime, one can hope that an appetite for democratic decision making and an attitude and understanding of its importance persist.

3. Further, there is preliminary evidence that children and adolescents who participate in democratic classrooms or alternative schools show significant gains in moral reasoning (Rundle 1977, Wasserman 1977). Such gains approach a half-stage increase in moral reasoning, roughly double the amount of gain achieved in most moral education courses within the existing curriculum. Much more comprehensive data to be collected longitudinally over the next two years on students at the SWS, the Cluster School in Cambridge, and the Civic Education units in Pittsburg will clarify these highly preliminary but promising data on the effects of a more democratic environment on moral and ego development. And the data will be available for very different groups of adolescents. An extension of development and research in Brookline into the effects of democratic classrooms on younger children similarly will help to clarify Rundle's (1977) pioneering study with fifth-grade students. In addition, there is clinical evidence from the Cluster School that the incidence of stealing within the school has decreased to the point where the students no longer steal from one another nor in the larger school. This very significant and tangible change in their moral behavior has not been generalized to the "street," however. The issue of whether changes in students' moral reasoning have consequences for their behavior in and out of school is obviously of great theoretical and practical importance.

Now (Second) the Paradoxes

First, I believe that we need to avoid certain definitional mistakes in our research on school democracy:

1. For example, it would be easy to equate school democracy with studies of the effects on students of participating in the governance of alternative schools or classrooms. That may be as much or

more than it is realistic, in the near term, to accomplish in most school democracy projects. If our understanding of the truly democratic school is that it is a community providing the governance, social, and educative conditions supportive of the full development of every student, then we will need to conceptualize and create such schools. Self-government will be but one aspect of such a school.

2. And so will moral development. I believe it would be a mistake to reduce school democracy to a means (albeit a sophisticated one) to stimulate the moral development of students. God knows moral reasoning and behavior are critically missing in our present education of children and adolescents, but morality is not—repeat, not—all there is to being human.

3. I think there is a danger that we may focus too exclusively on efforts to democratize the school and pay insufficient attention to opportunities for learning about (and promoting) democracy in other institutions in the community. While I accept the dictum of "Physician—heal thyself" (that is, educators should democratize schools first), Newmann's (1972) argument for education in democracy and social action in the community is incontrovertible, as is Stanley's (1976) pioneering study of educating families to be democratic.

Second, I believe there are real constraints that operate on democracy in school:

1. Students will understand and be democratic in qualitatively different ways depending on their stage of development. If stage theories have any validity at all, it follows that these points of view (whether moral or personal) significantly affect one's understanding of self-government, democracy, school rules, student rights and obligations, community, justice, and so on (Scharf 1977).

   Approximately one-fourth to one-third of the students at the SWS have given continuous commitment and leadership to school governance and the standing committees. They may be the students best able to understand and to state arguments about the complex moral and policy issues in governing the school and to see the importance of majority will as well as to tolerate the "mickey mouse" of management. Another one-fourth to one-third of the students were reasonably dutiful citizens (attended Town Meeting with some regularity, spoke infrequently). Nearly one-half the students, as noted, were marginal or nonparticipators. The relationship between participation in school governance and the student's stage of development is obviously a real issue in the vitality and applicability of such projects (as well as an empirical question on which we are now gathering data). And even when participation is mandatory, as it now is, we would expect the student's stage to delimit his or her ability both to understand democracy and to be democratic.

2. What we have said about the students applies as well to teachers. Certainly, we can expect many teachers to be genuinely attracted to the rhetoric of democracy. Most teachers are assumed to be at the conventional level of moral reasoning (Stages 3 and 4). A significant core of their thinking will have to do with authority, rule maintenance, discipline, and the order of the school class- room (even if the issue becomes jealousness in defense of a new order or disagreements as to who possesses the true gospel of the just community). Where variation in stage development among teachers is greater, different conceptions of school democracy might be expected. Further, the concept of a school where teachers know and care about one another, where the emphasis is on the quality of their relationships, may also figure prominently in the thinking of many teachers and counselors. For them com- munity is likely to be more important than democracy or justice. Finally, the "free schooler" teachers whose thinking reflects the radical educators' passionate desire to liberate mankind from culture with its patterns and authority will be ambivalent about the obligations a democratic school will require of students for the common good. What this says is that not all—perhaps not even a majority—of teachers will be comfortable with school democracy, nor will they all have the same conception of it. All of the projects to date have encountered this issue. This ob- servation underscores the essential nature of teacher selection and education for projects in school democracy.

3. As an extension of points 1 and 2 above, it seems probable to me that groups of students and teachers will create qualitatively dif- ferent democratic schools or just communities, depending on the predominant state of moral and ego development. Some of the possible differences have already been alluded to. For example, I would expect a predominantly Stage 3 school to be much pre- occupied with the students' social relationships with some, but by no means all, peers and with the teachers. Having and being with close friends and knowing teachers intimately—"a more personal education"— would be important reasons for belonging. I would expect such students to be little troubled by school rules and teacher authority that are seen as well intentioned and persona- lized. One would work very hard, academically or otherwise, to please and to be liked by such teachers who know and care about him or her. Such a group might be more likely to respond to an

effort to create a caring community—that is, to expand the friend-ship group—to add to the number of students and faculty "who know and care about me" than to build a legislative, rule-maintaining, self-governing community.

The other side of this could be that the school would be divided into cliques, perhaps allied with particular teachers, to some degree exclusive of one another and certainly so of outsiders. Self and peer group (one's sorority) would take precedence over the community as a whole. Further, a student's popularity or attitude rather than the rightness of arguments or the objective "wrongness" of school behavior could become critical in the community's decision making. Students would be loath to discipline friends or to bind them to broader community obliga-tions, because one's social perspective and bond really only ex-tend to one's immanent social group.

By contrast, students predominantly at Stage 4 understand that policy and rules are necessary for the school to exist as a com-munity, that they protect the student's rights and freedoms as well as impartiality in discipline, and that they have moral force and should be obeyed even if one's friends, teachers, or parents will never know. There is a recognition that if the school through the Town Meeting makes policy, it has to be respected: "It's important to get everyone to come to Town Meeting so that the rules are seen as having real power." Otherwise, both the rules and the process of making them are subverted. Thus, the delibera-tion and deciding of school policy and rules is a serious business, even when its content is mickey mouse. It is a critical process in identifying and legislating the common interests that bind the community. There is a realization that it is better for people to be authorities over themselves than to leave it to teachers (even trustworthy ones) and an intuitive sense that being in authority (for example, as chairperson of Town Meeting or as a member of a standing committee) can be rewarding. The obverse side of this may be an excess of debate, of speechmaking, of procedural rules, or of legislation. This kind of procedural orgy can bore or frustrate many students or faculty.

Conclusions

As a practical matter, we have miles to go before we sleep in understanding the complex consequences of (and constraints on) school democracy experiments even at the present scale. Nor do we know how to vitalize representative school government, which is the predominant form of student government in the U.S. high school. The question of the effective operational unit (the classroom, the alternative school, the "house," the student council) within the existing school in which to experiment with democracy is also moot.

I have no doubt that the way in which, and the inertia with which, public schools are presently managed by professional "administrators" who set budgets, appoint and reward faculty, establish school regulations, administer discipline, adjudicate student rights, and so on, is the major and formidable obstacle to all that this chapter presages.* As for organization, Scharf (1977) states the problem well:

> The increase in "comprehensive" schools over the
> past thirty years implies a size and organization
> which makes meaningful democracy improbable.
> Schools of 2,000 or more are simply too large to
> have effective student participation. The division
> of the academic day by periods and subjects prohibits
> the development of a sense of community likely to
> make democracy plausible or desirable. Similarly,
> the hierarchical model of management found in
> comprehensive schools makes student participation
> likely to appear as a threat to the principal's politi-
> cal control of the school. [P. 11]

My intuition is that the classroom is the most likely and practical place to promote democracy in the school. Why? Because it is of a size to permit individual participation and genuine common purposes; because it is the basic organizational unit of the school; and because much of what happens in classrooms goes on behind closed doors and so is protected from management. Further, there is encouraging word as to what happens when elementary classrooms are democratic (see Lickona 1977; Rundle 1977). If we are not heard from for another two years, while others are espousing democracy as the new laetrile for schools, it will be, in part, because we are trying to learn more about both its promise and its problems in the classroom.

---

*This happens, incidentally, under the muddy influence of systems development models copied from IBM or the Harvard Business School.

7

BEYOND JUSTICE:
A CURRICULUM FOR COOPERATION

Thomas Lickona

Heilbroner (1974), in a well-known essay on the future of human-kind, reaches this conclusion: "The outlook for man, I believe, is painful, difficult, perhaps desperate, and the hope that can be held out for his future prospect is very slim indeed" (p. 22). Heilbroner's grim prophecy calls to mind the following story:

An old priest was dying. As he prayed for the repose of his soul, he was troubled about Heaven and Hell. What, he wondered, were they really like?

Then, dimly, he saw two figures at the foot of his bed. He recognized one as Moses, the other as St. Peter. When they beckoned him, he got up and followed, walking through the wall of his bedroom. Silently, they led him through the galaxies of the night sky.

In a far-off place, they stopped before a big house. "The kingdom of God is made of many mansions," St. Peter explained, "So, too, is Hell. Step inside. We will show you the first room of Satan's Palace."

As the priest walked in, his ears were assaulted by a babble of complaints. Many people were seated at a large table. In the center, there was a big pot of the priest's favorite dish, beef stew. Although everyone in Hell had a spoon and could reach the pot, the people were starving. The spoon handles that were attached to their hands were twice as long as their arms. They could catch the stew, but they couldn't bring it to their lips. The cries

of the starving were so loud that the priest begged
to be taken away.

St. Peter and Moses then took him to another
mansion in a distant place. Moses invited the priest
to step inside the outer room of Heaven. There the
priest saw a similar large table surrounded by many
people. In the center, as before, was a huge pot of
beef stew. The spoon handles were again too long
for human arms, but there were no cries of complaint, for no one was starving. The people were all
feeding each other.

This parable teaches us that we make our own heaven and our
own hell. If we choose to pursue our own ends independently, we
seal our common doom. If, however, we choose to pursue our common interests together, we ensure our collective and individual survival.

Enlightened cooperation is not only our best hope for avoiding
the global horrors of war and famine that Heilbroner and others en-
vision, it is also essential for promoting human welfare in all spheres
of life. As a volunteer marriage and family counselor, I see couples
and families who are in trouble at least partly because they have
little or no idea of how to orchestrate their separate needs and desires
in a way that fosters their mutual happiness. As a college professor,
I have seen faculties unable to rise above differences and distrust to
move forward toward a common aim. In society at large, the evidence
is everywhere around us of what happens when people pursue their
own interest with little conception of or concern for the common good.
You need only pick up the paper or turn on the news to find fresh
examples of this group or that bent on maximizing its own gain—driving
the inflationary spiral still higher, dealing another blow to the environment, or thwarting efforts to conserve dwindling resources. To
cooperate, then, to act in concert with others for mutual benefit, is
an imperative in human affairs whatever the scale: whether as
partners in a marriage, coworkers on the job, citizens of the same
society, or inhabitants of the same planet.

You might grant that cooperation is prudent—a sensible adaptation to the human condition—but still ask, What makes it moral?
It may, in the long run, serve our self-interest to recognize common
goals and work together to achieve them, but are we really obligated
to cooperate? Obviously, there are many times when we act alone
and when it makes good sense to do so. Cooperation becomes a
matter of moral obligation when the attainment of a moral and requires
cooperation or when others suffer unjustly because we fail to cooperate.
If my marriage or family life deteriorates because I refuse to sit

down with my wife and talk about our problems and how to solve them, that refusal to cooperate is immoral. If school morale and programs for students suffer because faculty and administration pursue an adversary relationship rather than a cooperative one, that failure to cooperate is immoral. If I, as an individual, teach in such a way that shuts off open dialogue and cooperative interaction with my students and makes me insensitive to their needs as learners, that behavior is immoral. If a strike continues and the public welfare suffers because management and labor do not cooperate fully to achieve a just solution, that failure to cooperate is immoral. If an energy crisis worsens because a president and a Congress will not work together to mount an effective national program or because individual citizens refuse to cooperate with the effort to conserve energy, those failures to cooperate are immoral. If people anywhere, whether in a distant land or a nearby ghetto, are deprived of their human rights or go hungry or ill-housed or without medical care because I and others fail to support efforts to improve their lot and achieve social justice, that failure, too, judged by the standard of cooperation is immoral.

Cooperation clearly requires not only that we avoid doing harm to others but also that we take positive steps to prevent and alleviate conditions hostile to human welfare. Such cooperation may take the form of working together toward a shared goal (as when marriage partners strive for their mutual happiness) or the form of one person helping another where there is little likelihood of reciprocity (as when a well-off person contributes to the poor). Even if a particular helping act is unilateral in its immediate context, it can be cooperative when seen in a larger social context. Individual acts of altruism, though they be separate in time and space, constitute an invisible partnership to establish human environments in which people feel a decent measure of responsibility for each other's lives.

Why do people not cooperate more than they do? Sometimes they would if they could, but they do not know how. The spirit is willing, but the skills are weak. All too often, however, the will to cooperate is weak or absent as well. Underlying this failure of will, I believe, is a moral malaise that is one of the most troubling social conditions of our times: a lack of a sense of community, of bonds, or of felt connections with other human beings. When this sense of community is missing, one feels no responsibility for the welfare of others and no obligation to become involved in their lives. Perhaps the most chilling example of this kind of alienated detachment is bystander inaction in the face of another's critical need. Consider these all too familiar news reports:

> Kitty Genovese is set upon by a maniac as she returns
> home from work at 3:00 a.m. Thirty-eight of her

neighbors in Kew Gardens came to their windows when she cries out in terror; none comes to her assistance even though her stalker takes over half an hour to murder her. No one even so much as calls the police. She dies. [Darley and Latane 1968, p. 428]

An eighteen-year-old switchboard operator, alone in her office in the Bronx, is raped and beaten. Escaping momentarily, she runs naked and bleeding to the street, screaming for help. A crowd of 40 passersby gathers and watches as, in broad daylight, the rapist tries to drag her back upstairs. No one interferes. [P. 428]

A fifty-seven-year-old Benedictine monk suffers a severe fall in British Columbia's Golden Ears Park. Ron Zwall, sixteen, and his fourteen-year-old sister race down a rugged mountain trail hoping to alert Search and Rescue officials in time. Exhausted from their run, they ask several groups of hikers whom they pass to take over the call for help. All ignore their plea. By the time a parks official is located and a search team sent in, Father Damascus is dead. Vancouver Sun 1978, [pp. A1-A2].

Youths riding a B.C. Hydro bus harass and assault two Simon Fraser University students from Bangladesh. They strike Abdullah Al-Mamun in the face, hit Azizul Hoq Bhniya over the head with a glass jug and kick him. Both men require hospital treatment. More than a dozen other passengers on the bus and the driver watched the incident; no one protested the harassment or tried to restrain the assailants. [SFU Week 1978]

Two social psychologists, Darley and Batson (1973), wondered if such behavior is typical of all groups of people. To increase the likelihood of a helpful response in an emergency situation, they selected seminarians as subjects. Moreover, they asked each seminarian to write a sermon on the meaning of the parable of the Good Samaritan to be delivered to an audience of faculty and peers. While walking across campus to the lecture hall, each seminarian came across a person slumped in an alleyway. This individual, in reality an actor, coughed and groaned and cried out for help.

How did the seminarians, sermon in hand, respond? Of the 40, 24 simply passed by. The experimenters reported: "Indeed, on several occasions a seminary student going to give his talk on the parable of the Good Samaritan literally stepped over the victim as he hurried on his way" (p. 107).

Would children respond any differently if they were cast in the role of bystander to another's distress? To find out, Staub (1970) conducted a study with some 200 children. He escorted each individual child into a room, asked the child to draw a picture, then excused himself to "get some more crayons"—adding that there was a little girl playing in the next room and he hoped she would be careful. After the experimenter left the child, there came from the adjoining room the loud noise of a falling chair, follwed by a girl's severe crying (in fact a tape), which lasted for a full minute and a half.

Among kindergarteners, 19 percent went to see what the trouble was. Among second-graders, helping rose to 51 percent. But among sixth-graders, the percentage of helping children fell to a low of 15 percent. Comments from some of these sixth-grade children indicated that they did not want to risk getting yelled at by the experimenter for leaving the room. Disturbingly, Staub's study suggests that the roots of bystander unresponsiveness may reach far back into childhood.

There are many ways to read the data on bystander inaction. I think it is one of the uglier by-products of an individualist ethic, one which says that it is "OK," even smart, to look out for "Number 1" and forget about your neighbor—he should look out for himself. It is an ethic that is preached in a wave of popular literature. And it is an ethic that militates against a consciousness that no man is an island and that we are all members of the same human family, linked by our common humanity and equally vulnerable to the assorted problems and perils of the human condition. How does one develop that sort of consciousness—what I call a cooperative ethic? How do you inject it into the cultural bloodstream, into the moral marrow of the individual human being? There are surely many ways. I would like to offer cooperative moral education as one of them.

COOPERATIVE MORAL EDUCATION

Cooperative moral education has three goals: (1) to help people become aware of their interdependence and their common interests; (2) to teach them the skills and attitudes—such as mutual respect, group decision making, dividing labor, and coordinating actions—that they will need to engage in effective cooperative effort toward common goals; and (3) to develop the will to cooperate, so that capacity is translated into performance.

Although human beings obviously have an enormous capacity for egocentrism and selfishness, it is clearly not foreign to our natures to cooperate. Even young children do it. Garvey and Hogan report that "when pairs of three-and-a-half to five-year-olds play together, much of their speech and nonverbal behavior is mutually adaptive, reflecting sensitivity to and concern with one another's motives and behavior" (Hogan 1975, p. 537). In our own work, teachers of kindergarten and even nursery children find that when a task demanding cooperation is scaled to the children's level, they respond with competence and enthusiasm, often working better than they do when involved in solitary pursuits.

While students, even young ones, are capable of this kind of interaction, it is also clear that the school (like other social institutions) does very little to promote cooperation and a good deal to discourage it. In one of his first books, The Moral Judgment of the Child, Piaget (1965) roundly criticized schools for acting as if their goal were "the preparation of pupils for competitive examinations rather than for life" (p. 405). The school's determination to "shut the child up in work that is strictly individual" Piaget regarded as "contrary to the most obvious requirements of intellectual and moral development" (p. 405). You do not learn to cooperate, Piaget was saying, by working alone. Nearly 50 years after Piaget's indictment of competitive, individualistic education, however, it is still very hard to find classrooms where children are working together on an assignment or project. As a supervisor of student teachers and a father of two sons, I have been in a good many public school classrooms, and I can count on one hand the number of times I have seen students involved in collaborative effort. Even "progressive" schools seem to be unwitting captives of traditional individualism: their students may not compete as often or as fiercely, but they work separately on their "individualized" curriculum, with cooperative interaction either precluded or left to chance.

What would classrooms look like if they took seriously the development of a cooperative ethic in their students? What would teachers do differently? Having made the case for cooperation as an indispensable means to basic human goals, I would like to turn now to practical strategies for the classroom. Following that, I will discuss the contribution that cooperative activity makes to moral stage development as Piaget, Kohlberg, and other stage theorists describe it. Finally, I will attempt to clarify the difference and relationship between a cooperative ethic and a justice ethic, since I believe that education for cooperation takes an important step beyond education for justice.

TEACHER STRATEGIES FOR COOPERATIVE MORAL EDUCATION

The following 12 strategies for cooperative moral education have come directly from my interaction with classroom teachers. For the last eight years, I have been privileged to work with early childhood, elementary, and, most recently, secondary teachers who deserve most of the credit for translating the ideal of cooperative learning into a variety of imaginative educational practices. These practices demonstrate how a teacher can make cooperation a governing ethic in the life of the classroom, pervading its tone and texture, something that is stitched into the fabric of everyday events and activities in the students' lives. Taken together, these strategies constitute a curriculum for cooperation.

Strategy 1: Use Group Projects That Require Students to Work Together Toward a Common Goal

"I had always prided myself on the ways that I encouraged children to help and work with each other," wrote one kindergarten teacher, "until I came across the following idea in my reading: in a cooperative goal structure, students work together to produce one project; if students are each producing a project that they do not integrate into one, the goal structure is not cooperative (Johnson and Johnson 1975). Although I had thought I was using a cooperative structure, in reality I was not because the children all produced their own project. I began reflecting on how seldom children are given the opportunity to work together to produce one thing" (Kur 1977, p. 3).

This teacher wondered if requiring her youngsters to work together on one thing would improve the behavior of several especially aggressive children. She started simply by giving groups of four children craft sticks, glue, and a piece of cardboard and telling them to build a structure—one structure—of their choice. To her surpise, she found that though some groups floundered for a while, "the children on the whole worked much better together than when they were at a table together, but each working on his own thing. Only three arguments occurred" (p. 4).

With time, Kur saw an increase in her children's ability to cooperate on such projects. In the beginning, dominant children "ran the show" while less assertive children tended to hang back. Later, however, "leaders became less important, shy children began to assert themselves, and decision-making became a shared responsibility." She reports the following exchange among three children who were making a spring picture together. Robert was "a bright, aggressive boy who until this time had made the decisions in the group"; John was "a quiet, withdrawn child, easily dominated"; Anna was "a girl who had had trouble relating to others."

John: Hey, Robert, what's that supposed to be?

Robert: The top of the swing set.

John: It sure doesn't look like that.

Robert: Well, what should I do with it?

Anna: You could make it into a tree.

Robert: How can I do that?

John: You could draw a line like this.

Robert: Hey, yeah. Who has the brown? [Emphasis added]

The teacher wrote, "I was especially pleased by this interaction. Anna made a constructive suggestion—previously rare for her. John, once withdrawn, offered instruction that was positively received by Robert. Robert was beginning to relate to the other members of his group as persons with something valuable to contribute" (p. 5).

A "we" orientation also grew stronger in the groups. "I could hear children telling others to stop scribbling because 'You are wrecking our picture!" The children were also becoming less dependent, calling on me only to see what they had done. There was very little idle chatter in the groups, most talk centering on the task at hand. I think this is because they were enjoying what they were doing. Every day now, my children ask if we can play 'those group games.'"

Children were not only enjoying this new kind of activity but were also developing important insights into the nature of cooperation—insights that would ordinarily be considered remarkable for five- and six-year-olds. When the teacher asked at a class meeting, "What does it mean to cooperate?" these were some of the responses:

It means to help with the work, like, you know, don't goof off.

You gotta talk nice, or no one will listen to you.

You can't be too bossy—everybody has to have a turn.

You help people do things, like if they can't make a tree, you show them how.

Equally impressive were the generalized effects of the cooperative projects. "My children are kinder people now," the teacher said, "more attentive to each other's needs." A little girl who was an aggressive behavior problem before the projects, for example, took the lead in befriending a newcomer to the class. When a job needed to be done, all pitched in. "Clean-up time," the teacher reported, "has been cut in half since the projects began."

This teacher's strategy of having children make something together is an excellent way to introduce cooperative learning at any age level. Making something with your hands is usually highly involving and is nonthreatening when there are many hands and heads to share the work. Karen Van Fleet,* a second-grade teacher, recounts her children's enthusiasm for a project in cooperative "Monster-Making": "I began by asking the children to each draw a part—any part—of a monster while they were still at their seats. When they had drawn, colored, and cut out a part of the monster, I randomly divided them into groups by counting off. The groups were then to pool whatever parts the children had constructed on their own, draw missing parts if needed, and create a whole monster from the assorted contributions.

"The cooperation," reports teacher Van Fleet, "was wonderful to see." Here are some comments recorded from one group's interaction:

> Van: You draw better than I do, you draw the body and I'll paste.
>
> J. J.: Look, Mrs. Van Fleet, we're taking turns! [This said as if it were his own wonderful idea.]
>
> Kim: You guys can share my crayons.
>
> Kelly: Everybody should color, so we can all have the same to do.
>
> Johnny: You can make one leg, and I'll make the other.

---

*This teacher's report and those of other teachers quoted later in the text are taken from accounts submitted to me as the instructor of a course or workshop in which the teachers participated. These are not available as formal papers; hence, I have not provided citations and references in the usual fashion.

When the groups were finished with their monsters, the teacher gathered everyone together for a class meeting to share the results of their labors. This kind of whole-group sharing is itself an important stragegy, since it provides an appropriate culminating activity and a chance for the class to respond appreciatively to each group's efforts. That sort of experience, in turn, contributes to a strengthened sense of community within a class. In their class meeting, teacher Van Fleet says, "Each group stood up laughing and giggling, delighted to show their funny monster. And everyone in the group made sure that each member was holding up at least one corner of the big paper on which their monster was mounted—another show of cooperation and community.

"It was a special joy," this teacher concludes, "to see a little boy and girl who do not ordinarily get along be randomly assigned to the same group and actively cooperate on a project." This teacher discovered that a cooperative group task provides a needed support structure that helps children relate to each other in positive ways and to develop social-moral skills they can use in other situations as well. Too often, when children do not relate well, we assume that they are too immature to do so, that they lack the requisite developmental equipment. Instead, we should experiment to find the right support structure that will elicit those capacities, however fragile or partially developed, that children do have within their repertoire.

Strategy 2: Set the Stage for Cooperation

Contrary to the impression these stories may convey, it is not always all sweetness and light when you first try to do cooperative projects with a class. In particular, junior-high and high-school teahhers sometimes find that interpersonal hostilities spill over into the small groups and work against a cooperative spirit. Or the students may assimilate the cooperative assignment to old habits of thinking and behaving. This is what happened to Priscilla Williams, a fourth-grade teacher, when she set up what she hoped would be cooperative math groups. Instead of children helping each other with the set of problems their group was assigned, she found them bickering in a tense atmosphere of group-against-group competition. "Come on, stupid, you're gonna make our team lose!" was one boy's comment to another—though the teacher had said nothing to give them the idea that this was any sort of competitive contest.

Teacher Williams saw clearly that her children needed to be prepared for cooperative activity, needed a different "mental set" to break free from their well-reinforced habits of competition. So she took two basic steps for setting the stage that comprise a crucial strategy in cooperative moral education. First, she called a class meeting to discuss cooperation. Such a meeting is an opportunity to ask students, What does it mean to cooperate? and to explain that the next activity requires cooperation. A teacher can also ask at this point, What rules do we need in order to have good cooperation? A list can be made and posted of these rules (for example, share materials, try to use everyone's ideas, make sure everybody has a job to do) that the class agrees are necessary if people are to cooperate successfully.

Then the teacher told her children, "When you complete your task, I'll ask each member of every group to write an answer to these four questions: (1) How did your group cooperate? (2) What did you do to fulfill your responsibility as a member of the group? (3) Did you offer help to anyone? (4) What changes would you make to improve your group?" These questions served two purposes. First, they conveyed in concrete terms the idea that successful group cooperation requires responsible contributions from every individual member. Second, they held the child accountable to the rules of cooperation by letting them know in advance that everyone would have to evaluate his group's work and his contribution to it. In effect, this teacher was saying, "Make no mistake about it, I'm serious about this business of cooperating."

Did it work? Teacher Williams tried the mathematics groups again with wholly different results. "Organization was smooth and the atmosphere very pleasant. Some groups chose to be democratic and took votes to determine who would do what problems. Another group divided up the problems equally and assigned them by picking numbers out of a hat. Others flipped coins. One group simply had volunteers, until all problems were assigned. As children worked, I heard frequent comments such as 'Shawn, could you see if this is right?' and 'Yeah, Mike, it's fine!' A few people politely reminded fellow group members of the agreement to number and initial completed problems."

Setting the stage for cooperation, as this teacher found, can make all the difference. In this case, the support structure consisted of rules for cooperation and a system of accountability.

Strategy 3: Hold an Evaluation or Feedback Meeting after a Cooperative Project

The feedback meeting is a logical correlate of the stage-setting strategy. Before they begin work, the class resolves to cooperate; after they finish work, they meet in small groups or all together to discuss how well they carried out their good intentions. Teacher Williams used this kind of follow-up session after a social studies project in which each group invented and constructed a game. This account of one group's interaction conveys the give-and-take spirit of the game-making enterprise:

> One group of four boys decided to make a racetrack. Each chose to concentrate on one aspect such as the track, the spinner, or the race cars. Eric liked the idea of using a tic-tac-toe board. The other three vetoed that as the main idea for a game, but agreed that if he made it, they would "use it somehow." Treavor added, "I know, it can be in the center, and we'll have to win at that before we can enter the starting gate!" Eric beamed. Jimmy suggested the name "Blackjack" for the game. "Like gambling," said Dean, "maybe we can make bets on our race cars!" "Yeah, but let's not use real money," said Treavor. "Okay," said Dean, and added, "Blackjack— that's real tough!"

The teacher was impressed by the mutual respect displayed within this group and by their effort to integrate and build on each other's ideas. "They were extremely pleased by the outcome," she wrote, "and each was eager to point out his contribution." During the evaluation meeting, the teacher gathered all the groups together to discuss and reflect on their experience:

Teacher: How did we cooperate?

Ray: It's like the Wright Brothers. They worked together and stuck it out until they finally made an airplane.

Teacher: Do you all agree with Ray?

Eric: It's true, we worked together.

Teacher: And for what?

Mike: To understand better.

Amy: To get something done—our game.

John: Another example is that puzzle over there [pointing to a jigsaw on the table]. One person just can't go over and put it together. People get stuck, and they need other people to put it together, too.

> Kim: And if you work together, you get done faster!
>
> Teacher: I see, so it's like the old saying, "Two heads are better than one!"

After this meeting, the teacher observed that "the children are now looking at the class as a functional group. Each person has become an integral part, each depending on the others to obtain a common goal." Follow-up discussions, like the one above, not only are a measure of a group's growing solidarity but also contribute to it. They give the class a chance to celebrate its cooperative success. Just as important, they make public and explicit the meanings of the shared experience, the insights gained, and the lessons learned. Raising important learning into consciousness is essential, since all of us in T. S. Eliot's phrase can "have the experience but miss the meaning."

The evaluation meeting serves another important function, one that is especially critical in the early stages of cooperative work: helping students identify problems they may have had in working together. Kathy Rogers used a small-group evaluation meeting to find the trouble spots in a group of her first-graders. She had given them a measurement activity where their task was to (1) decide which three things to measure; (2) decide how to measure (they had a string, part of an egg carton, and straws); and (3) decide who would record the information. The teacher observed that not all members of the one group had participated actively, and when the group finished its task, she initiated the following conversation with them:

> Teacher: Did you have any problems working together?
>
> Joe: Yeah, Troy didn't want to measure the first three things.
>
> Teacher: So how did you decide on what to measure?
>
> Joe: We found something he wanted to measure and everybody else said yes.
>
> Teacher: Troy, why didn't you want to measure the first three things?
>
> Troy: They were too long [pointing out, for example, that they couldn't reach the top of the door].
>
> Teacher: Is there anyone in the group who didn't work together?
>
> Group: No.

Teacher: Was there anyone who did all the work?

Veronica: Yeah.

Teacher: Who?

Joe: We each had a chance to draw this, three of us.

Teacher: Three drew on paper?

Troy: I didn't.

Veronica: I didn't.

Joe: Three of us did, I know that!

"Joe kept insisting that three of the people helped to do the work," the teacher commented, "but actually Joe and Mike did it all. Troy and Veronica let Joe know during our discussion that they did not get a chance. Joe would not accept this. Finally, I said that perhaps tomorrow, when they measured three things outdoors, the group could try to cooperate more so that everyone would feel a part of the activity."

The next day, when the class was measuring outside, the teacher kept an eye on the same group. "This time Joe was trying to include all in the work, though he still assumed the leadership role." At the end of the activity, the teacher approached this group for a brief evaluation of their second effort:

Teacher: How was it working in a group today?

All: Good!

Joe: Everybody got to do something, right?
[appealing to the group for agreement].
Troy, you got to do something, and Veronica
and Mike did, too.

Troy: Yeah!

This group improved quickly as a result of its first evaluation session; others may take longer. But even if children do not have any difficulty cooperating, they stand to benefit on several levels from the evaluation meeting. It offers an opportunity for the kind of reflection that Dewey regarded as essential for wresting the full value from an educational experience. It enables students to analyze how they worked together, to bask in the glow of their collective achievements, to learn from their mistakes, and to grow in their ability and desire to engage in cooperative endeavor.

Strategy 4: Use the Group to Identify and Reinforce Cooperation

Gloria Norton, a kindergarten teacher, describes how she used group discussion to highlight examples of cooperative behavior and to give children public recognition for such actions. She began with a class meeting, hoping that their recent unit on "Community Helpers" would help the children define what it means to cooperate.

> Teacher: Think of people who cooperate. Who can give an example?
>
> Betty: Firemen cooperate.
>
> Brian: So do policemen.
>
> Matthew: So does the emergency squad.
>
> Teacher: How do all of those people cooperate?
>
> Betty: By working together.
>
> Teacher: And why is it important for them to work together?
>
> Tracy: If firemen didn't work together, the people would get burned up.
>
> Jason: Policemen work together to catch crooks and put them in jail.

The class agreed on this definition of cooperation: "People working together to do something." At the end of the meeting before free play began, the teacher said to the children, "Watch to see if people in our room do something that is cooperating."

When free play and "pick up" were over, Teacher Norton gathered the children into a circle once again and initiated this discussion:

> Teacher: Remember our discussion of cooperation? Who noticed someone cooperating during "free play" or "pick up"?
>
> Betty: Ruth and I worked together to put the shapes back in the bucket.
>
> Teacher: Ruth and Betty cooperated by putting the shapes back in the bucket together. Betty, did you see someone else cooperating?
>
> Betty: Yes, I saw Jonah, Brian, and Jason put away the puzzles together.

Teacher: Jonah, Brian, and Jason cooperated during
pick-up time by putting away puzzles. Let's
show Betty and Ruth, and Jonah, Brian,
and Jason that we appreciate their work by
applauding them. [The five children stood
as the group applauded and appeared very
pleased.] Brian, did you see someone
cooperate?

"Brian responded as the others had," the teacher reports, "and
I continued in a linking fashion, asking the person who was mentioned
for cooperating if he could in turn identify someone else. My thought
was that children would be more likely to mention someone else's
cooperation if they themselves had just felt the warmth of group
praise."

The teacher continued to use this linking strategy in class meetings held each day for about five minutes after cleanup time. "To
close the meeting," she says, "the children even added a group
cheer: 'It-sure-feels-great-to-co-operate!'"

What was the effect of all this on the children's day-to-day
behavior? The teacher made observations over a three-week period.
"prior to my research," she says, "I rarely heard comments such as
'Richard and Kevin picked up the block corner—it looks good.' Now
I hear about five to ten comments like that not only during pick-up
time but throughout the day. These comments show that the children are aware of community—aware of each other and their contributions to the group."

Another yardstick of this emerging sense of community was
the children's participation at pick-up time. "Before the group discussions of cooperation," the teacher says, "there were nine people
who consistently did very little to help. By the end of three weeks,
three of these people became full participants, four participated more
frequently, and only two remained reluctant to help." Interestingly,
one little girl who had helped some of the time before the class
emphasis on cooperation made a clear point of not ever helping after
cooperation became a class theme. With a strongly independent
child, the teacher needs to find a way to support the child's autonomy
while at the same time inducing the child to enter into cooperative
participation: for example, "Everyone must do her fair share to help
with clean-up, Laura, but I can see that you wish to choose your own
way of helping. Let me know in a few minutes the special way that
you've decided to help today."

"On the basis of my research," Teacher Norton concluded,
"I have seen how the clearly expressed goals of the group can become
in almost every case, the goals of the individual. I learned I feel

much better when I'm not continually enforcing the rules ('It's time
to pickup'). Group reinforcement proved much more effective
than teacher reinforcement had ever been. The children wanted their
friends to notice what they were doing to cooperate, and as a result,
they became more aware of their membership in the group."

Is this kind of growth of the group achieved at the expense of
individual development? This teacher did not see it that way. Rather,
she saw the group as a support structure for individual growth: "It
seems to me that children feel more personal strength when they
are part of a group. They become more willing to contribute when
the emphasis is on what they do contribute rather than on what they
don't. The group structure is especially helpful, I believe, to the
child who lacks an internal locus of control."

What about this teacher's use or reinforcement as a means to
achieve her goals? Moral educators tend to flinch at the idea of reinforcement, linked as it is to a technology that commonly seeks to
manipulate behavior rather than to develop the person. To reject
reinforcement altogether as a tool for moral education, however, is
to ignore the fact that in life we are always reinforced for something.
The important questions are, What kinds of reinforcers are being
used and For what ends? Gloria Norton used positive peer feedback
to develop her children's ability to cooperate. And once again, with
the help of the right environmental conditions, children who are
usually characterized in the developmental literature as prisoners of
their egocentrism demonstrated that they could indeed take significant steps toward cooperative morality.

Another teacher, Debbie Wilcox, found group reinforcement to
be highly effective in promoting cooperation among her fifth-graders.
She instituted a practice called "Appreciation Time," a short session
at the end of the day when class members could tell about something
that another had done that they appreciated. At one meeting, for
example, one girl said, "I appreciate Julie for loaning me some
paper when I forgot mine. All I did was say I didn't have any, and
there was Julie offering me some of hers." Another girl said, 'I'd
like to appreciate Martha for helping me study for my spelling test.
That was the first time I ever got 100!" Teacher Wilcox reports that
"Appreciation Time has become the most popular thing we do. If I
ever forget it, the children are sure to remind me." An activity
like Appreciation Time not only fosters mutual helping among classmates but also provides many opportunities for them to practice an
important social skill: giving and receiving positive feedback. When
people are able to give and receive positive feedback, their ability to
cooperate successfully is greatly enhanced.

Strategy 5: Provide Opportunities for Work in Pairs

Many teachers think that paired activity, a smaller social
unit, is the easiest way to begin. Assigning children an academic
task to work on with a partner is also a good way to begin integrating
cooperation into the regular school curriculum. Debby Boyes, a
third-grade teacher, shares her first experiment with paired learning:

> I gave each pair of children a record sheet with measur-
> ing activities on it. All of the questions revolved
> around the children themselves and their playground:
> How far can you jump on the sidewalk? How far
> apart can you spread your feet? How high can you
> reach on the building? How long is the teeter-
> totter? I suggested that when one partner jumped,
> the other mark off the leap with chalk, and that
> way they could measure each other's jumps,
> stretches, and so on. So, off we trooped, armed
> with record sheets, chalk, rulers, and ourselves,
> to the playground.
>   The children jumped and measured their hearts
> out. They were laughing, relaxed, and extremely busy.
> Those who got mixed up on their measuring were
> helped by their partner or another twosome. They
> agreed, argued, rechecked their calculations, and
> looked to me with a lot of pride in their eyes.

This teacher observed a side benefit of cooperative learning
that secondary, as well as elementary, teachers have reported:
a marked increase in students' enthusiasm for the task at hand.
Writes teacher Boyes: "The forty-five minute period flew by.
Where I once struggled to keep the children's minds on their work,
that day I heard groans when it was time to stop. On the way into
school, Jennifer looked up at me and said, 'That was so much fun,
Miss Boyes. We didn't do any work today!' The truth of the matter
was they had worked more and understood better in that one period
than they usually did in an entire week."

Working outdoors on a concrete activity surely contributed to
the children's enjoyment of the measuring but so, the teacher believed, did their collaboration as partners. A ninth-grade English
teacher in an inner-city school offers a clue to explain why collaboration increases the appeal of a task: "I thought my students had an
attention span of about five minutes," he said, "until I started having
them work in pairs. When they had a partner, they could go the

whole period and still stay on task." Teachers say there are times, especially with some students, when partners can distract each other from the job to be done. But on the whole, working in pairs helps to focus attention and thus to sustain it.

Strategy 6: Extend Cooperative Learning throughout the Curriculum

Debby Boyes's cooperative measuring project, combining moral development with mathematics, suggests an answer to the teacher who asks, How can I make time for social-moral education when I have trouble getting through the basic skills curriculum as it is? Strategy 6 goes a step further and challenges us to take the whole academic curriculum as a vehicle for developing cooperation. How to do this is described by Sister Paul Barno, a Catholic nun teaching in a parochial school. She began with the premise that "there are no skills more important to a human being than the skills of cooperative interaction" and set out to provide opportunities for students to work together throughout the school day.

In science children worked in pairs to construct and balance mobiles: "One would hold the stick while the other balanced it, sliding the string closer to or further from the center. If a pair had great difficulty, a third person offered help or suggestions on how to make it balance easier." In art murals quickly became a favorite project. Children working in a group first had to decide what they would illustrate. Then, some would draw together, while others preferred to separate their sections initially and later blend them with the drawings of the others. In another art project, children designed and decorated a quiet "Meditation Corner" for the room.

The crowning cooperative achievement came in social studies where the whole class collaborated on a unit on Mexico as their contribution to the school's "Festival of Many Lands." The teacher writes:

> The children were excited to work on this project. They eagerly settled into their tasks, were able to talk out most disagreements, and objected if one person tried to take over. As they worked on maps, charts, and displays of people, places, and things, it was enlightening for me to hear them discuss new points of view, reconsider their own, and alter their first opinion.
>
> The fruit of our labors included an enriching day on which many parents joined us as we discussed what we learned, danced, ate tacos, and broke piñatas. The children were able to view their efforts on TV and in the

newspapers. More than this, we all felt a new unity
among us that this cooperative experience had made
possible. One tangible result was the change in a
little boy who had not been well-accepted before. His
mother is a Mexican. Eddie, who rarely offered answers
in class, participated readily in this project. He in-
structed us in life in Mexico, since he had visited
there. On the final day of the project, his family came
in with Mexican gems and silver, and Eddie proudly
wore a toreador's costume made by his mother's hand.

Under this teacher's skillful guidance, cooperative learning
became the medium for another kind of moral education that teachers
often find difficult: helping children learn to accept those who are
different and to value those differences. Curriculum content alone
will not necessarily bring about this kind of attitude change in children. Sister Paul succeeded in generating mutual respect among her
children, I think, because she combined the content of her unit on
Mexico with the process of cooperative learning. Social studies became social development.

The projects I have described thus far depict the teacher as the
careful choreographer of cooperative learning—setting the stage,
assigning the task, and monitoring the outcome. This sort of
teacher-structured interactive learning is a core component of the
cooperative curriculum, but it is not the only kind of cooperation that
can and should occur in a classroom. If a teacher primes the pump
through structured tasks and otherwise fosters a climate for cooperation, many students will spontaneously work together when allowed to
do so. Ann Caren recounts a month-long activity, dubbed the
Dinosaur Project, that was entirely initiated and sustained by her
second- and third-graders:

One boy brought a bag of plastic dinosaurs to school
and decided to set up a scene. Other boys soon
contributed their dinosaurs. Questions arose:
Where did dinosaurs live? When did they live?
What did they eat? After looking all this up in
books, the children set up one ice-age environment
and one woodland and field environment with a large
body of water. For materials they used twigs,
rocks, grasses, and sand gathered from the school
grounds. The children made charts illustrating
different ages, and did many dinosaur drawings and
paintings. Endless discussions took place about

which dinosaurs were the oldest and where the various
types lived.

Teacher Caren recommends stocking the environment with
materials— "blocks, lincoln logs, lego, animals, plants, clay, scrap
materials, and pletny of paper and pencils—that naturally stimulate
children to work together on activities that are meaningful to them."
Crafts are especially good; one boy learned how to macrame and
taught other children how to do it for three straight days.

Strategy 7: Provide Opportunities for Students to Teach Each Other

Peer teaching, which often occurs spontaneously when the environment encourages it, can be used as a deliberate strategy for
fostering cooperation. The excellent book Children Teach Children
(Gartner, Kohler, and Riessman 1971) documents that children-
teaching-children is an idea with a long history and proved benefits.
In addition to enhancing the ego development of the children who teach,
it changes the school from a place where students must always compete against each other for good grades to one where they can help
each other succeed.

Children-teaching-children can take many forms: an older
student tutoring a younger one; a child who is strong in a skill or subject helping a classmate who is not; or a student serving as teacher
of a small group or the entire class. A way to help students step into
the role of teacher of the whole class is described by Mary Hogan.
She established "Hobby Time," a period each day when one of her
second-graders could teach the rest of the class how to do something.
Children were eager to sign up for their turn. Hobbies that were
taught included drawing, making a crocheted rope, magic tricks,
knot-tying, fortune-telling, making God's eyes, collecting shells,
and potting a plant. Writes teacher Hogan: "I learned that students can be great teachers, and that children give their undivided
attention when one of their own is teaching or helping them. The
peer teacher even went around and gave suggestions on how to improve an individual child's attempt at the teacher's hobby. What an
ego booster it was for a child to be able to teach others something he
could do."

Some hobbies, like making God's eyes or fortune-telling, proved
to be difficult for a child to explain. In those cases, the teacher
gently assisted, careful not to upstage the peer instructor. After all
the children had had their turn, the teacher reflected that the next
time she undertook this project with a class, she would ask the group
for a constructive critique of each child's performance "in order to

help the child know what he did well and what he could improve on. "
That kind of supportive group feedback to the individual adds another
dimension of cooperation to the peer teaching experience.

When the children have the opportunity to teach each other, they
enter into a vital kind of helping relationship. Within that relationship,
they can feel a measure of responsibility for the welfare of another,
an attitude that is at the psychological center of cooperative morality.
That being a teacher does indeed heighten a child's general sense of
responsibility to others was the finding of an elegant little study by
Staub, Leavy, and Shortsleeves (1974). These researchers taught
fifth- and sixth-grade girls how to make their own puzzles. Half of
these children then practiced by themselves what they had learned,
while half taught puzzle making to a second-grade girl. A week later,
when given the chance to write letters to hospitalized children, those
girls who had been teachers wrote significantly more letters than
those girls who had not been teachers. That helping another child make
a puzzle could increase compassion for hospitalized children is a
hopeful indication that children can develop a morality of cooperation
that transcends specific situations.

A growing number of schools have incorporated cross-age teaching into their programs. Students who teach younger children are
reported to gain in their self-esteem, interest in school, and ability
to cooperate with their classmates (Gartner, Kohler, and Riessman
1971). Student participation in teaching should not stop with cross-
age tutoring, however, since the opportunities for peer teaching within
the individual classroom are endless. Students can help each other
with homework, study for a test together, correct each other's work,
counsel each other on a problem, or share a special skill. Students
should move frequently between the roles of teacher and learner;
being the teacher should certainly not be a privilege limited to the
academically bright. Every child has something he can teach another,
and every child has a right to the uniquely valuable experience of helping another person learn. What is more, all children have a need for
the bonds of caring and community that such experience creates.

Strategy 8: Use Cooperative Test Taking

One of my favorite examples of cooperative learning comes from
a junior high school home economics teacher, Sylvia Cole. She was
the first teacher to take seriously my suggestion that students should
not only study together but should also take at least some of their
tests together.

This teacher decided to give team testing a try with a class of
ninth-grade girls. She gave each student a test paper but explained

that she would accept only one paper from each pair. They could discuss answers and were to agree on the one answer to each question that they wanted to appear on their joint paper. The teacher describes what followed:

> The girls immediately spread out into different areas
> of the room. Only one pair, however, began openly
> discussing the questions as a way of arriving at
> agreed-upon answers. In the other pairs, each girl
> worked independently on her own paper. After about
> ten minutes, these girls began to slide their test
> papers across the table so the other could read what
> was written. Later, they would point to questions
> and answers, still without saying anything. Finally,
> they succeeded in communicating openly. One pair,
> however, had become such expert cheaters that I was
> never aware of their collaborating during the test!
> They relied upon their old means of communication
> and were very pleased with their combined answers.

When the test was completed, the teacher says, "The girls were happy and excited. They asked how soon I could have the papers corrected. Usually they don't even care if they are returned!"

To elicit the students' feelings about the team testing, Sylvia Cole asked them three questions: (1) How did you feel as you took the test? (2) How would you feel if your partner had not known any of the answers but still would be given the same grade as you? and (3) How would you feel if you had not known any of the answers but your partner had known them all? Their responses to these questions, the teacher says, reflected strong agreement. They were not sure if it was "exactly fair" for the partner who knew nothing to receive the same grade, but they reasoned she may have learned something from the experience. If they were responsible for teaching her some information, then that was "OK." If, however, they had been the one who knew nothing on the test, they agreed it would be so embarrassing that they would definitely study harder for the next one.

"One girl," the teacher continued, "mentioned that working together eliminated all desire to cheat. I asked if that desire was strong on other tests, and she replied that it certainly was. Then everyone in the class began talking at once about how they usually cheated on all tests. I asked if they felt cheating was right and they all agreed it was not, that they felt guilty, but that they would probably continue to cheat in all subjects!" The candid revelations of these girls are consistent with what dozens of empirical studies have shown: on any given examination, even at the college level, most of the students, if given the opportunity, will cheat (Burton 1976).

Fascinated with the results of her first experiment, the teacher was curious to see what would happen when she tried team testing with a group of seventh-graders. One difference was striking: unlike the ninth-graders, the younger students immediately paired off and openly discussed their answers to the test questions. Their natural cooperative tendencies were still quite close to the surface. Like their older counterparts, the seventh-graders said they "loved taking a test this way and wanted to know how soon they could have another! During the test, one girl who had an excuse to leave early to go to the nurse actually asked if she could stay to work on the answers some more."

These experiences led this teacher to decide that cooperative test taking deserved a permanent place in her classroom. She intended to use individual testing as well but came to see that working with a partner on a test had both social and intellectual benefits for her students. She added, "When I decided to try team testing, I was not a believer. The results I experienced completely surprised me. The atmosphere was absolutely electrifying."

Strategy 9: Use Class or Community Meetings to Develop a Sense of Collective Responsibility

All of the strategies thus far discussed contribute in some way to a sense of community in a classroom, to a feeling of being part of a larger whole. In particular, many of them develop a feeling of interdependence and mutual responsibility. The next strategy, the class or community problem-solving meeting, is in my judgment the most powerful way to crystallize feelings of community and interdependence into a clear sense of collective responsibility.

Collective responsibility means that one person's problem, one person's suffering, is everybody's problem. It is an idea that gains expression in the belief that we are only as free as the least free among us and that when one person's dignity is demeaned, we are all demeaned. It gains expression in all metaphors, secular or religious, that assert the brotherhood of man.

In moral education, collective responsibility means all of the students share with the staff the responsibility for the quality of life and learning in the school. The class or community meeting can institute this kind of shared responsibility by presenting to the group problems that can be seen as community issues. When, for example, a girl in Kohlberg's Just Community High School had her pocketbook and $15 stolen, other students at first wanted to deal quickly with the

incident by making a rule about the consequences of stealing if you
were caught. Not satisifed with this, the staff used the community
meeting to help the students see that they had a responsibility, as a
community, to help prevent such theft and to compensate the victim
of such behavior. A collection was subsequently proposed and taken
up by the students, and the girl was reimbursed for her loss.

One of my sons, a sixth-grader, recently underwnet the harrass-
ment that children frequently experience as newcomers to a school.
A teacher can attempt to avoid such situations by calling a class meeting and putting the challenge to the group, "How can we help new
students feel at home here? What can each of us do to help them feel
part of the class?"* Even young children can respond to this kind of
appeal. Nell Woodmancy, a kindergarten teacher, found, in fact, that
her children listened and communicated best in their circle meetings
when she posed this question: "Who has a problem they would like
other people to help them solve?" All the discussion then focused
on the one child's problem until a solution was reached.

How collective responsibility works in a classroom is illustrated
by the following transcript of a class meeting conducted by Kathy
Rogers with her first-graders. When six of them complained that
class meetings were "too boring," she invited them to bring up
problems they would like to discuss, and the whole class would help
to work out a solution.

> Mark: My problem is I don't have any place to
> park my bike because the bike rack is
> full.
>
> Teacher: You feel bad because the bike rack is full
> when you get to school in the morning.
>
> Mark: Yes, and if you leave your bike on the grass,
> Mr. Bashaw [the principal] will get mad
> and take it away.
>
> Teacher: Well, we certainly don't want to lose our
> bikes. How can we help solve Mark's
> problem?
>
> Kevin: Let's build another bike rack.

---

*I would like to thank Lawrence Kohlberg for this suggestion as
well as for other helpful comments about the ideas expressed in this
chapter.

Teacher: Could we build a bike rack?

Joe: No, it's made of metal. But maybe my Dad [the school janitor] could build one.

Erin: Yeah, or we could give each kid a name where his bike goes.

Jeff: Maybe we could talk to Mr. Bashaw.

Robbie: All you got to do, Mark, is to come to school earlier!

Troy: I know, Mark, you could move someone else's bike and put yours there [laughing]!

Teacher: What do you think about that?

Robbie & Joe: No.

Teacher: Why not?

Robbie: It wouldn't be fair.

Teacher: Why wouldn't it be fair?

Troy: 'Cause if everyone moved someone else's bike, no one would be able to find their own bike.

Teacher: So how do you think we should solve Mark's problem?

Jeff: I still think we should go talk to Mr. Bashaw [followed by general agreement].

The teacher went to Mr. Bashaw on behalf of the children. Mr. Bashaw, to his credit, found out that the high school had an extra bike rack and had it moved to the elementary school. Mark's problem was thereby solved.

The teacher who uses the class meeting to develop a sense of collective responsibility teaches important skills as well: how to talk and listen in a group, how to reach group decisions, and how to cooperate with the teacher as the moral leader of the group. Children are no longer condemned, in Piaget's phrase, "to wage war against authority." The teacher remains the moral authority—the person who holds the group accountable to the standard of fairness—but through the class meeting joins the students in a genuine partnership to ensure the welfare of all. Students who experience that kind of creative cooperation with a teacher learn a way of relating to and using authority that can serve them the rest of their lives.

Strategy 10: Teach the Behavioral Skills Required for Cooperative
Interaction

As teachers will attest, class meetings do not necessarily improve the moral atmosphere of a classroom. Done badly, they can
even worsen it. If students interrupt, put each other down, or otherwise demonstrate disrespect for each other as persons, the class
meeting can be a moral setback for both students and teacher. That
is why it is crucial in undertaking this kind of meeting to have the
group agree at the outset on rules for good talking and listening and a
system for enforcing them. In the early stages of class meetings, a
teacher's major goal is to firmly establish such rules for communication and to help students develop habits of listening and speaking with
respect for others.

Any form of cooperation requires communication skills. When
students lack such skills, as they often do, it falls to the teacher to
devise a way of teaching them, of helping students practice the specific competencies they lack. Stressing the importance of good communication in the class meeting and reinforcing it when it occurs are
helpful strategies, but they are often not enough. A second-grade
teacher, Peggy Manring, tells what she did when mere exhortation
failed to improve the behavior of a group of children whose social
relations had steadily deteriorated. There had been a rash of fist
fights, pencil jabbings, and kickings; making children aware of their
behavior had not decreased such actions but only increased tattling.
The teacher reports:

> I brought in a bag of wood scraps from the local toy
> factory. There were cubes, rectangles, wedges,
> and slivers. I dumped these on the rug within
> everyone's reach, and asked the children to make
> a model of the classroom, working as a group.
> I tried to focus on their skills in cooperation as
> these became a problem. Here is an excerpt
> from the dialogue that took place:
>
> David: That is the dumbest chalkboard, Martha.
>   You put it in a stupid place.
>
> Teacher: David, you think Martha should put the
>   block in a different place. Would you
>   like to suggest to her where she might
>   put it?
>
> David: Yeah, right there! The chalkboard is
>   behind the table.

Teacher: Martha, if you accept David's suggestion, you may move your block. If you like it where you put it, you may leave it right there. [to David] When you don't use the words "stupid" and "dumb," people like to listen to you. You had an interesting point to make about the chalkboard.

Martha moved the block, smiled at David, and the next time David wanted to say something, he said, "Paul, I suggest you look where the art table is. It's parallel to the teacher's desk," Paul picked up on the "I suggest"; so did Eddie and Alan—all three volatile kids. All eighteen children seemed to be stretching to cooperate. Several said, "You know, Mrs. Manring, we've been trying to cooperate for eighteen turns" and "It feels pretty good here, even though we're having a little trouble."

After 30 minutes in the circle and many compliments from her, teacher Manring reports, the children parted to play in groups of two, three, or four. "They built amazing cities, parks, and buildings. I stayed to keep my finger on a few pulses. Some rejection and a few tears, but no one gave up."

This teacher used a direct, didactic approach to skill development—giving children the words to say ("I suggest") that evoke a cooperative response in another. One such intervention turned out not to be enough, however, and it rarely is. Interpersonal skills are as slow to develop as any other skills, if not considerably slower, and require practice in many situations. They are also as basic to human functioning as any other skills, and a movement that ignores them does so at its peril.

Strategy 11: Use Competition in a Way That Supports Cooperation

Whenever I speak to groups about a curriculum for cooperation, people ask, "What about competition? Does it have any place in the classroom or school, or are you ruling it out?" Competition is not evil in a cooperative moral environment, any more than individual work is. Indeed, with a little thought, one can see that competition—as in a game played for mutual enjoyment according to agreed-upon rules—can itself be a form of cooperation.

The relevant question is, What kind of competition? As we all know, there are many ways to compete, some of which are immoral and antithetical to a cooperative ethic and some of which are not.

One can, for example, seek to humiliate one's opponent in defeat, or one can seek to preserve his dignity. I urge teachers to foster a kind of competition that contributes to, rather than detracts from, the cooperative ethos of the classroom or school. There are different ways to do this; one of them is described by Toni Romano, a fourth-grade teacher.

Here is the scene: her children come bursting into the classroom after gym, flushed with the triumph of winning the soccer championship against the toughest class in the school. The teacher's first thought is "How can I settle them down?" Then she remembers her goal of fostering cooperation and community. She says to the class, "It's obvious that you won—congratulations! How does winning make you feel?" A roar goes up. The teacher waits for the din to subside, then asks, "How do you think the losing team feels?" Another cacophony of sounds, these appropriate to the agonies of defeat. The teacher's next question: "What can we do to help the other team feel better?"

After some discussion, the class decided to send complimentary letters to the losing team. "In groups of five the children tried to think of good things that happened in the game besides the final score. Each group had a secretary to record their remarks." Here are the letters written by three of the groups:

> We think that both classes played fair, and all
> played well. Melissa blocked good kicks. Gretchen
> was a good goalie and tried hard. All of Patricia's
> headballs were in the right direction. The rest of
> the class played a good game. All were good sports.
> [Group 1]
>
> It was really fun to challenge your class. Your
> goalie was terrific and so were all your players.
> You had a real good chance to win. Most of our
> goals were made by penalty shots, and they usually
> aren't caught. So you can't help that. Remember,
> soccer isn't everything in the world, and you always
> have more chances.
>
> > Heather
> > Tracey
> > Chris
> > Sharon
>
> P.S. Just remember, you are in second place.
> [Group 2]
>
> Thank you for not calling us cheaters for winning.
> You made a nice team to challenge. We are sorry

you didn't win, but we do hope we can play you again
sometime.

> Steve
> Lonnie
> Tina [Group 5]

The teacher then suggested that the children might deliver the
letters personally and read them to the losing class. The class agreed
to this, and one person from each group volunteered to read the
letters.

"My children came back bewildered," teacher Romano reports.
These were some of their comments:

> Steve: Jeff shook my hand as I was leaving the
> room! That's a switch!

> Lonnie: They really liked the letters. I'm glad
> we made them feel better.

> Heather: Mrs. Romano, Jodie had tears in her eyes!

"The whole atmosphere in our room changed," the teacher
says. "The children were very proud of what they had done. I feel
sure they are richer because of this experience."

This teacher helped her children recognize that they and the
losing team really had a common need: to feel good about the game
they played. She helped them achieve that empathic insight and then
act upon it in a way that fostered goodwill and mutual respect between
the two teams. In so doing, she infused competition with the spirit
of cooperation. With an eye to the right opportunity, any other teacher
can do as much.

Strategy 12: Foster Altruistic Cooperation

Some of the foregoing strategies foster cooperation that serves
the immediate mutual interests of the cooperators (as when students
take a test together or work together on a project). Other strategies
foster cooperation that involves helping another (as when one student
teaches another, or the class helps an individual member solve a
problem) with the expectation that the help-giver will eventually receive similar help in return. Different from both of these, however,
is a third kind of cooperation: working together to help someone without the expectation of reciprocity (as when the fourth-grade soccer
champions helped the losing team feel pride despite defeat). This
form of helping takes cooperation beyond the boundaries of self-
interest and into the realm of altruism.

Patti Brody, a second-grade teacher, describes how she and her class came to be involved in altruistic cooperation. She had been working on fostering other kinds of cooperative activity for several weeks. The children had met regularly in class meetings to solve problems and make the classroom a good place for everyone to be. They had worked together on a class play. These orchestrated activities had had spin-offs in the form of spontaneous cooperation on the playground, as when the boys and the girls played together for the first time and built a marvelous snow fort.

Then one day the teacher read the class a story about a man who lived in a circle of love. When he asked another person to come into this circle, the person refused. Instead of being hurt or discouraged, the man said, "Well, if you won't come into my circle of love, I'll just have to make it bigger so it will go around you!" "This gave me a wonderful idea," the teacher says, "for stimulating cooperation and moral development." She relates what happened next:

> I asked the children if they would like to be in a club. They responded with applause, so at a class meeting we set up our club. After much brainstorming and voting, we named it "The Love Circle." We made badges out of circles with the word LOVE in the center. On the opposite side of the badge, each person wrote one way he or she promised to help the club in the way they lived, and shared this with a partner.
>
> Each month we try to think up a special way to enlarge our love circle. This month it is putting on a play for the people in the nursing home down the road from our school. We are also being "Secret Pals" for each other until Christmas. Each day we do something nice for our Secret Pal without anyone seeing it.

Did this teacher's efforts to foster golden-rule morality really "take" with her class? She thinks it did. She observed a greater sensitivity in the children toward each other's needs. This was most evident, she says, in their attitude toward one boy who had been somewhat of an outcast.

> This boy is very poor and not always clean when he comes to school. In the beginning of the year, he was the butt of many jokes and comments. Now I have seen a change. It isn't always daily, but it is coming. I saw one boy, Matt, helping this poor boy with his math.

No one had asked him to. He was even sitting in the
seat with him. It really brought tears to my eyes.
I had almost given up on anyone's being nice to this
child. But other children have noticed Matt's effort,
and now this boy has almost become the center of
attention in our room. If he's missing a pencil or
something else he needs, someone is right there to
help out. If he doesn't let me know himself about a
problem he's having, someone else will. They
truly are becoming a group of caring and concerned
children.

At the secondary level, altruistic cooperation can take the form
of citizen action—students studying and then attempting to ameliorate
a real social problem such as vandalism, pollution, hardships of the
elderly, or unfair business practices toward the poor (see Newmann
[1971] for examples of projects like these). Whatever form it takes,
and whether it goes on within the school or in the larger community,
altruistic cooperation has an important place in the moral curriculum. Perhaps more than anything else, it develops a disinterested
concern for the common good—a caring about the needs of others
without the worry about what is in it for me.

COOPERATION AND MORAL STAGE DEVELOPMENT

How does cooperative moral education contribute to moral stage
development* as described by Piaget (1965), Kohlberg (1976), Damon
(1977), and other developmentalists? It seems to me there are four
ways that cooperation stimulates progress through the stages of moral
reasoning. I think it important to spell these out, since I believe
development through the moral stages to be an important educational
goal in its own right. Further, I would like to dispel any notion that
education for cooperation is at odds with education for mature moral
reasoning. I believe that cooperation, far from being antithetical to
stage development, is in fact essential to it.
First, a "stage" is held to be a way of looking at the world that
is not implanted in the child by social agents but actively constructed

*For a full discussion of these issues in this volume, see
Chapters 12 and 13 by Scharf and Samson, respectively.

by the child as he interacts with and tries to make sense of his world. To move, for example, from Piaget's heteronomous moral stage—where the child does not grasp the social origin and function of moral rules—to Piaget's autonomous stage—where he does understand these things—the child must experience the need for morality. To understand why people must be honest, keep agreements, and help each other, he must learn firsthand, from his own social relationships and interactions, that these behaviors are necessary for people to be able to live together and get along.

Cooperative living and learning give students this opportunity to "construct morality" for themselves. Through class or community meetings, for example, they are able to create rules and solutions to problems. They are able to understand these social arrangements as just that—mutual agreements among people about how to organize their social life for the benefit of all. "Rules imposed by external constraint," Piaget (1965) wrote, "remain external to the child's spirit. Rules due to mutual agreement and cooperation, on the contrary, take root inside the child's mind" (p. 362). And again, "In the moral as in the intellectual realm, we really possess only what we have conquered ourselves" (p. 366).

In short, constructivism, the action of the mind on the environment, can be viewed as the force that keeps a person moving through the stages—toward a better understanding of the nature and purpose of morality. This constructivism is most fully called into play in a classroom or school where students work together to build an intellectual and moral community.

Second, development through the stages of moral reasoning can be considered a process of getting better and better at dealing simultaneously and fairly with conflicting perspectives on what is right in any given situation. It is, to use Piaget's term, a process of "decentering." Cooperation demands such decentering, because it necessarily involves people in comparing their ideas and coordinating their actions toward common ends. When students work on a project together, they must jointly decide what to do and how, and then carry out their plan. They must learn, as an English colleague aptly put it, "how to make a mesh of things."

Under the steady pressure of cooperation, Piaget believed, the child's natural egocentrism breaks down. "It is only through contact with the judgments and evaluations of others that this intellectual and affective anomie will gradually yield to the pressure of collective logical and moral laws" (p. 401). "Thanks to the mutual control which cooperation introduces, it suppresses both the spontaneous conviction that characterizes egocentrism and the blind faith in adult authority. . . . A new morality follows upon that of pure duty.

Obedience withdraws in favor of the idea of justice and mutual service, now the source of all obligations" (pp. 403-4).

In a similar vein, Kohlberg (1976) argues that development through his moral stages depends on opportunities for "role-taking"—"taking the attitude of others, becoming aware of their thoughts and feelings, putting oneself in their place" (p. 49). "The higher an individual child's participation in a social group or institution," he writes, "the more opportunities he has to take the social perspectives of others. . . . Not only is participation necessary, but mutuality of role-taking is also necessary" (p. 50). Cooperative moral education can be seen as an effort to maximize social participation and mutual role taking.

Studies of extreme environments bear out the importance of cooperation to moral stage development. "Of all the environments we have studied," Kohlberg reports, "the American orphanage had children at the lowest level, Stages 1 and 2, even through adolescence. Of all environments studied, an Israeli kibbutz had children at the highest level, with adolescents mainly at Stage 4 and with a considerable percentage at Stage 5" (p. 50). The U.S. orphanage, Kohlberg says, "involved very little communication and role-taking between staff adults and children. Relations among the children themselves were fragmentary, with very little communication and no stimulation or supervision of peer interaction by the staff. . . . In contrast, children in the kibbutz engaged in intense peer interaction supervised by a group leader who was concerned with bringing the young people into the kibbutz community as active dedicated participants. Discussing, reasoning, communicating feelings, and making group decisions were central everyday activities" (p. 50). To summarize, cooperative social interaction stimulates mutual perspective taking, and this in turn stimulates development through the moral stages.

Third, Rest (1979) maintains that Kohlberg's moral stages can be understood not only as ways to think about justice but also as ways to think about cooperation. Each stage, Rest says, provides a different answer to the question, What does it mean to cooperate? At Stage 1, to cooperate means to submit without understanding to the dictates of authority. At Stage 2, to cooperate means to be fair to those who are fair to you. At Stage 3, to cooperate means to live up to the ideal of a "good person" that is held by significant others and to practice golden-rule morality in one's interpersonal relations. At Stage 4, one cooperates not only in personal relations but also in a broader social context—by being a good citizen and a loyal member of one's social institutions. At Stage 5, the level of principled morality, one cooperates by keeping one's freely made social contracts and by helping to develop laws and institutions that maximize human welfare. If, indeed, the stages of moral reasoning are ways

of thinking about one's responsibilites to others, one's role in the
social network, then children and adolescents need social experiences
that make cooperation a salient theme, central to their moral consciousness.

The consciousness of cooperation, I think, is especially important at Kohlberg's postconventional level of morality. A postconventional thinker, at Stage 5 or 6, has rejected convention as a basis
for deciding what is right in favor of "self-chosen ethical principles"
such as justice and liberty (p. 35). Rejecting convention should not
means rejecting community, however, and moral autonomy should
not be confused with moral independence. Although these confusions
are not part of Kohlberg's theory, I think they are often part of
the moral psychology of individual persons. There is a dangerous
tendency at the post conventional levels for a subtle kind of moral
isolationism to set in. All of us know post conventional moral thinkers
whose lives bespeak detachment from the human community and its
problems. Cooperative moral education provides a strong antidote
to the very human and lifelong tendency to slip away from our social
responsibilities into the concerns of self.

And fourth, a final connection between cooperation and moral
stage development centers on the idea that conflict stimulates development. Kohlberg et al. (1975) hold that moral controversy or conflict
may stimulate developmental stage advance by calling into question the
adequacy of one's existing moral perspective. A colleague of Kohlberg
who believes that the role of the developmental educator is to "maximize conflict" cast a skeptical eye on my proposal for maximizing
cooperation. My response to his skepticism is that if you seriously
seek to increase cooperation in a classroom or school, you will also
increase conflict. Elsewhere (Lickona 1978), I have related the
experience of an elemetary-school teacher whose cooperative bean-
growing project came to a temporary halt when some partners found
their bean plants sabotaged by others. They met as a class to talk
about what had gone wrong, resolved the crisis, and went on to build
a greenhouse together for the school. This teacher's experience, and
that of others, indicates that when people work closely together for
very long, some degree of conflict is almost inevitable—a natural
by-product of the intensified interaction.

Teachers who set out to implement a curriculum for cooperation, therefore, need not worry about depriving their students of the
dose of conflict needed for optimal development of moral reasoning.
Moreover, the conflict that occurs when people are genuinely trying
to cooperate has a special value, since it occurs in a context that
tends to inspire conflict resolution in the direction of renewed
efforts to cooperate for the achievement of the common goal. Here
is another valuable moral lesson for students to learn: Even when

persons are in conflict, they can and should search out their common ground—what unites them as well as what divides them—and use that ground as a basis for resolving differences. In the absence of a governing cooperative ethic, conflict can easily become a regressive rather than a progressive influence on the social functioning of groups and the moral development and behavior of individuals.

THE RELATIONSHIP AND DIFFERENCE BETWEEN COOPERATION AND JUSTICE

"I see nothing moral about cooperation," said an educator who listened to my case for cooperative classrooms and schools "Two people can cooperate to slash my tires, or to murder me." One might add that people also cooperate to make war. Clearly, cooperation, to be good, must have a good or just end. In that sense, justice is the principle that regulates cooperation and gives it its moral meaning.

In a profound sense, however, a cooperative ethic goes beyond the requirements of justice as we ordinarily understand them. A justice ethic arises from and attempts to regulate individualism. It recognizes that as I pursue my individual interests and you pursue yours, these interests will sometimes conflict. In moral education, a current metaphor for this conflict-of-interests model of human affairs is the moral dilemma, in which one person's interests are typically pitted against another's. Heinz wants the drug in order to save his dying wife; the druggist wants to hold out for a higher price in order to maximize his profits. Justice is needed to arbitrate such conflicts, to see to it that everyone gets a fair shake—that no one is abused or exploited. In this sense, justice is a negative ethic, a limiting principle that protects us from each other.

A cooperative ethic, by contrast, is much more positive with a wider view of human affairs. It recognizes that we have vital common interests as well as conflicting ones. It sees individualism, even when regulated by justice, as inadequate. It says not only "Do not hurt" but also "Do help." It holds that we are obligated not merely to be fair to each other but also to take positive steps to cooperate in at least two ways: first, by identifying our common goals and, second, by working together to achieve them. One student offered this image: a justice ethic is what keeps you off my back; a cooperative ethic causes us to join hands.

A cooperative ethic asserts that our destinies are intertwined and we must see them so. It asserts with John Dewey that schools must "make ceaseless and intelligently organized effort to develop

above all else the will for cooperation" and that the goal of education
is to develop a "society of free individuals in which all, through their
own work, contribute to the liberation and enrichment of the lives of
others" (Dewey 1934, in Archambault 1964, pp. 12-13, emphasis
added).* It asserts that we need cooperative moral education if we
are to develop persons who can come together to build such a
society—to find ways to help people do meaningful work and lead
meaningful lives, to create and preserve life-enhancing environments,
to control and prevent war, to reduce the spiritual violence we do to
each other, and to work out the immense problem of wisely using the
scarce resources of a small planet. A cooperative ethic asserts,
finally, that to educate our children to cooperate is necessary to ensure the survival of humankind.

---

*For an excellent discussion of Dewey's ideas about democracy
as a cooperative enterprise and an account of a democratic alternative
high school project, see Chapter 6 by Ralph Mosher.

3

MORAL EDUCATION IN THE FAMILY

8
FAMILY STRUCTURE AND MORAL EDUCATION

Gail B. Peterson
Larry Peterson
Richard Hey

The family is a social group in which moral issues are raised and discussed frequently, and moral decisions are made every day. Family decisions reflect moral values and a family's particular style of reasoning, feeling, and acting. Family members decide and enforce a series of rules that govern their relationships. These rules may be overt—such as stating the time children are to return home from evening activities—or they may be covert—such as allowing only one particular person— (say, the father) to bring up important issues. These rules govern interaction, social order, and distancing among members and serve as the basis for family communication.

Family members struggle with many moral issues, such as fairness, sharing, respect, cooperation, growth toward self-awareness, and reciprocity. These issues are a part of the dynamic interaction among family members but are rarely focused on as ethical or moral concerns. Family life, and parenting in particular, involves making a great many decisions that affect other very vulnerable human beings. Families are in the business of making moral decisions and judgments, often without being aware of decisions being made or the impact of the decisions on themselves and other family members. We believe that family living is, in large measure, a series of moral choices made by, for, or among family members and that much of the family life can best be understood by examining a particular family as a set of persons, with each person viewing moral issues from a unique, sometimes conflicting, perspective.

In this chapter, we will focus on Kohlberg's model of stages of moral development in conjunction with some family development concepts to help explain how families function. Thomas Lickona's chapter (Chapter 10) offers parents specific ways to facilitate development of moral reasoning and behavior in children. As part of a practical approach to moral education, it is also important to raise questions that help gain insight into the institution most suited to facilitate the development of children and adults—the family. We hope this chapter raises such issues and questions, leading to some practical suggestions to enhance development.

MORAL DEVELOPMENT PSYCHOLOGY

Kohlberg's model of moral development is explicated by Samson (Chapter 13) and Scharf (Chapter 12) elsewhere in this volume. But to summarize briefly, Kohlberg contends that the capacity to reason about ethical concerns progresses through a series of invariant, sequential stages that are not specifically related to chronological age or stage of cognitive development. The stages include: Stage 0—total focus on fulfilling personal needs and desires, a stage that can characterize people as diverse as an infant and the classic sociopath; Stage 1—obedience and punishment oriented; Stage 2—utilitarian or "instrumental hedonist" orientation: Stage 3—"goodboy - nice girl" approval orientation; Stage 4—"law and order" - stability orientation; Stage 5—social contract - negotiation; and Stage 6—universal principles (Briskin 1975, Kohlberg 1969). An adult may function at Stage 0, as a sociopathic killer, or at Stage 6, like Gandhi, but more frequently will function in Stages 1 through 5. Chronological age and higher cognitive development are necessary but not sufficient conditions of higher moral development. A 30-year-old person who deals in formal operations all day may be a Stage 1 person in terms of reasoning about moral issues and social relationships. Family members, even as adults, may have differing capacities for complex reasoning about ethical issues.

THE FAMILY AS A SYSTEM

Families operate as social systems with each member, no matter how young or old, playing an important part in shaping the family structure. The organization and complexity of family life depend upon the number and the ages of persons in the group. A family consisting of husband and wife involves only one relationship to develop, and each member has only one other person to consult when making a decision. It is relatively easy to discuss and reflect upon a decision that affects only one other person. But if this couple had had six children and one of the adult's parents living with them, there would have been nine persons to consult and the interests of nine persons to think about when reflecting on the impact of a particular

decision. A woman deciding to work out of the home may have an
easier time deciding if she has only a husband to consult and consider
rather than a husband, a mother-in-law, and six children. Economi-
cally, it may be an easier decision for the second woman, but in terms
of examining the impact it could have, both positive and negative,
such a woman would be dealing with a much more complex set of
factors.

Family members are interdependent. This means that an
action on one person's part affects all other persons in the family.
In Peoplemaking , Satir (1972) compares this idea of interdependence among family members to being all tied together with
ropes around the waists. If one person moves, all the others feel the
pull. Families operate in a similar way, although the ties that bind
are invisible, psychological connections. Even when children have
grown up and are living hundreds of miles away from "home," if a
parent becomes ill and "pulls" on the psychological ropes, the children respond to the tension in the system by returning home or calling
home more frequently. Psychological ropes may be like loose elastic,
like clotheslines, or like metal pipes depending on the rigidity or
flexibility, or the distance or closeness, they create in family interaction. Some families allow a great deal of flexibility and independence
but yet remain close as if bound together with elastic. Other families
organize relationships as if the members were bound together with
pipes—that is, there is only one right way to act and members do not
become psychologically either close or distanced from each other.
These familieis may seem to be stuck in a rut. The "clothesline"
families are like most families in that they are somewhat flexible—able
to achieve both closeness and distance among members.

Most families are organized in ways that allow them to be capable
of flexibility and change. At the same time, families try to maintain a
balance in the system that does not easily allow either for rapid, sudden change or for changes in family members that violate family values
or family rules. Most families find change and transition to be somewhat stressful because each member needs to seek new ways to act
to adapt to the change. One such change may occur in families with a
newly dating adolescent. Each person in the system is affected by this
change of identity from "girl" to "young woman." This marker of
changing identity may be greeted with a certain amount of tension
until the new identity is recognized, established, and adapted to by
other family members. A father may tease his daughter or openly
disapprove of her choice of date; a sibling may threaten to reveal her
secrets to the date; or a mother may become involved in dating and
social etiquette tips. All these would be ways of indicating they
recognize a shift and are somewhat ambivalent about what it means
to the new dater and to themselves in relationship to her.

After the family adapts to the new role and concludes that it is one that is here to stay, they may simply ask where, when, and with whom she is going tonight. Families go through transitions whenever a family member reaches such an important marker.

Some of these markers are consistent among families and have been used as indicators of a family's stage in the family life cycle. Although family professionals use the term stage to designate separate time segments in a family's life, the term is not used in the same way as psychologists use it. A family stage is a period of time in the life of a nuclear family that is demarcated by marriage, birth of the first child, death of a spouse, and the chronological age of the first child:

Stage 1: Marriage, before children,
Stage 2: Birth of the first child through age 2 years,
Stage 3: Preschool,
Stage 4: School age,
Stage 5: Adolescent,
Stage 6: Launching families,
Stage 7: Empty nest (or freedom years), and
Stage 8: Retirement to death.

The stages are usually sequential but are not necessarily so. A couple may never have children but might go through career phases that affect family life as much as the presence of children. One may marry a spouse who already has children and start married life somewhere in Stages 2 through 6. One may leave a spouse with school-age children to marry a new spouse, thus moving from Stage 4 to Stage 1. The chronological age of the first child is the critical factor in determining family stage: although a child may not function at the level of a 13-year-old, if the child is 13, the family will be considered an "adolescent family" (Aldous 1978; Duvall 1971; Hill and Hansen 1969).

The family development framework points out that most families change over time in an orderly fashion—that families are not static social groups. The framework also points to periods of heightened tensions and stress during transitional periods. It suggests that the process of learning new roles, reacting to external pressure to assume new roles, and responding to internal cues for growth and change may all converge for an individual at one point and that families are similar in these critical transition points. For example, all families experience stress in the transition to parenthood because they are learning new roles and are adjusting to each other's playing new roles. These developmental transition points (Stages 1 through 8) may be anticipated and planned for by families. On the other hand, there are many other transition points and markers of changes in identities and family living arrangements, such as divorce, geographic relocation or occupational mobility. These are not predictable or sequential or experienced by all nuclear families; consequently, they are not markers of new stages in this framework, even though they are important family and individual indicators of change.

MORAL DEVELOPMENT IN THE FAMILY SYSTEM

When we use Kohlberg's moral stage model to examine family life, one of the first things we notice is the similarity of ages between those associated with important transitions for individual moral development and those associated with transition points for the family. From the list of family stages, we can see that the changes the oldest child goes through in the transition points of the family life cycle are closely related to the stages that both Piaget and Kohlberg indicate are periods of growing, changing, consolidating, and dramatic restructuring of the child's thought process and moral judgments. The internal maturation and new socially imposed normative expectations based on the child's chronlogical age seem to converge to create an optimal time for development. The child's struggle toward growth in turn creates changes in the entire family system. Each person learns to accommodate and adapt to the individual's change or finds a mechanism to impede the cognitive growth and maintain the established equilibrium. We have two separate theories, one of individual stage development and the other of family development, each indicating that there are critical points for persons and families that are similar. Individual growth affects families, and families affect an individual's ability to grow.

We have little research that addresses the issue of individual growth affecting family structure. It is difficult to complete longitudinal research that would allow a researcher to examine a family system when the oldest child is 10 years old and then compare that family when the child is 14 years old. In such long-term research, many other variables, such as physical, emotional, and social maturation, would need to be disentangled. It would be difficult to attribute the family change to any one particular change in the child. A series of studies have been completed that indicate that in a small group setting designed to enhance moral development, children do move into new stages of moral judgment. We are not aware of any research that examines how families react to the changes the children make as a result of these programs.

There has been much research completed on some of the family characteristics that create an environment that facilitates moral development. Moral development is enhanced when parents use democratic decision-making strategies (Peck and Havighurst 1960); when parents utilize inductive reasoning in controlling children's behavior (Hoffman and Saltzstein 1967; Holstein 1968; G. Peterson 1976; Schoffeitt 1971; when parents discuss moral issues for a longer period of time (Holstein 1968; G. Peterson 1976); when parents use a high level of support (G. Peterson 1976); and when parents themselves are postconventional (Holstein 1968; G. Peterson 1976). A supportive, nurturing environment in which parents explain rules to children or allow children to help establish family rules is related to increased levels of moral development. Perhaps the key factor here is that these parents allow a child to live in a safe environment: safe enough to explore possibilities and risk failure while being assured of remaining accepted and cared for by the family.

If we examine the family as a system that attempts to find a balance among members, we may see a group of individuals, each trying to convince others to reason as he or she does. We have some evidence that marital satisfaction is related to similarity of stages of moral development between spouses (Russell et al. 1975). Satisfaction is higher when, for example, a husband and wife are both conventional thinkers than when one is conventional and the other is either pre- or post-conventional. Cognitive style in reasoning about decisions involving social relationships and moral issues such as "fairness" seems to be important between spouses for maintaining satisfaction. Perhaps this balance is also a goal among parents and children, and parents encourage children to think as they do but inhibit growth if the child shows signs of moving beyond them. For example, a child with conventional reasoning may live in an environment that is supportive and where control is through reasoning and democratic decision making while he moves into conventional thinking. If this child is exposed to post-conventional thought, his parents may feel left out or threatened and may seek to regain balance in the system through a series of sanctions whose purpose is to "get the child in line." Perhaps it was this kind of family imbalance on a large scale during the Vietnam War that led to the perception of a generation gap. As young men and women came to grips with a world situation that directly affected them, they may have reflected and found new peer support for post-conventional responses to the war much to the dismay of their conventional, and previously supportive, parents. Perhaps much of the teasing, astonishment, name calling, conflict, and tension between generations was a result of the children en masse moving ahead due to the large-scale stimulus of the war.*

---

*Student activists have been studied by Keniston (1970) but especially by Haan (1971, 1975), Block and Haan (1969), and Haan, Smith, and Block (1968).

Again, we have little research that touches on the effects of individual moral development on family systems or of cultural events on both individuals and families, but we can raise interesting issues and questions to discuss and speculate about. As a premise, we believe that educators and parents must be aware that a change in any one family member ultimately affects all family members.

IMPLICATIONS

Thomas Lickona, in Chapter 10, gives the reader some helpful suggestions for enhancing moral development. He suggests setting a good example for children to model and holding family fairness meetings to arrive at a definition of fair. In addition, he advocates conducting democratic family meetings to help achieve mutually satisfying family decisions, creating positive affective relationships among parents and children, sensitizing the child to viewing the world through a social lens, and using Turiel's "plus-one" strategy for maximizing moral stage development of children. All of these suggestions are important in developing a moral atmosphere and in helping children develop a style of moral thinking, feeling, and behaving. We would suggest that these ideas also help the adults focus on moral issues, values, and decision making and remind them that parenting, business, teaching, or other occupations also involve ethical, moral decisions in that they affect the lives of many persons. We might well wonder if executives of Ford Motor Company had been involved in Lickona's family fairness meetings whether they still would have decided that it was more "cost-effective" to risk 300 burn deaths and serious burn injuries from rear-end collisions than to spend $137 million to repair faulty gas tanks on Ford Pintos.*

---

*According to James Warren and Brian Kelly of the Chicago Suntimes, Ford knew in the spring of 1969, 16 months before the Pinto was marketed, that its fuel tank would not withstand a 20-mile per hour rear-end collision. Kelly and Warren (1979) quote a 1973 letter from Ford to the highway safety administration in which Ford analysts argued against stricter fuel leakage standards on the grounds that safety modifications would cost $137 million whereas the estimated "cost" (!) of 300 burn deaths and serious burn injuries was only $50 million.

Perhaps more issues and questions to stimulate our imaginations are raised than answered by giving the family a careful examination. It is much easier to say that the family is intimately involved in the development of moral sensitivites than it is to pinpoint exactly how that is true or to examine all of its implications. It seems as if increasing a person's level of moral decision making should be an unconditionally positive thing to do, but we believe that parents and teachers must first examine the intimate social environment—the family—to see if the results are always beneficial. In this section, we offer some speculations on four issues concerning the relationship between the family and moral development.

One issue that has already been alluded to is whether we as teachers and family members have the right to raise the developmental levels of others without some conscientious soul-searching first. If the family is indeed a set of interdependent persons, and one changes, then other family members must either also change or work very hard at inhibiting the change. The late Don Jackson and other early family therapists were instrumental in showing that in order to create change that could be maintained, a therapist had to work with the entire family system. In cases where one member was removed for residential treatment for alcoholism or schizophrenia, the person's initial symptoms would reoccur shortly after returning to the family environment. The interdependent system needed an "identified patient" to maintain its balance and worked at regaining balance, much to the detriment of one member. The family that has found a balance may work in the same way to hold a member back. If a school system or church values post-conventional thought in its adolescents and structures the curriculum to achieve that goal, it may unwittingly increase family tensions by placing a post-conventional child in a position where conventional parents are in power. If these same school and church systems facilitate the adolescent's development in a home where the parents are postconventional, they have done that family a service by supporting a movement that helps parents and child reason together more easily (although not necessarily agree more often). Perhaps in such a group, parents themselves should be intimately involved. Special instruction would be given to parents who did not "understand." If we value higher moral development, we may be raising the child's ability to use abstract moral reasoning beyond the parents' levels. A certain amount of stress is probably normal whenever a child is changing, and this stress is probably amplified in families where the child goes beyond the parents. We need to be aware of these possibilities and assume some responsibility in helping the family cope with this situation.

A second issue is parent-sibling and sibling-sibling interaction. A family is a set of people operating at differing moral stage levels.

Quite frequently, parents comment that siblings go through periods of great cooperation and companionship only to be followed by periods of conflict and seemingly continual negativism. Other parents have observed that their children were always "at each other's throats" but became close friends in late adolescence or early adulthood. An examination of sibling relationships using the moral stage model could perhaps illuminate this. Children may operate at times in similar levels and thus will be able to understand each other's motivations, intentions, reasoning, and concept of _fair_. As one sibling shifts and tries to explain motivations in terms that the other cannot understand or explains _fair_ in a way that is not understood by the younger sibling, there may be a great deal of tension. If an older sibling tries to explain that acting in a certain way is important in order to "fit in" with peers (Stage 3), and the younger one acts according to "what's in it" (Stage 2) or out of "fear" (Stage 1), the younger child will not understand and will try to force the older sibling to revert to preconventional reasoning by teasing, name calling, or conflict of some sort. As the younger sibling shifts into conventional reasoning and begins to be concerned with others' opinions, the siblings may again view the world through similar lenses and rediscover their friendship. They may go through cycles of changing, catching up, and changing that resolve themselves when they each achieve the parents' levels and, if all goes well, when they share similar cognitive styles, values, and experiences that allow collegial relationships to develop among all family members.

The families that seem to experience continual conflict until the children reach adulthood may have siblings who never are solidly in the same stage at the same time until adulthood. There are, of course, other intervening factors in sibling relationships that are important, but the stage shifts should be studied to see if this is, in fact, one of the processes that occurs in sibling relationships.

A third issue, previously referred to, is the possible relation between marital satisfaction and similarity of moral development stages between spouses. The statement that "I've outgrown him" may indeed be true in the sense that one person has shifted from conventional to postconventional thinking while the other has not. One result of the women's movement has been the growth of a supportive environment for women to expand, explore, and challenge old orders and rules, all with group and media support. This encouragement may have facilitated the movement for many women into new ways of viewing social relationships as negotiable contracts rather than as social rules. Women have been encouraged recently to be role makers and not role takers. Some of the results may have been harmful to men, marriage, and family by supporting the change of one part of an interdependent system without recognizing and supporting the changes in

the other elements of the system. The male liberation movement and
men as house spouses have not received the same support from the
media that women's issues have. Perhaps educators and parents need
to be cognizant of, and work harder at encouraging, male liberation.

Female spouses may need to develop patience and slow the pace
of change at times. Quite frequently, we see a sudden change in one
partner, the woman in this case, and she decides that she has outgrown the relationship and wishes to terminate it. She becomes im-
patient, expecting and desiring a quick change in her husband's ability
to handle issues that she has been brooding about over a period of
years. Developmental change comes slowly and needs support and
patience to allow its growth. We, as spouses, educators, and
parents, are all involved in some ways as therapeutic agents for those
in our environment, and being alert to the pace and tensions of developmental change can heighten our awareness of the ambivalence and
tension that sometimes surround this growth.

Along with this idea of developing patience, it seems well to
remeber that different social environments function in different levels.
Briskin (1975) suggests that although each new stage is an integrated
whole, or "gestalt," there are elements of each lower stage that allow
the person to understand the reasonings of persons operating at lower
levels. Sometimes patience is also needed while a family member
switches gears to operate at different stages. A husband working in
a competitive, dog-eat-dog business environment may need a period
of time to begin to function in a cooperative, supportive way in the
family. He may need even more time to gear up and discuss with
wife and children the new role contracts that they would like to establish. In the same way, a parent who has tried to help Stage 2 siblings
understand fairness may take a while to move into Stage 5 discussion
of fairness. The jump from dividing an Oreo exactly in half, including counting out an equal number of crumbs, to a discussion of how to
fairly manage time over several years is indeed a big leap and one
that sometimes takes a while to accomplish. Sometimes spouses need
considerable patience and understanding as their mates make cognitive jumps or describe the stress involved in not being able to function with superiors or children at the highest stage possible. Sometimes the difficulty in making people understand is exactly this kind
of situation—how do you make a Stage 2, "what's-in-it-for-me" execu-
tive understand that burning and killing people in unsafe autos is un-
ethical even if the changes would cost the company more?

A fourth and final issue to note is that changing family roles may
be a result of development of one or more members. Probably the
impact on other family members will depend on the extent to which
the person's role is pivotal. If a mother, father, or 1 of 2 siblings
moves in the stage hierarchy, the impact on others will be greater

than if the middle child in a family of 13 children shifts. A change in family roles may also be a stimulus for development. Quite frequently, after the death of a parent, a divorce, or other major shift in family structure, family members reflect on life and on the family. Through new responsibilities and reflection, they may begin thinking about important issues in different, broader way and may shift into the next stage of development. Because the family is made up of persons reflecting different stage levels, each person sees the actions and behaviors of others through his or her own moral lens. Roles in the family may be a moral issue. For example, a parent, watching a child work through new alternatives to marriage and new role patterns, may be fearful and threatened of "everyone doing his own thing," because he or she is not at the same level of contract and negotiation. New "radical" forms of marriage and role relationships may not be understood as a contract two persons have agreed upon but only as a threat to the traditional nuclear family.* Intergenerational conflict may be viewed in some cases as misunderstanding because family roles are not seen through similar moral stage lenses by parents and their grown children.

In conclusion, it seems to us that as parents and educators we can raise and examine questions and issues in family life by seeing the family as a system that teaches moral values and styles of making moral decisions. By heightening our awareness, we may affect more positive moral values rather than indifference, and we may work more conscientiously at enhancing the level of moral judgment in all family members. It is important to families that educators and church curriculum advisers at least explore the possibilities that these programs might increase family stress and that they might need to take some responsibility in helping decrease it. The contextual variables affected by open, lengthy communication, democratic decision making, support, and control through reasoning are important to note. It is also important—perhaps sobering—to recognize that few children manage to transcend the level of development that their parents achieved. It is time to address the issue working with parents rather than with children to increase levels of moral stage development in families.

_____

*Family historians suggest that it is only in the past 200 years that middle-class families have taken the form that we now refer to as <u>traditional</u> (Shorter 1975).

9
PARENT BEHAVIOR AND MORAL EDUCATION

John T. Hower

The influence of parents on moral character seems to be primarily related to their behavior in a multitude of daily interactions with their children. When considering moral education, many parents think immediately of the talks they have with their children disseminating information as to what is right and wrong and why. While such lectures are without doubt important, they play a relatively minor part in the overall moral education of the children to whom they are given. Most parents are very concerned that their children learn the difference between right and wrong, and the available evidence indicates that almost all children do in fact learn this distinction. For example, a study by Gordon et al. (1963) found no differences in the degree to which six groups of teenage boys (black and white; delinquent and nondelinquent; lower-class, middle-class) understood the applicability of middle-class norms. Problems in moral behavior seem to lie in learning to live by the rules rather than simply learning the rules. The purpose of this chapter is to identify parental behaviors that have been shown to be relevant and salient in fostering good moral character development in children.

Moral character as used here refers to an integrated orientation that would include a general behavioral conformity factor to the basic expectations of society, an interpersonal orientation of empathy and cooperation, and a sense of autonomy and independence of judgment. Mere conformity is generally not considered evidence of good moral development, and the orientation to the needs and feelings of others could by itself simply indicate feelings of insecurity and inferiority rather than moral maturity. Keniston (1970) has also pointed out the disconcerting fact that it is possible to find high levels of moral reasoning on a cognitive level, while behavioral and affective components are lacking. Thus, moral development is best viewed as a manifestation of an integrated process of personality development including self-control, empathy toward the needs and feelings of others, and initiative and independence. Hogan (1973) has worked extensively to develop a concept of moral character that combines these several aspects of personality within the individual. From this standpoint, it is not surprising that good moral development takes place in the context of good personal, social, and intellectual development. Parents should not think of moral development as a separate entity that can be imparted to their children regardless of other aspects of their lives. Much research has focused on the parent-child interactions found to be present in families of children who are well developed morally. The findings are strikingly similar to those related to good general adjustment and high self-esteem.

Research has also been directed toward identifying the critical aspects of the parent-child interaction. Of the literally hundreds of factors examined, there appear to be several general clusters that represent the salient dimensions of the parent-child exchange. The first and most crucial dimension is the child's perception of love and acceptance by his parents. The opposite end of this dimension would be represented by the child's feeling rejected by the parent. The other major dimension in parenting style is one of control (firm versus lax). Specific variations relating to the manner in which the control is administered will be examined later. The basic differences in styles of parenting can be conceptualized in terms of this two-dimensional model of acceptance and control. A permissive parent can be seen as accepting with lax control, an authoritarian parent as low in acceptance and high in control, the neglecting parent as low in acceptance and low in control, and the authoritative parent as high in both acceptance and control (Baumrind 1971). (See Figure 9.1.)

PARENTAL ACCEPTANCE

Each of these general dimensions has been shown to be associated with different manifestations of moral behavior in the children of parents exhibiting these styles. The most important finding of the majority of studies in this area is that the love-rejection dimension is by far the most crucial factor, regardless of the degree of parental firmness. Parental acceptance has been repeatedly associated with healthy moral development, while rejection is associated with the opposite. Becker (1963), after reviewing the literature on the consequences of parental discipline, concluded that parental warmth was the basic factor influencing personality functioning, regardless of the method of discipline used. Discipline techniques were related to specific pathology, but the single variable of parental warmth distinguished normals from pathological samples. Sears, Maccoby,

FIGURE 9.1

Parental Dimensions and Styles

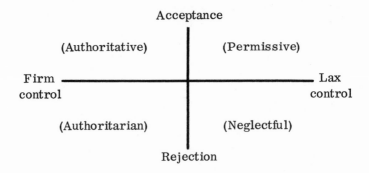

Source: Constructed by the author.

and Levin (1957) found conscience development (defined by confession of transgression) to be positively related to love-oriented child-rearing practices and negatively related to object-oriented techniques (tangible rewards, physical punishment, and deprivation of privileges). The love-oriented pattern was effective only when mothers showed frequent expressions of affection. McCord and McCord [1958) studying criminals and their sons found that boys whose fathers were criminals were less apt to become criminals if accepted by their fathers than if rejected by them. In this study, parental acceptance was associated with conformity to social norms even when the parental model was a criminal. Hoffman (1963), in a review of the literature, found parental acceptance to be related to moral internalization. Acceptance has also been shown to relate positively to the development of self-esteem (Coopersmith 1967) and negatively to alienation in high school students (Rode 1971). The cumulative research findings are essentially in agreement that parental acceptance is associated with moral development as well as with general personality development.

PARENTAL CONTROL

Frequently when there is news of an act of vandalism or other misdeed, parents can be heard lamenting that there is just not any control anymore. If those "kids" were under their roof, the law would be laid down. Ironically, such gross failures in moral behavior are more often attributable to a lack of relationship than to a lack of control. This does not mean that the control dimension is unimportant, but it must be evaluated in the context of the climate of the parent-child relationship. If the child feels accepted, the parents' control measures are much more likely to be useful.

I will never forget an experience I had while working at a day care center, one that demonstrates the interplay of the acceptance and control dimensions. I was enforcing a "time out" procedure (incidentally a power-assertive technique) that required a four- or five-year-old boy to stay on his cot. I do not recall the details of his infraction, but he was very upset at being limited to his cot. What I will never forget is his howling at the top of his lungs, "You don't even like me!" I do not think this was an attempt to even the score with me, but, rather, it was a very serious and mournful expression that seemed to come straight from his heart. Regardless of how justified I might have been or how deserving he was of the punishment, he was primarily feeling rejected, and I doubt very much that the incident did anything to stimulate his moral development or his development as a person. How could it be that I, who was studying to be a therapist, could leave a child feeling rejected? Yet as I reflected on my interaction with Robbie, I had to admit that my relating to him and my feelings about him were not usually that warm. More often than not, I was correcting him and less often I was involved in coming to know and appreciate him as a person. Prior to this incident, had I been asked whether I accepted Robbie, my reply would have been an instant "Of course!"

Most of us simply do not think it possible that a child could walk away from us feeling rejected. I have met very few parents who are able to admit that their relating to their children could be in any way rejecting in nature. A parent may not feel hateful toward his child, but the behavior exhibited in relating to the child may affect the child with the feeling of being rejected or the sense of nonaffirmation. It seems that the experience of the realtionship from the child's point of view is supremely important. In numerous studies, we have found a significant correlation between children's assessment of parents' behavior and their adjustment (Hower 1976).

In the model presented earlier, the authoritarian combination of high control and low acceptance seems to be the most destructive. Cumulative research findings quite consistently indicate negative relationships between authoritarian parenting and moral development (Baumrind 1971; Hoffman 1963; Hower and Edwards 1979). One variation from this trend is the finding that a strong, rigid, and compartmentalized type of moral character can be a product of autocratic parenting (Peck 1958). Seemingly high levels of control exacerbate a relationship that may already be perceived as rejecting. It may also be true that the high degree of control contributes directly to the

child's feeling unaccepted. Rejecting and noncontrolling conditions
are also negatively related to the moral indices, though the relationship was not as strong in our study (Hower and Edwards 1979). Since
the neglectful parent is not as intrusive in the relationship as the
authoritarian, perhaps any aversive affect is less apparent to the
child.

In the context of warm, accepting parental conditions, the desirable degree of control is the subject of some debate. Baumrind
(1971) reports that with four-year-old subjects the authoritative position is associated with much better child development than the permissive position. Among younger subjects, the absence of any parental control has been associated with increased aggression (Hollenburg
and Sperry 1951) and low levels of self-reliance and self-control
(Baumrind 1971). In contrast to this, a study involving 18- and
19-year-olds indicated that those classified as most socialized and
empathic rated their parents as permissive (Hower and Edwards 1979).
These differences can probably be best explained in terms of developmental trends. While at least moderate levels of control are apparently helpful with younger children, as they grow older and more capable
of higher levels of thought and interaction, high levels of control become irrelevant if not destructive. This shift is noted in a study of
four- six- and eight-year-old children on resistance to temptation
(Jensen and Buhanan 1974). Four-year-olds deviated less under
promised punishment, six-year-olds deviated less under promised
rewards, and eight-year-olds performed as well or better when
motivated by more intrinsic empathy-oriented instructions.

There is evidence that most parents follow this pattern of
gradually relinquishing control as the child gorws older (Armentrout
and Burger 1972; Burger, Lamp, and Rogers 1975). The challenge
for parents is trying to stay in step with their children's development
progress. It appears questionable for a parent to maintain the same
level of control throughout the growing-up years. A good parent for
preschool children may be unable to move out of that controlling mode
and then experience difficulties in dealing with the more independent
child. This is probably a source of a number of parent-child conflicts that are notorious in the teenage years. Under ideal conditions,
the accepting parent would direct the child and enforce controls in
the earlier years, moving toward a position of less and less overt
control as the child grows older. As this is happening, the child
should be developing internal controls through verbal interactions
with his parents and peers. When they impose controls, wise parents
are mindful of their long-range goal for their children: independent
moral functioning.

The movement of parenting stance from the authoritative quadrant to the permissive quadrant presupposes the development of a

healthy moral internalization in the child. A unique set of problems arises when a child grows from childhood to adolescence without adequate internal controls. Therapists working with adolescents and their families are frequently faced with this dilemma. The teenager wants to be treated with a permissive respect and trust, and the research indicates that this would be appropriate for a child of that age. Such a young person, however, facing a complex social world with poor impulse control and poor moral judgment, will frequently act irresponsibly under permissive conditions. Many parents, feeling they have no other choice at that point, swing to a more authoritarian stance that would appear to have a poor prognosis for success in fostering internal control. This is a difficult dilemma for which there are no easy solutions. It is difficult for parents to maintain love-oriented interactions when their adolescent is behaving irresponsibly, and it is difficult for the adolescent to maintain his composure while controls are being tightened. While undoubtedly some controls must be applied, parents should realize that an unsevered supportive relationship is in the long run the most potent means of influencing their child.

Sometimes families in this predicament find it helpful to come to very clear agreements as to what behaviors bring what privileges and consequences (De Risi and Butz 1975). If infractions occur, the parents and the adolescent can refer to the agreement rather than to the particular judgment of the parents. This frequently defuses the power struggle. Family therapy is often helpful in this type of impasse as well because it fosters a more democratic atmosphere in which there is a sense that "we" have a problem rather than "you," the adolescent, have a problem.

TYPE OF CONTROL

In addition to the degree of control, research has shown that the manner in which control is administered has a bearing on moral development. Researchers have identified three major classes of control interventions that are primarily relevant to the discipline encounter (Hoffman 1970). Power assertion refers to an approach to parenting that is oriented to the use of force in a threatened or actual fashion, including punishment techniques such as spanking, deprivation of desired physical resources, and any interaction in which the parent makes use of his superior power to control the child and the environment. The general category of love withdrawal includes temporary rejection techniques such as ignoring, withholding affection, or expressing dislike for the child. The flavor of this technique is captured in the phenomenon of shunning among certain religious groups. Nonconformers are essentially cut off from the group until proper restitution is made. The third class of parental interventions is <u>induction</u>. Inductive techniques include verbal inter-action and reasoning, especially explaining the effects of a child's be-havior on others and attempting to engage the internal controls of the child rather than forcing conformity through external controls.

Before discussing each of these types of control separately, it should be noted that it is essentially impossible to separate these techniques from each other. Any discipline encounter between parent and child would have some degree of each of the three elements, no matter what the parent does. The fact that the parents are trying to say something to children or in some way intervene is to some degree an assertion of power. There are also elements of love withdrawal, because children know that parents are not completely happy with their current behavior, and inklings of induction even with the most blunt punishments in that there are implied messages that children should not be doing what they are doing. Although many parents will use all three types of interventions in different situations or even use elements of all three in one incident, they are classified on the basis of their predominant style of intervention technique. It has been use-ful to look at the child behavior associated with the predominance of each of these styles.

Power assertion has consistently been shown to be negatively related to moral internalization (Hoffman 1970). Children whose parents use power-assertive techniques tend to be externally oriented (aware of punitive consequences rather than having internal moral standards). Even with preschool children, Hoffman (1960) found that children whose parents used unqualified power assertion were hostile to other children, power assertive toward other children, and resistant to parental influence. Power assertion can produce an immediate, though short-term, suppression of antisocial responses (Parke and Walters 1967); however, in light of developmental trends, power-assertive techniques would appear to become more and more in-appropriate as the child matures.

The effects of love-withdrawing techniques do not show con-sistent patterns. In most studies, the love-withdrawing behavior of the parent was unrelated to the moral indices, and the few significant findings follow no clear patterns (Hoffman 1970). It is reasonable to conclude that the effects of love-withdrawal techniques are not as clearly negative as the power-assertive techniques, but any benefi-cial effects have not been adequately demonstrated at this point, perhaps because of the unpredictable nature of a love-withdrawing maneuver. Children are temporarily cut off from their source of direction and understanding and left to figure out why their behavior caused the rift and what they must do to correct it.

Just as power-oriented techniques are clearly associated with negative influence, inductive-reasoning approaches have been associated with facilitation of moral development. When parents explain to children how their behavior hurts someone else, they appeal to children's internal capacity for empathy and self-control. Children are often willing to alter their behavior if they feel they have a meaningful reason to do so. Parents using inductive techniques provide cognitive means with which children can learn to understand their environment and control themselves accordingly.

The use of inductive techniques may also have a direct bearing on the development of a strong affective bond between parent and child. In a factor analysis of our data on adolescents, there was a mutual loading of acceptance and induction on the same factor (Hower and Edwards 1978). For this sample, the use of inductive techniques and the feeling of acceptance could almost be seen as synonymous in the experience of the child. It may be that using inductive techniques is one way that parents communicate acceptance. This notion has an intuitive appeal that parents who take the time to explain their rules will be perceived by their children as accepting. There is also an implication that good parenting can be a single integrated process of relating to the child in which acceptance and control fit together quite naturally.

The proverbial example of the child's life temporarily stopping for the horrible experience of going for discipline to the woodshed pictures a compartmentalized relationship of discipline and wrath, on the one hand, and acceptance for the child when he is back from the woodshed, on the other. When parents relate to their children empathically trying to understand the pressures, temptations, or jealousies they feel, the children are likely to feel that they are dealing with fair people. In this atmosphere, parents have a better chance of explaining their points of view regarding the children's actions or desires to do something. Children treated in this way are more likely to perceive any controls as reasonable demands. Pikas (1961) found with adolescents that differences occurred in the acceptance of parental authority, depending on the reason for the directive. Authority based on rational concern for the child's welfare was accepted, but arbitrary and domineering or exploitative authority was rejected. Elder (1963) found with adolescents that conformity to parental rules typified adolescents who saw their parents as democratic and providing explanations for their rules.

In our research, the parental characteristics could be condensed into one set of interactions that was positively related to moral development and one that was negatively related (Hower and Edwards

1979). The accepting, inducting, and noncontrolling characteristics were positively related to the moral indices; and the rejecting, controlling, and power-oriented techniques were negatively related. It seems that one group of parents was able to relate successfully to the children and the other was not. The successful parents were rated as low in control: perhaps the relationship felt noncontrolling to the adolescents because these parents were able to administer the control in such a way that it was not seen as insulting or rejecting. These parents did not try to control their children but rather to support their development and understanding as individuals. Presumably, these parents applied some controls especially in the early years, but perhaps since they were applied against the backdrop of acceptance, children perceived the controls as reasonable.

BEHAVIOR MODIFICATION AND MORAL DEVELOPMENT

In recent years, an enormous body of literature has appeared documenting the efficacy of shaping children's behavior through the use of behavior modification techniques (systematic use of reinforcement). The strategy attempts to increase the frequency of desired behaviors and decrease the frequency of undesirable behaviors through the differential use of reinforcers. The literature indicates—and my own experience confirms—that these techniques are extremely useful in shaping behavior, especially with children ages four to ten. It seems to me that these procedures are too effective to be ignored by moral educators, since morality ultimately deals with the proper regulation of behavior.

The troubling aspect of these behavioral techniques is the tendency to minimize the verbal interaction between parent and child. The incident given earlier of Robbie was an example of a time-out procedure. The theory is that when a child misbehaves, he usually receives some form of reinforcement from his environment (for example, seeing other children laugh) that makes him likely to repeat his behavior on some other occasion. The time-out procedure involves removing the child to a specified location that is as free as possible of any source of stimulation and thus reinforcement and having him stay for up to five minutes (Patterson 1971). Thus, following the misbehaving act, the child is removed from the situation promptly and with minimal discussion (which might be reinforcing) and placed by himself in a neutral place. It seems that the employment of such a procedure misses an opportunity to interact with the child inductively regarding the reasons why the behavior was inappropriate and the feelings of others who might have been involved. Such a discussion could stimulate the development of empathy and any number of other internally mediated responses relevant to moral maturity. The time-out procedure also seems to incorporate both power assertion and love withdrawal as leverage on the child; and, as mentioned earlier, neither of these styles has proved particularly effective in stimulating more internalization.

Nevertheless, the time-out procedure and other behavioral procedures appear to be very effective in changing behavior. Behavior modifiers argue, I think rightly, that children and parents are happier and freer to develop the all-important, warm, accepting relationship when the children's behavior is well controlled and the household is free of nagging and bickering. Also, behavioral techniques are usually recommended for younger children, and the literature seems to indicate the more overtly controlling techniques are more appropriate then than in later years. The use of positive reinforcers, which comprises much of the behavioral literature, is generally more palatable to the moral educator because these positive reinforcers are directly affirming of the child and do not remove him from his sources of interaction. It would seem wise for any parent using behavioral techniques to take the time after a time-out period, or after he has given positive reinforcement, to explain the meaning of the situation to the child. It is dangerously easy to simply monitor behaviors and reinforcement and neglect the internal sources of self-control and interpersonal sensitivity that must be developed if the child is to become a morally mature individual.

PRACTICAL IMPLICATIONS

In light of the material presented here, what then are the practical implications for parents interested in stimulating moral development in their children?

The first implication that parents should be aware of is the potency of their relationship with their children. Aside from any specific techniques employed or lectures given, children's experience of a warm, accepting relationship will do more toward sending them to moral maturity than any other single thing. Their failure to experience that relationship will do more to hamper their moral progress than anything else.

A second implication for parents is a recognition of the developmental progress of the child. All children of all ages need to feel accepted, but the degree of control needs to progress at the pace of the child's capacity for autonomy. Preschool children need firm controls and clear expectations for behavior. By the time they are through their adolescent years, the parental stance should have moved toward permissiveness. There is no formula for determining what controls should be lifted at what age. This depends on individual circumstances, but children should be encouraged to use self-control and judgment whenever possible. Parents should be aiming at ultimately relinquishing control rather than trying to be in charge as long as possible. Parents who are too controlling for too long run the risk of losing their place as consultants in later, more independent years. Too much control tends to close the doors of communication.

And third, the approach to administering parental control should be aimed at the internal sense of self-control and understanding within the child rather than at mere conformity. Inductive-reasoning approaches have been associated with the greatest levels of moral internalization, while power-assertive techniques and love-withdrawing techniques have been less effective, if not harmful. It is particularly wise to focus on how children's behavior affects others. This will stimulate the development of empathy and will orient them to thinking of others in a cooperative fashion, which is the essence of the golden rule. If any behavior modification techniques are used, parents should take special care to explain the reasons and implications of children's actions. Behavior shaping is not enough.

CONCLUSION

Early in this chapter, moral character was defined in terms of conformity, empathy, and autonomy. An individual who conforms to social expectations and is empathic toward others is an asset to any society, but it is of special interest to find an individual who has these cooperative characteristics but who also has a sense of autonomy—an ability to stand apart from the crowd if need be. In our study (Hower 1976), there was a slight difference in the parental picture in the group of subjects who were both well socialized and autonomous versus the group that was simply well socialized. Both groups rated their parents as accepting and noncontrolling, but the autonomous group expressed a greater sense of experiencing the accepting and non-controlling relationship. This is a small finding dealing with one sample in one study, but it seems to capture the thrust of this chapter. The experience of a strong relationship is the most character-producing influence a parent can give.

10

FOSTERING MORAL
DEVELOPMENT IN THE FAMILY

Thomas Lickona

During the trial of Adolph Eichmann, Rabbi Harold Schulweis of Oakland, California, was struck by the lone testimony given about a Christian who had rescued Jews from a Nazi concentration camp. Rabbi Schulweis saw in this testimony a "glimmer of redemption" from the "horrendous image of man" that emerged from the trial. He wrote a magazine article urging that rescuers be identified and honored. On Christmas day, in 1962, NBC commentator Chet Huntley presented a network television documentary in which some rescuers were interviewed and their stories told. With the help of this publicity, Rabbi Schulweis was able to recruit and fund a team of psychologists to investigate the backgrounds of these persons who had risked their lives to save Jews from the holocaust.

One such courageous individual was a once-wealthy German businessman. In the interview, he reported how he had become involved in the business of rescue: "I was believing in 1942 that the war will be another year. It cannot be any longer. It's impossible. I was then a rich man. I had about 300,000 or 400,000 marks, and I started with one person, then six people, from there to 50, then 100. . . . People came to me—maybe they like my looks, I don't know what it was—asking me very bluntly and very frankly, 'Will you save me?'" (London 1970, p. 243).

The first request for help came from his secretary, who said that the Germans were going to kill her Jewish husband. He thought at first that she was crazy and said, "Germans don't do things like that!" But she insisted that they would, and so he agreed to keep the husband in his office over the weekend. As he became convinced that the fears of Jews were justified, he became more and more deeply involved. By the war's end, he had spent four years and all of his fortune to save more than 200 Jews.

"I come from a poor family," he told the interviewers. "My mother came from Hesse, which was mainly small farmers. . . . I believe that is part of my personality. You inherit something from your parents, from the grandparents. My mother said to me when we were small, and even when we were bigger, 'Regardless of what you do with your life, be honest. When it comes to the day you have to make a decision, make the right one. It could be a hard one. But even the hard ones should be the right ones.' I didn't know what it means" (p. 243).

He went on to talk about his mother in glowing terms—about how she had told him to live, how she had taught him morals, and how she had exemplified morality for him. "Always in life she gave me so much philosophy. She didn't go to high school, only elementary school, but so smart a woman, wisdom, you know" (p. 243).

This man's childhood proved to be the rule among rescuers rather than the exception. Other rescuers remembered their parents in similar ways: as strong, good people who both preached and lived morality. The lesson of this extraordinary study is obvious: Conscience is not formed in a vacuum. Parents can have a profound influence on the moral development of their children.

Teachers, of course, have long known this to be true. The children they see in classrooms come to them not as blank moral slates but with many habits of mind and conduct that bear the stamp of their family environment. "I had a little girl who was stealing constantly," a second-grade teacher told me recently. The teacher spoke with the girl's father. "She comes by it naturally," he explained apologetically. "I just got out of the penitentiary." Similarly, the child who experiences a concern for respect and fairness and honesty at home is likely to carry those values into his relationships at school.

The public, at least as represented by the American Gallup Poll, is quite willing to let the schools have a hand in the teaching of morals and moral behavior. But wise parents also know, as one mother said, that "we cannot inflict the total responsibility for this education upon the school. Moral education must be a joint effort between the school and the home." What is the part that parents can play in the moral development of their children? Can they—should they—approach their role as moral educators as deliberately and systematically as teachers should approach theirs? I believe that children would be the beneficiaries if parents did. I would like to share strategies for fostering moral development in the family and to review some of the research on parents' role as moral educators of their children.

Throughout this chapter, I use moral development broadly to mean growing out of egocentrism toward relations of cooperation, fairness, and mutual respect. This definition is intended to encompass three interrelated strands of moral growth: the development of moral thinking (reasoning about right and wrong), the development of moral feeling (wanting to do the right thing and feeling bad when you do not), and the development of moral behavior (translating thought and feeling into action). The development of all three of these— thinking, feeling, and behavior— is what defines the child's progress toward moral maturity.

STRATEGY 1: SET A GOOD EXAMPLE

Strategy 1 is the homiest of advice. I call it the "grandmother's strategy" because our grandmothers knew the importance of good example long before social learning theorists made official pronouncements about modeling and observation learning. Children are from their tenderest years greatly affected by what they see important others do. The already cited study of the rescuers points to the power of positive models, just as the voluminous research on television plainly demonstrates the bad effects of negative social models on children's social and moral behavior (see Liebert, Neale, and Davidson [1973] and Liebert and Poulos [1976] for documentation of the assorted evils that can be laid at the door of television).

Testimony to the positive impact of parental example also comes from an investigation into the families of young U.S. civil rights workers who spent a year or more in the Deep South in the early 1960s at a time when "nigger lovers" were in danger of "turning up dead" (Rosenhan 1969). Persons who took this degree of risk were classified by the researchers as "fully committed" to the civil rights movement. They were compared to "partially committed" students, who had taken only one or two low-risk "freedom rides" and whose commitment seemed more talk than action.

Partially committed students, the interviews disclosed, usually disliked their parents. They frequently remembered them as preaching one thing and practicing another, especially toward members of outgroups. One student, for example, went on a tirade about how easily his father condoned dishonesty when the victims were people he did not like.

Fully committed civil rights workers, on the other hand, typically looked up to their parents as persons who lived by their moral ideals. One young man remembered vividly how his father had carried him on his shoulders in a parade to protest the execution of Sacco and Vanzetti, two political radicals believed by many to have been framed for murder. Another student recalled how his father, outraged by the Nazi atrocities, had signed up for service in World War II despite bad health and old age.

The examples we set for our children need not always be the stuff of moral protest or profiles in courage. The way we relate to them on an everyday basis surely matters at least as much. Piaget suggested in <u>The Moral Judgment of the Child</u> (1965) that if we wish to rear a moral child, we should begin by treating the child morally. He recommended that parents place themselves "on the child's own level, and give him a feeling of equality by drawing attention to one's own needs, one's own difficulties, even one's own blunders, thus creating an atmosphere of mutual help and understanding" (pp. 137-38). A parent can say, for example, "This has been a tough day for me. I'm not in a very good mood, and I need your help." Or, "I lost my temper when I hit you. That was not right to do, and I'm sorry." Piaget wrote that "if a parent preaches by example rather than by precept," he exercises "an enormous influence" on the child's progress toward moral maturity (p. 319). By example a parent can teach a child that morality is "not a system of commands requiring ritualistic and external obedience but a system of social relations such that everyone does his best to obey the same obligations, and does so out of mutual respect" (p. 138). Children thus learn that rules bind everyone, big and small.

STRATEGY 2: USE A FAIRNESS APPROACH TO RULES AND DISCIPLINE

For the last three years I have had the opportunity to do volunteer family counseling. One family I saw for several weeks consisted of a mother in her early forties (separated from her husband), a 12-year-old girl, Janet, a nine-year-old boy, Bobby, and a younger sister (the names have been changed). In one session I remember well, Janet repeatedly put her sneakered foot up on the arm of Bobby's chair, then slowly inched it toward his hand until he reacted by shouting, "Cut it out!" and tried to slap her leg as it was quickly withdrawn. The mother responded to this little game with mounting annoyance, making first one threat, then another: "Knock it off if you know what's good for you!" "I'm going to slap you silly!" And, finally, "When we get home, it'll be the belt!" After the third round of this interaction, I interrupted the mother's account of their latest family crisis at home to call attention to the situation at hand. "Look," I said to Janet and Bobby, "do you understand what your mother is saying? Do you really <u>want</u> her to punish you? Janet grinned sheepishly and said, "If you never get punished, it gets kind of boring!"

This was clearly a case where the children had the mother well trained. They were accomplished at provoking her to provide the punishments and threats that added a desired degree of danger to their otherwise routine existence. Such punishments, however, added nothing to their moral development. Indeed, they may have actively impeded it—since punishment often has the effect of letting children off the hook. In a remarkably candid discussion of lying, a group of sixth-graders revealed that they saw punishment as "the luck of the game . . . , the price they paid for their lies. Once the price was paid, they were free to lie again" (Glasser 1969, p. 190). Punishment is undesirable for other reasons as well: it sets a bad example (teaching children to use power to settle a conflict of wills); it often causes children to feel sorry for themselves rather than for the victim of their misdeed; it teaches them to be more careful rather than more moral; and it fails to develop a positive alternative to the offensive behavior.

A positive alternative to punishment, what I call a "fairness approach" to rules and discipline, has been used with equal effectiveness by parents and teachers. The basic rationale for this approach is the idea that all children, even young ones, come equipped with at least a beginning sense of fairness and that the continuing development of that sense of fairness is a crucial part of moral development. The fairness approach requires parent and child to pool their ideas in a cooperative effort to solve the problem at hand.

To establish a fairness approach in the home, parents I have worked with find it helpful to hold a structured ten-step fairness meeting. The ten steps of the fairness meeting are listed in Figure 10.1. Steps 1 through 6 are aimed at achieving mutual understanding between parent and child as the foundation for the problem-solving steps. These first six steps require the participants to engage in the kind of systematic role taking that Piaget (1965) and Kohlberg (1976) regard as the sine qua non of moral development. Steps 7 through 9 are aimed at solving the problem. Step 10 is aimed at evaluating the solution after it has been implemented to see how well it is working and what can be done, if necessary, to make it work better.

As an example of how a fairness meeting can work even with young children, consider the following account by a mother. She describes her first fairness meeting with her two children, James, age seven, and Elizabeth, age five. "The problem we discussed is one that has been disturbing to our family for quite a while."

[Step 1—parent states purpose of meeting]

    <u>Mother:</u> James and Elizabeth, we're having a problem with you two getting along. I'd like to talk with you about it and see if we can come up with a fair solution.

FIGURE 10.1

Steps in a Fairness Meeting

Achieving Mutual Understanding

1. State the purpose of the meeting (to find a fair solution).

2. State intent to understand each other's feelings about problem.

3. State your feelings about the problem.

4. Ask your child for his feelings about the problem.

5. Paraphrase your child's feelings to show understanding.

6. Ask your child to paraphrase your feelings.

Solving the Problem

7. Together brainstorm fair solutions to the problem.

8. Agree upon a solution that everyone thinks fair; sign a "fairness agreement."

9. Plan implementation of solution and follow-up; evaluate meeting.

Evaluating the Solution

10. Hold a follow-up meeting to evaluate how the solution is working.

Source: Constructed by the author.

[Step 2—parent states intent to achieve understanding]

Mother: First, I want you to know and understand how I feel about this situation, and then I want to find out how each of you feel.

[Step 3—parent states feelings about problem]

Mother: Kids, I get so irritated when I see the two of you fighting with each other or hitting one another. When I get irritated I start to yell at you, and everything becomes upset. I would like to see the two of you try a little harder to get along.

[Step 4—parent elicits children's feelings]

Mother: Now, I've told you how I feel. I'd like to hear each of your feelings about this.

James: Elizabeth always wants to do everything I do. She wants to sit in the same seat that I do and she wants to play with the same toys. Sometimes she hits me, too.

Elizabeth: James punches me. He makes me cry. He won't play with me. I don't like it when you yell, Mommy.

[Step 5—parent paraphrases children's feelings]

Mother: Okay, I want to make sure that I understand what you said. James, you feel Elizabeth is always in your way—wanting to sit with you and play with you. Also, you don't like it when she hits you. Elizabeth, you say that James makes you cry when he hits you and won't play with you. And you don't want me to yell because it upsets you.

[Step 6—children paraphrase parent's feelings]

Mother: Can you remember what I said about the situation?

James: You want us to try not to fight because it upsets you and everybody else. Right?

Mother: That's right, James. Elizabeth, do you understand that?

Elizabeth: Yes.

[Step 7—all brainstorm fair solutions]

Mother: You know what I'd like us to do together? I'd like us to make a list of all the things we can do to try to make this situation better. All the things we put on the list have to be fair to everyone. Okay? [Children nod.] Elizabeth, do you understand what "fair" means?

Elizabeth: Yes, Mommy. It means everybody has to like it.

Together we came up with these possible solutions:

1. Don't hit.
2. James should try to teach Elizabeth some of his games.
3. Mommy shouldn't yell.
4. Elizabeth should try to find things to do by herself sometimes.
5. Everyone should try to say and do nice things.

[Step 8—all reach and sign a fairness agreement]

We agreed on the following solutions as being fair:

1. No hitting or yelling by anyone—Mommy, James, or Elizabeth.
2. James should try to play with Elizabeth at least once a day.
3. Elizabeth should try to play by herself sometimes.
4. Everyone should try to say and do nice things.

We all signed our contract and promised to try our best.

[Step 9—all plan implementation and follow-up; evaluate meeting]

We decided to post our solutions on the refrigerator where all could see them. Next to our solutions we put a paper to be used to keep a list of nice things said and

done during the next two days. James agreed to write
down whatever Elizabeth wished to have recorded on
the list.

We agreed to start immediately with our plan and
to inform Dad about it when he got home. We decided
we would meet again in two days to see how our plan was
progressing.

I asked the children how they liked our fairness
meeting. They said they were glad to know that I cared
about them. They were also pleased to know that I realized I had to change, too. They weren't the only ones
who had been acting badly.

[Step 10—follow-up meeting to evaluate solution]

In our follow-up meeting we began by reading the list of
nice things that people had said and done during the last
two days. We decided that everyone had indeed tried to
be kinder. Then we went over each of our solutions,
and we all contributed a comment about how well the
plan was working:

> <u>Mother</u>: James, I'm so pleased that you've been
> trying to include Elizabeth in your playing.
> Do you realize that I've had to speak to you
> only twice in two days? I think that's quite
> an improvement. And Elizabeth, you are
> certainly trying to be nicer to everyone.

> <u>James</u>: I'm glad you're not yelling, Mommy. And
> I don't think Elizabeth has hit me at all.

> <u>Elizabeth</u>: James played with me, and he let me sit in
> the bean bag with him yesterday.

To the questions, "Is our plan working?" and "Are we
all trying to be fair?" we all answered with a resounding
yes. To the question, "Can we make our plan work
even better?" we answered that we would remind ourselves of our agreement at the beginning of each day and
would have another meeting in a week's time to see if
we were each still following our plan.

This mother concluded:

Our household is now a much happier one. We continue
to add to the list of nice things said to and done for others,

and even Dad has gotten involved. I can foresee using
this method in dealing with other problems that come up
with my children and even with my husband. The fairness meeting seems to be a good way to get things out
into the open. Often we do not think about how the other
person views a situation, and it does us good to hear the
other side of the story.

Does a parent always need to go through the full ten steps that
this mother followed? It depends on the problem and on a family's
experience in using a fairness approach to conflicts. With simple
problems or with long experience, the process can be abbreviated.
Sometimes one can begin with Step 7 (brainstorming fair solutions).
Sometimes a fairness meeting can be a single step: a quick, on-the-
spot settlement. For example, a five-year-old wanted to play for
30 minutes with his ten-year-old brother, while the older brother
wanted to have private time. With brief parental mediation, they
agreed to 15 minutes of play and 15 minutes of private time as a fair
compromise.

Does a fairness approach to rules and discipline mean that
children never suffer any negative consequences for their lapses?
Not at all. Consequences, even stiff ones, can be built into the fairness agreement: pick up your toys after you have been playing with
them or they are taken away for a week; have the car home by mid-
night or lose driving privileges for a month. The critical condition
is that the consequences be agreed upon as fair by both parent and
child. If children consent to the fairness of consequences in advance,
they are much more likely to accept them as their just dessert should
they break their agreement. If they do protest the justice of their
fate, the parent can ask, "What did we agree was a fair consequence
for not living up to the agreement?"

The most important ingredient in the successful use of a fairness approach is tenacity. Parents must follow through—must invest
the time and energy necessary to hold everyone accountable to what
they agreed was fair. After a while, fairness will be "in the air,"
part of the moral atmosphere that the family breathes. One mother
of several adolescents described how the climate of their home had
changed: "Just using the word 'fair' has helped to defuse a lot of
emotional situations in our house. Attitudes in our family are improving. There's less use of authority, more input from the children."

How does a fairness approach foster moral development? It
does so in many ways. First of all, it requires children to think
morally—to "decenter" and consider the needs of others as well as
their own. It sets a good example for children by treating them with
respect for their rights and feelings as people and by showing that

reason rather than power can be used to resolve conflicts. It teaches a child responsibility by making him an active partner in the solution of conflicts. Finally, a fairness approach gives children valuable practice in the skills of communication and problem solving. It thereby equips them to deal effectively and justify with the myriad problems they will encounter as they make their way in their widening social and moral world.

STRATEGY 3: CONDUCT DEMOCRATIC FAMILY MEETINGS

A family meeting is similar to a fairness meeting in several ways. Both seek to foster the values of equality, fairness, and cooperation in the family. Both enable children to grow in their ability to understand problems and solve them fairly. The similarity between these two kinds of meetings can be seen in the following interchange among members of the same family (the "Browns") that I used to illustrate the fairness approach. The cast of characters is the same, except that the father has now joined the group. The problem is whether watching television during dinnertime is acceptable.

> Mother: I'd like to see if we can reach a solution for this problem together. I, for one, don't like the TV on while we're eating dinner.
>
> James: Well, Mom, you always have dinner ready during our favorite program. Why can't we eat earlier?
>
> Father: I don't get home from work until 4:30, so we can't eat earlier. How about if we just turn the TV off while we're eating?
>
> Elizabeth: Then we'll miss "Adam 12." I have an idea. We can put the TV on the table. Then we can all watch and eat without moving.
>
> Mother: I don't want the TV on at all while we're eating. Perhaps I could plan dinner for after your program. The only thing is, then I'll be tied up in the kitchen later every night.
>
> Father: How about if we all helped with the cleaning up and doing dishes? Then it wouldn't take as long.

> Mother: I'd be willing to try this if everyone else is willing. What do you think, kids? I'll have dinner later if you all help me clean up so we won't be too late in the kitchen. Is this fair?

> Elizabeth: Yes.

> James: It's fair.

This particular meeting is clearly a kind of a fairness meeting, only done with the entire family. The fact that the whole family is involved, however, takes the situation an important step beyond the typical fairness meeting between a parent and one or two children. In a family meeting, the child has more perspectives to consider, more feelings to take into account. Moreover, the family meeting can be used to encourage children to take a qualitatively new perspective—that of the group. Questions can be raised such as, What can we do to make this a happier family? What does it mean to be a family? Asking children to take the perspective of the family as a group stretches their moral thinking in new ways. They must not only keep in mind the different viewpoints of individual family members but must also coordinate these viewpoints and think of what is good for the family as a whole. What will help keep the family peace? What will facilitate family communication? What will foster feelings of mutual support and togetherness? Children who share in dealing with questions like these are involved in the fundamentally cooperative and creative activity of _making_ a family.

For this reason, a family meeting is an ideal context for fostering what I have described in Chapter 7 as a "cooperative ethic." Such an ethic involves a feeling of shared purpose and a strong sense of collective responsibility for the common good. When a cooperative ethic surrounds and supports a family's negotiation of fair solutions to problems, it makes all the difference. With it, families can readily reach equitable solutions; generosity oils the wheels of justice. Without a cooperative ethic, fairness negotiations can turn into a self-protective, me-centered process with more "take" than "give."

A cooperative spirit was very much at work in the Brown family's solving of the television problem, as evidenced by the generous offers of both the mother (to change the dinnertime) and the rest of the family (to help with cleanup each night). This spirit of cooperation, the mother felt, was no accident. It had been deliberately cultivated in a previous family meeting that followed steps (see Figure 10.2) that I recommend as a way to begin family meetings. The leader opens with a statement of the purpose of the meeting and then

FIGURE 10.2

How to Begin Family Meetings

The First Meeting

1. Explain the purpose of a family meeting: "to communicate thoughts and feelings in a positive way. When families do this, they become happier and able to solve their problems."
2. Ask, "What rules for talking and listening do we need in order to have a good family meeting?" Write down the agreed-upon rules.
3. Say, "Let's each think of something that someone else in the family did for us recently that we really appreciated."
4. Invite each person to tell the family what it was that he or she appreciated.
5. Ask, "How did it feel to hear someone express appreciation for something you did?"
6. Ask each person to think of something he or she can do to make the family happier and to write this down (a parent or older sibling can help a child who cannot write).
7. Invite each person to read what he or she has written; decide when each of you will begin to do something that will make the family happier.
8. Agree upon a time for a follow-up meeting.
9. Close with, "What was something we each liked about this family meeting?"

The Second Meeting

1. Review the rules for talking and listening.
2. Ask, "What did we each do since the last family meeting to try to make the family happier?"
3. Ask, "Is there a problem in our family that we could solve fairly by talking together?" Choose a problem and follow Steps 7 through 10 of the fairness meeting.

Source: Constructed by the author.

elicits agreed-upon rules for talking and listening that will help the
family have a good discussion. The next step is for each person to
think of an appreciated action by another family member and to express that appreciation before the group. (One procedure is to write
down on a index card what it was that you appreciated; the cards are
then exchanged, with each person reading aloud another person's
statement.)

These expressions of appreciation call to mind the "Appreciation Time" that teachers have used to create a caring community in
their classrooms (see Chapter 7). It is a simple but powerful process, one that sets a positive tone for whatever discussion follows.
In the first family meeting held by the Browns, appreciations went
like this:

> Elizabeth: James let me get in bed with him last
> night.
>
> James: Mom gave me enough money to buy double
> pizza for lunch today. I appreciated that.
>
> Father: James and Elizabeth, I appreciated your
> helping me with the dishes the other night
> when Mon wasn't feeling well.
>
> Mother: I thank all of you for letting me lie down
> and rest the other night while you all did
> the dishes.

"After we all had spoken," the mother reports, "we agreed that it
felt good to hear someone say something nice about us. The children
were especially pleased with the notes of appreciation they received."

Once family members feel appreciated by others, they are more
disposed to take the next recommended step of answering the question,
What is something I can do to make the family happier? Each person's decision can then be written down, including a commitment to
a time for putting the new resolutions into practice.

The second family meeting should be a follow-up to the first.
It should begin with a recognition of improvements in the family, however modest, since the first meeting. If no improvements have been
made, each person should be invited to comment on reasons for his
or her failure to carry out the resolution made in the first meeting,
and a plan should be made for doing better. If some progress has
been made, the family can move on to tackling a group issue—such
as television at dinnertime—that requires group problem solving.
This kind of group problem solving is a good deal easier if it has been
preceded by visible efforts on everyone's part to contribute to the
family's well-being. That was in fact the experience of the Browns.

To keep family meetings from going stale, they should range over a wide variety of topics. Sentence stems that families have found useful for varying the subject of the meeting include: "I wish . . . ," "I feel . . . ," "Something that's on my mind is . . . ," and "Something I like to do together as a family is . . . ." Family meetings have also been used to:

Democratically establish rules for family living (for example, the division of chores, bedtime, curfew),
Deal with infractions of family rules,
Negotiate new privileges,
Air and defuse feelings (anxieties, pressures, anger, frustrations),
Plan (for example, a birthday party, a vacation, how to get through a rainy Saturday), and
Discuss an abstract issue (for example, "What's the difference between fairness and love? Why are both important in a family?" or "What does it mean to have a democratic family?").

Handled correctly—in an atmosphere of mutual respect—all of these issues can serve to foster both the growth of the family as a moral community and the individual moral growth of its members.

Whenever possible, a family should reach consensus on how to solve a problem rather than voting. Voting tends to foster divisiveness and a feeling among those in the minority of having lost the argument. Striving for consensus compels cooperation by requiring all members to try to understand everyone else's perspective in an effort to achieve agreement. Rotating the leadership is another effective strategy that stimulates the child's development by giving him a more responsible role to play in the family. Even a five-year-old can be coached to conduct a family meeting. The child can be given the words to say to the group—for example, "Everyone take a turn and tell your point of view about the problem" followed by "Everyone tell how you think the problem should be solved." A parent or older child can record the various viewpoints and solutions as they are offered and then read them back as a review of everything that has been said. I have found that writing things down helps considerably to focus thinking and discussion and move the meeting steadily toward a conclusion. (For further discussions of family meetings, see Dreikurs, Gould and Corsini [1974] and Lickona [n.d.]).

My own work with families has generated informal documentation of the effects of family meetings on relationships between parents and children and the moral atmosphere of the home. Formal research on family meetings and their effects on the moral development

of adolescents has been carried out by Stanley and reported in her
excellent chapter, "The Family and Moral Education" (1979; see also
1976). Stanley conducted a ten-week course for ten parents and seven
ninth- and tenth-grade adolescents (five families). Part one of the
course taught parents and their adolescents how to talk with one another, particularly about rules and conflicts. They saw, modeled,
and practiced skills of empathic listening and confrontation. Especially valuable, Stanley reports, was a session in which participants
were asked to write down the family rules and how they were decided.

In the second part of the course, families were taught through
role playing how to conduct family meetings. As homework, each
family conducted a family meeting and tape-recorded the first and
last of their meetings. Holding such discussions with their children
was no small step for many parents. "I can't let a twelve-year-old
tell me how to run my life!" was the way one man expressed his fear
of losing control over family decision making.

In the third part of the course, families learned a systematic,
six-step democratic approach to conflict resolution (similar to a
fairness meeting) adapted from the work of T. Gordon (1970). In
the fourth and final section of the course, parents and adolescents
discussed personal moral dilemmas (for example, what should you do
if you see a friend doing something that you think is wrong, like cheating or stealing?). They also discussed differences in values between
parents and children as revealed by an exercise that asked each
family member to rank his or her own values and to predict the
rankings of other family members. Parents who ranked values
such as broad-mindedness, love, and forgiveness as being most important to them were shocked to find out that their children believed
that they would rank, as most important, values such as politeness,
obedience, and cleanliness.

What were the effects of Stanley's moral curriculum for the
family? First, she found that by the end of the course parents had
become significantly more egalitarian in their attitudes toward family
decision making, as measured by a parental attitude inventory.
Second, by analyzing tapes of first and last family meetings, she
found that parents talked less as the course progressed and spent
more time eliciting the opinions and feelings of their children. This
shift was accompanied by an increase in a family's effectiveness at
making decisions. Finally, the adolescents in the course showed a
significant advance in moral reasoning, as measured by the Kohlberg
moral judgment interview. A control group showed no such advance.
Moreover, the experimental subjects increased their advantage over
controls on a posttest one year later.

Because the family meetings were intertwined with other activities and influences in the course, it is impossible to say for certain

that the positive outcomes were due to the meetings. But the family decision-making sessions were the major intervention of the course, and it seems likely that they accounted for a good deal of the change. I take Stanley's data as supporting the testimony of individual families I have worked with regarding the value of family meetings. One father summarized the benefits this way: "Looking back, I think one of our most important achievements has been learning to share our ideas and to listen to and respect each other's point of view. Some important decisions affecting the family are now being arrived at by all the members and not just Mom and Dad. We have decided that when any member of the family is having a problem, he or she may call a meeting so that everyone can help try to solve that person's problem. Our family is growing closer together." It seems reasonable to hope that children who develop deeply rooted concern for the rights and needs of others within their own family will come someday to feel a similar concern for all members of the human family.

STRATEGY 4: DEVELOP A POSITIVE AFFECTIVE RELATIONSHIP WITH THE CHILD

We know intuitively, I think, that there is something more basic than whether our parents set a good example, deal with us fairly, or include us in democratic decision making, important as all of these things are. We sense that beneath or prior to these influences is something still more fundamental on which everything else builds. I submit that what may be prior to morality is love.

Recall the warm, glowing terms in which the German rescuer spoke of his mother. Recall the affection that the fully committed civil rights workers felt for their parents. These are not isolated findings. Parental warmth, while not the only antecedent of mature conscience, has been consistently and positively linked in the research literature to children's moral development (see, for example, Hoffman 1970; Staub 1976, 1978).

A study that points to the importance of a positive parent-child relationship to moral development was conducted by Mantell (1974), a clinical psychologist. Mantell probed into the family backgrounds of two groups of young men with diametrically opposed attitudes toward the Vietnam War: 25 War Resisters and an equal number of Green Berets. The soldiers were randomly selected from a Special Forces detachment stationed in Germany; 20 had previously served in Vietnam. The War Resisters were randomly chosen from members of the New York City-based War Resisters League; they were usually deeply involved in public protest of the war and many faced jail sentences for refusing induction, burning their draft cards, and the like. Each subject underwent intensive interviewing, lasting 5 to 15 hours.

The Resisters and Green Berets came from stable homes; divorce had occurred in only one out of six families. But there the similarity ended. In Green Beret families, the fathers laid down the law, demanded unquestioning obedience, and responded to deviations with physical punishment, often severe. The War Resisters' fathers, by contrast, set fewer and more flexible rules and relied chiefly on praise, reasoning, and reward to encourage desired behavior.

The differences in moral development between Resisters and Berets were evident in their recollected adolescence. Green Berets had defied authority often but when no one was looking. They had engaged in frequent drunken driving, petty theft, and vandalism. War Resisters had also defied authority but did so openly and because of deeply held moral beliefs that conflicted with authority's rules or behavior.

Most striking were the differences in the overall relationship between father and son. While discussions of varied topics were common in War Resisters' families, they hardly ever occurred in the families of Green Berets. Only three Green Beret fathers were remembered as understanding and only three as affectionate. Nearly half of the Green Berets could not recall ever sharing an interest with their father. War Resisters' fathers, on the other hand, typically took a strong interest in their son's hobbies, schoolwork, and thoughts. Most of the War Resisters continued to feel deep affection for their fathers, despite whatever faults they attributed to them. These profiles suggest strongly that the positive relationships that War Resisters enjoyed with their fathers provided strong supports for the development of a principles conscience.

Another study, carried out in a very different context, fits the same pattern. Holstein (1972) studied 53 families with eighth-grade youngsters in an upper-middle-class community in San Francisco. First, she individually interviewed the parents and the children to determine their major stage of moral reasoning. Then, in individual interviews, she asked the parents and their eighth-grader to discuss a moral dilemma that they had each solved in different ways.

Holstein discovered that parents who scored at Kohlberg's post-conventional level (Stage 5) valued democratic process in their family discussion of the dilemma. They took their adolescent's opinion seriously and tried to incorporate it and reach genuine consensus. Parents who had scored at Stage 3 or 4 of Kohlberg's scale behaved very differently; they were likely to explain to their child that they were right and then expect the child to conform to their judgment.

Not surprisingly, children of higher-stage parents turned out to be farther along in their moral judgment development than children of lower-stage parents.

Holstein then looked at the relationship between the child's stage of moral reasoning and that of each parent. She found that all of the principled, Stage 5 mothers had children who had progressed from preconventional moral reasoning (Stages 1 and 2) to conventional moral reasoning (Stages 3 and 4). For fathers, however, there appeared to be no such relationship at all. Principled fathers were just as likely to have preconventional children as they were to have conventional-level children.

Puzzled by this, Holstein probed further. She compared what she called "unsuccessful fathers" (principled themselves but with children still reasoning at a preconventional level) with "successful fathers" (principled themselves and with children who had developed to the conventional moral stages). When the children of both groups of fathers were asked to rate how often their fathers showed affection to them or played with them, the successful fathers emerged as much warmer than unsuccessful fathers and as much more involved with their child. Thus, Holstein's findings lend further support to the idea that a child's moral development is affected by the nature of the total relationship between parent and child. Morality appears to grow best when it is nurtured by love.

Why this is so is a matter of theoretical speculation. It may be that close relationships provide more frequent opportunities for the various kinds of role-taking experiences that are held to be crucial for the development of moral reasoning. I suspect it goes deeper than that. Consider the following passage from an essay by Barnard (1974), originator of the heart transplant:

> Whenever we were ill, my father got up at night to doctor us. I suffered from festering toenails that pained so much I would cry in bed. My father used to draw out the fester with a poultice made of milk and bread crumbs, or Sunlight soap and sugar. And when I had a cold, he would rub my chest with Vicks and cover it with a red flannel cloth. Sunday afternoons we walked together to the top of the hill by the dam. Once there we would sit on a rock and look down at the town below us. Then I would tell my problems to my father, and he would speak of his to me. [p. 21]

To me, this passage bespeaks a tenderness, an intimacy, and a depth of affection between father and son that make further comment almost superfluous. We nod as we read it; we know in our hearts that this is good. Indeed, that is where the impact of such a relationship is—on the human heart. For a son to have such a father is to have a person to love, to identify with, to want to be like. I think the old notion of "identification" with the parent deserves another look as we try to understand the nature and causes of moral development in children. Identification, or something like it, may provide much of the emotional force behind the process of moral growth. Stages of cognitive moral reasoning such as Kohlberg's help the growing child answer the question, How should I be moral? (by being obedient to authority, by making fair deals, by pleasing others). Stages do not, however, answer the more basic existential question, <u>Why</u> be moral? I may be perfectly capable of high moral reasoning but not care enough to use it when I face a moral problem in the real world. To understand why some people care deeply about being good and others hardly at all would require us to look at many factors. One of them, I think, is the quality of the affective bond between parent and child.*

STRATEGY 5: HELP THE CHILD SEE THE WORLD THROUGH A MORAL LENS

This last strategy puts the accent on something that is part of the other strategies as well: helping children see the world through a moral lens. The goal here is to sensitize children to questions of right and wrong—to open their eyes to the moral dimensions of any human situation.

---

*The optimal amount of parental affection may vary with the sex of the child. Bronfenbrenner (1961) reports that adolescent girls rated high on moral responsibility received less parental affection and less discipline than girls rated low on moral responsibility; boys rated high on responsibility received more affection and discipline than boys rated low.

Similarly, the optimal degree of identification with a parent may vary as the child moves through the stages toward moral autonomy. Haan, Smith, and Block (1968) found that principled moral reasoners in the Berkeley sit-in disagreed moderately with their parents on social issues, whereas conventional-stage reasoners expressed virtually no disagreement with their parents' views. Strong identification with the parent may be optimal in childhood when the child is progressing toward conventional morality; less strong identification may be optimal in adolescence when the task is to progress toward postconventional morality.

One way to do this is to discuss moral questions in the home on a regular basis. The opportunities for moral discussions are endless. There are all the problems and conflicts within a family that can be discussed in moral terms. What are the rights and obligations of parents? What are the rights and obligations of children? There are all the situations a child encounters at school and with his peers. Is it right to let a friend copy your homework? What should you do if your friends ostracize or ridicule another child? And there are all the moral conflicts and crises in the news about the world at large. Should hospital workers go on strike? Should nuclear power plants be allowed to operate in densely populated areas? Should capital punishment be restored? Should the drinking age be raised to 21?

In our own family—we have two boys, ages 11 and 6—we have used the dinnertime to discuss moral issues. We have found the newspaper "advice column" (for example, "Dear Abby") to be a good source of real-life dilemmas that are both challenging to the mind and easy on the stomach. One of us reads the letter aloud but not the advice. What should a grandmother do who finds her three young grandchildren to be extremely jealous of her attentions? What should a mother do when her second-grade son says he does not have to tie his shoes because "Daddy don't"? Should children be made to visit relatives if they do not want to go? What should people do if they suspect their babysitter, the son of good friends, of stealing from their rare-coin collection? Should an eight-year-old girl be allowed to talk every night on the phone and go to the movies with a "boyfriend" she says she "loves"? Should a boy tell his teacher that he saw a classmate defacing school property? Our task has been to decide what advice we would given in these situations and why.

There is ample reserach documentation that classroom discussion of moral dilemmas and issues stimulates advance in students' moral reasoning (see Lockwood 1973, for a review). Within the family, Grimes (1974) found that a program of moral dilemma discussion between parents and their eleven-year-olds was followed by a shift in children's moral reasoning from Stage 2 to Stage 3 on Kohlberg's scale. Vertical stage development of this sort is obviously important and one of the significant benefits of engaging children in moral dialogue and debate. Equally important, however, is another kind of growth that is rarely discussed in the literature: namely, horizontal development. By horizontal development I mean the process of spreading out one's powers of moral reasoning to cover a widening range of life situations. The goal of horizontal development is that people will use what moral reasoning they have, that they will see the world around them in moral terms and make decisions that are moral decisions.

It may well be that the most serious moral deficiency in contemporary society is not that people ask moral questions and reach the
wrong conclusions but that they do not ask moral questions at all.
Halberstam, in his Pulitzer Prize winning book, The Best and the
Brightest (1969), reports that in all the councils of government that
charted the course of the Vietnam War, no one ever raised a moral
question about the war. The best intellects in the country never asked:
Is this right? Right to escalate the bombing? Right to napalm civi-
lians in South Vietnamese villages? Right to support a government
that imprisoned and tortued political opponents? Right to be involved
at all? The advisers and the decision makes asked only: Is this
smart? Can we get away with it? What will the military and political
consequences be?

The same amoral calculation has been depressingly evident in
U.S. domestic scandals as well. A Federal Bureau of Investigation
official who directed that agency's attempts in the 1960s to blackmail
Martin Luther King and sabotage the civil rights movement was subsequently asked, "Did you, at any time, stop to consider whether
what you were doing was right?" His response: "The question never
crossed my mind."

Why is moral blindness so common? Why do not people auto-
matically stop and ask themselves, Is this right? Self-interest is
surely one of the reasons. An active conscience can be a great inconvenience. It makes it more difficult to cheat on our income tax,
tell a self-serving lie, damage another person's reputation, or do
nothing when we see others being wronged. Fear of ridicule also
serves to stifle moral questions. Persons who are public about their
concern for others are called "do-gooders" or "bleeding hearts."
Expressing moral doubts about the Vietnam War, Halberstam tells
us, was regarded in the halls of power as weak or unmanly. Many
of us can remember sharply the discomfort we felt on those occasions when we revealed "moral scruples" about something those
around us considered merely the smart thing to do. It is certainly
a measure of the challenge before us as moral educators that the
human condition is such that we feel embarrassed when we try to be
good.

With self-interest and the world's scorn allied against morality,
children need to think and talk about moral questions until it becomes
second nature to do so. Only if moral discussion is part of their
everyday discourse will it be natural for them to ask consistently,
Is this right? Is it right to follow the crowd? Cheat on this test?
Take this drug? Exploit this boy or girl? By taking the time to discuss moral issues in the home, we say to our children, "Being a
good person matters. There is nothing more important in life than

doing what is right." Parents who make moral concerns central in the dialogue of the home are likely to have children who make morality central in their lives.

4

MORAL EDUCATION AND SPECIAL CONCERNS

11

SEX ROLE ASSIGNMENT IN FAMILY AND SCHOOL SYSTEMS: AN ISSUE OF JUSTICE

V. Lois Erickson

Children have moral claims on members of both the family and society to be cared for and guided toward becoming what they might become. Parents and teachers in particular have major moral responsibilities in these areas. This chapter focuses on an issue of justice: in our society, care and guidance "to become" is not often offered to children as unique individuals but to girl children and boy children according to the prevailing sex role assignments. In this chapter, I will examine this problem through the perspective of developmental and social theories, trace some of the limiting growth patterns that have resulted for girls and boys and for women and men, and stress that the restricting of human potential through sex role assignment is an issue of justice. In the conclusion, I will argue that solutions must rest in our own adult development—we parents and teachers must look at our own moral and ego conceptions of maleness and femaleness and rethink those conceptions that limit human growth.

THE PROBLEM: CONVENTIONAL SELF-ORGANIZATIONS IN MOST ADULTS

To be optimistic for a moment, I want to stress that some men and women do come to a level in their maturity where they recognize the mutuality of need and purpose between the sexes. They have a glimpse of understanding that their identities are separate yet inter-related and even come to cherish this separateness within a common humanity. They also recognize across sexes the common drama of the flesh and spirit and may even realize that the conflicts pitting males against females mark but a temporary moment in human history.

However, the problem before us is that most men and women do not capture this glimpse of the whole, or if they do, it is fleeting, or elusive, and does not affect their lives. Developmentally, most adults do not transcend the concrete traditions, roles, and rule systems of their society (Kohlberg 1973; Loevinger 1976). They settle for accepting what is, and never ask what might be or ought to be. Conformity to the is in a society such as our own limits both men and women; like lids upon our growth, the conventions of our social institutions, while offering security and predictability, stablize and cement our growth. Just what does this mean developmentally and how is this a different problem for women and men? In the following section, I review briefly how limiting sex-role conceptions may take hold in children and then not be transcended in the maturing process.

Kohlberg (1966) has created a theoretical framework to account for the acquisition of sex-typed attitudes and behaviors based on cognitive organization and development and on competency motivation. He theorizes that early sex labeling using the words "girl" and "boy" results in a self-categorization that initiates the sex-typing process in a young child. The child then actively selects and organizes perception, knowledge, and understanding along this sex-role dimension. The understanding of sex-role is concrete in the young child and is focused on physical differences in body structure. For example, the larger physical size and strength of most adult males results in the young child holding the belief by age 6-7 that males have more social power and prestige than females. Thus the theory suggest that universally-perceived sex differences in bodily structures and capacities create sex stereotypes: differences in body size, shape, function and strength between the sexes result in beliefs about what females and males are like, what they can do, what they should do, and how this is valued.

Kohlberg indicates that the motivational forces to build cognitive structures around this sexual self-concept are likely to be closely connected to competency motives (see White 1959). Kohlberg elaborates (in Erikson 1974), "A girl, cognitively perceiving herself as a female, therefore values what her society deems to be feminine attitudes, behaviors, and objects because of the gneral tendency to value and to be competent in dimensions consistent with one's perceived identity". Social reinforcement works in that "the girl asserts she is a girl, she wants to do girl things: therefore the opportunity to do girl things and the presence of feminine models is rewarding". Thus, the young girl views herself as a female like her mother; she wants to do the things that her mother does; and when she does these tasks with her mother, it is rewarding. Identification with the parent of the same sex, sex-differentiated roles, and social reinforcements to maintain these assigned roles then perpetuate the cognitive structures. However—and this is important—the press of the socialization process impinges differently on the two sexes. And, not surprisingly, the conventional sex assignments held by most adults are expressed in their practice of parenting and teaching such that boys and girls are socialized differently.

The evidence that shows that differential socialization in our society can and does result in major differences between the sexes is overwhelming (Block 1973, 1976; Maccoby and Jacklin 1974; Termon and Tyler 1954; Tyler 1965). I am content to report the work of Block (1973, 1976). Her research shows that boys are socialized with an emphasis on achievement and competition, insistence on control of feelings and expressions of affect, and concern for rule conformity. Girls are supposed to develop and maintain close interpersonal re-lationships; they are shown affection physically, given comfort and reassurance, and encouraged to talk about their problems and reflect on life. Block's research indicates that while the issues between parent and son appear to be those of authority and control, the parent-daughter themes emphasize relatedness, protection, and support. Her studies also suggest that fathers are more crucial than has been supposed in channeling the sex typing of both male and female children.

Let me summarize the major points before us so far. Early self-categorization as male or female leads to selective perception and organization along sex role dimensions. Because most adults are conventional in their conceptions of their roles, they perpetuate these sex role dichotomies in the socialization of their own children. The socialization pattern is different for boys and girls, and I argue later in this chapter that significant, though different, personal costs in psychological growth are paid by both sexes.

CONCEPTIONS OF MATURITY: THE LOEVINGER PARADIGM

Before further examining these concerns, it would be helpful to reflect on conceptions of maturity. What is maturity? How can the maturity process be described? Is the socialized conformist just an intermediate step toward full maturity? Are there growth stages that clearly transcend this? These sorts of important questions are in no way new. Socrates, in Plato's Apology (1914), raises such concerns with Callias:

If your two sons were only colts or bullocks, we could
have hired a trainer for them to make them beautiful
and good and all that they should be; and our trainer
would have been, I take it, a horseman or a farmer.

> But now that they are human beings, have you any trainer
> in your mind for them? Is there anyone who understands
> what a man [human] and a citizen outght to be?

In our own time, psychologists have proposed answers to such questions, making them the core of their developmental theories. Perhaps
the most comprehensive, well-researched paradigm of personality
development emerging in this era is that based on the ego development
work of Loevinger (1976).

Loevinger defines the ego as close to what the person thinks of
as the self. The striving to master, to integrate, to make sense of
experience is the essence of ego. She identifies the characteristics
of the ego as having a structure, functioning as a whole, and being
guided by purpose and meaning. Ego development can be seen as the
increase in complexity and differentiation, involving structural change
in thinking. The way we think about ourselves, others, and our experiences becomes more complex as the ego develops. Thus, a shift
from dichotomous thinking to appreciating multiple perspectives, the
use of exceptions and contengencies, the growing sense of having a
past and a future, and perspective taking of the viewpoints of others
all take place with ego development. These more adequate forms and
qualities of thought develop sequentially, in stages. (Table 11.1
places Loevinger's ego stages parallel to Kohlberg's stages of moral
judgment.)* But just how do conceptions of sex role assignments relate to stages of ego and moral development?

We know that at the conformity stage (3) socialization patterns
impinge differently on boys and girls: they channel most women into
a pattern of care and communion and most men into a pattern of
achievement and agency. Only in the higher stages do traditional sex
roles and rules for fairness become modified as the individual begins
to express a differentiated sense of self. At the self aware ego level
(3/4), the modal level for adults in our society, a questioning of sex
role assignments becomes at least a possiblity. At the next stages
(4 through 4/5) the conscientious person greatly increases tolerance

---

*The ego is considered to be the global essence of the conscious
personality, and moral judgment is considered a domain within it.
In Table 12.1, the Loevinger ego stages are paralleled with the
Kohlberg stages of moral judgment. Research indicates that the corresponding ego stage is a necessary but not sufficient condition for
moral stage.

TABLE 11.1

Approximate Correspondence of Ego and Moral Stages

Stage	Characteristic
Loevinger	
Stage 1: presocial	Distinguishes self from nonself
Stage 2: impulsive	Present orientation; dichotomous thinking
Transition stage Δ: self-protective	Guarded perceptions; opportunistic behavior
Stage 3: conformist	Identification with peer group; focuses on appearance or things
Transition stage 3/4: conscientious-conformist	Growing self-awareness, reflection, and introspection
Stage 4: conscientious	Rich and differentiated inner life; sense of personal choice
Transition stage 4/5: individualistic	Toleration and respect for individual differences
Stage 5: autonomous	Cherishing individual differences; toleration of ambiguity
Stage 6: integrated	Integration of identity; a sense of a common humanity
Kohlberg	
Stage 1: punishment and obedience (heteronomous morality)	Fear of punishment; obedience to power dominates; physical consequences prevail
Stage 2: naïve instrumental hedonism	Satisfaction of own needs; trade-off behavior
Stage 3: Interpersonal conformity	Loyalty and affection are predominant concerns
Stage 4: law and order	Societal maintenance; honor and duty through rules
Stage 5: social contract	No legal absolutes; rules are recognized as made by people
Stage 6: universal ethical principles	Universal principles of justice that hold for all people; transcend cultural rules

Source: Compiled by the author.

and respect for individual differences. Not only to accept but to cherish individuality is the mark of the autonomous ego stage (5). If also at a postconventional level of morality, the person sees the right to this individuality as an issue of justice and has the courage to acknowledge and deal with conflict. An autonomous person can unite and integrate ideas, tolerate ambiguity, and take a broad view of life as a whole. The highest ego stage (6), the integrated, is rare indeed, and a new element is present—the integration of identity across sexes within a common humanity.

With Table 11.1 before us, we can argue that both men and women must go through these qualitatively different, sequential stages if they are to reach the more adequate stages of autonomy and integration. However, because the effects of socialization emphasize self-achievement or agency for males and social orientation or communion for females, to transcend these polarities in reaching full maturity requires different tasks for each sex (Block 1973). Women must learn to integrate aspects of agentic self-assertion and self-expression with concern for communion. Men need to learn to balance their sense of the achieving self, or agency, with considerations of mutuality, interdepedence, and joint welfare. For an integration of agency and communion, or rights and responsibilities, occurs in an integrated person, man or woman (Bakan 1966; Block 1973).

PARENTING AND TEACHING: GENERATIVITY TASKS IN THE ERIKSON THEORY

If we can now visualize what maturity is and could be, and how both men and women are derailed in the process, we can approach the roles of parenting and teaching through the sequential perspective of psychosocial task theory. Most readers will recognize that there are qualitative differences in how adults conceptualize their parenting and teaching tasks. During the past three years, I have been studying task/ structure relationships across ego theories—asking the basic question: Do adults at varying ego levels (loevinger) approach their life tasks in an identifiably different way? Using Erikson's "Eight Ages of Man" (1963), I have studied the particularly adult ego qualities of identity, intimacy, generativity, and integrity and traced the varying conceptions of each psychosocial ego stage as seen through the lens of the successive ego structures.

Let us next briefly review Erikson's thinking on his familiar psychosocial tasks. Erikson's concept of ego identity is the sense of confidence that the inner sameness and continuity in the self, developed in the past, are matched by the sameness and continuity of one's meaning for others. Thus, a core consistency in the self is predictably

there. The danger of this stage is role confusion. The strengths acquired at this stage allow individuals to be eager to fuse their identities with those of others. Intimacy in Erikson's theory is viewed as
the capacity to commit oneself to concrete affiliations and partner-
ships and to develop the ethical strength to abide by such commitments,
even though this may call for significant sacrifices and compromises.
The avoidance of such experiences can lead to a deep sense of isolation.

Generativity is primarily the concern in establishing and guiding
the next generation, a quality that migh include but extends beyond
one's own offspring. One does not achieve generativity by the mere
fact of having children. A personal sense of loss or impoverishment
often pervades when this caring fails. Parenting and teaching, when
they are true expressions of guidance for the children of the world,
reflect a profound sense of generativity. Erikson stresses that while
the maturing process of youth needs guidance by mature adults,
mature adults also need to be needed. Erikson's last stage, ego
integrity versus despair, represents a new integration: an accepting
of one's own life at its given time in history as something that had to
be no matter how dear the cost. In this stage, an understanding of
some world order in a spiritual sense takes meaning. Erikson writes
that a "wise Indian, a true gentleman, and a mature peasant share
and recognize in one another the final phase of integrity" (1963).

Now that we have taken a broad look at growth theories and
tried to integrate them for a more comprehensive look at the concept
of maturity, let us go back to our specific concern of sex role assignment and issues of justice in family and school systems.

IDENTITY/IMTIMACY

Let us first try to capture the identity/intimacy constructions of
males and females as they develop toward increased maturity, according to Loevinger's theory. I want to clarify that identity and intimacy
represent a fluidness, a mutually ongoing development of the identity
and intimacy tasks.* So, with this acknowledgement of a fused

---

*Although Erikson clearly states that only through a successful
core resolution of identity can true intimacy be achieved, he also
says that the sequence is a bit different for women. A woman holds
her identity in abeyance as she prepares to find the man who will
rescue her from her emptiness and loneliness by filling what he calls
the "inner space" (Gilligan 1977). While for men he sees identity as

identity/intimacy resolution, let us review the related structural ego development.

People at preconventional 2 or Δego identity have likely not yet resolved the earlier stage of trust versus mistrust such that they can risk being vulnerable with people. Thus, they need to control others and assume people are all pitted against each other. Erikson's concept of a negative identity reaction, an identity in opposition to others, seems to fall into these preconventional Loevinger ego stages. Intimacy at these stages can amount to genital combat. Thus, the opposite sex is viewed in dichotomous, simplistic ways. Preconventional men view women as "goddess or devil," "virgin or whole." Preconventional women view men as "benevolent father" or "surly misogynist" "sugar daddy" or "rapist." While the maturity of the identity shapes the intimacy that seems possible, the process seems to be identity through intimacy. Indicative of such a stage are books which suggest that we "look out for number 1."

Persons at conformity stages of identity and intimacy have not yet sorted out their own uniqueness or the uniqueness of those they relate to. Identity is more a mirroring; intimacy is largely a search for the self. For women at a conformity stage, there has also been a negation of self in service of others, which lends to a "morality of responsibility." Gilligan (1977) argues that women are just learning to claim their own moral rights. She notes that the Western philosophy affirming the rights of the autonomous man has been accepted as a given in Kohlberg's stages of moral judgment. Gilligan argues that men, too, need a morality of greater care and responsibility. As stated above, this bridging of rights and responsibilities, agency and communion, is possible only at the higher stages of ego and moral integration.

Persons at a conscientious stage of identity/intimacy can reflect, introspect, and think about thinking. At this stage, they question identification with traditional sex roles and seek their own identities. This emerging conscientious identity/intimacy stage is captured in Scarlett O'Hara's words in Gone With the Wind:

> I'm tired of everlasting being unnatural and never doing
> anything I want to do. I'm tired of acting like I don't

---

preceding intimacy, for women he claims these tasks seem fused. Despite these observations on sex differences in human separation and attachment, Erikson's chart follows the male diagonal: women are considered the deviant sex. However, identity through intimacy is the experience of most women.

eat more than a bird and walking when I want to run,
and saying I feel faint after a waltz, when I could dance
for two days and never get tired. I'm tired of saying
"how wonderful you are" to fool men who haven't got
one half the sense I've got, and I'm tired of pretending
I don't know anything, so men can tell me things and
feel important while they're doing it. [Mitchell 1936]

The dialectic of identity/intimacy as understood by a person at
a postconventional (5 through 6) ego level is expressed in Gibran's
(1964) poem on marriage:

Let there be spaces in your togetherness,
And let the winds of the heavens dance between you

. . . For the pillars of the temple stand apart,
And the oak tree and the cypress grow not in each other's shadow.

GENERATIVITY

Erikson (1974) relates his developmental psychosocial tasks to
the conception of care: "In youth you find out what you care to do and
who you care to be. In young adulthood you learn whom you care to
be with. In adulthood you learn to know what and whom you can take
care of"
The concept of care in persons of fragile identity by necessity
reflects their own insecurity and self-protectiveness. To be generative requires seeing children as people separate from the self with
their own potential for transcending assigned roles toward their own
uniqueness. In The Great Gatsby, surely Daisy reveals her own
limited identity when she says:

She told me it was a girl, and I turned my head away'
and wept. "All right," I said, "I'm glad it's a girl.
And I hope she'll be a fool—that is the best thing a
girl can be in this world, a beautiful little fool."
[Fitzgerald, 1925]

This cannot be generativity by Erikson's definitions, nor is a
person at the next stage of conformity able to guide children in a truly
generative way. In Boslooper and Hayes's book, The Feminity Game
(1973) Chris Evert's mother is quoted as saying, "If my daughter ever
developed big leg muscles, she'd give up tennis" (p. 47). Now this

quotation may seem simplistic, but in the attempt to conform, to mirror the "right" appearances and customs, teachers and parents with conformity orientations often adjust children to a state inferior to their capacities. If a child remains Daddy's "little girl," the "chip off the ol' block," or "teacher's pet," the generativity process may be smooth but hardly growth producing—for either the child or the adult. Haan (1971) writes on the moral growth possible in families if both parents and children cope with the disequilibrium and conflict that occurs as family members seek their identities. But, if teachers and parents view their task as shaping children to duplicate their elders, then the concept of generativity is indeed limited.

By contrast, some humans progressively construct rather than merely reflect their experiences. Conscientious teachers and parents (those at Loevinger's stages 4 through 4/5) are able to discern how they ought to be generative, and they strive for a high standard of achievement. Teaching and rearing children is a serious responsibility not to be taken lightly. Even when parents undertake these responsibilities seriously, however, they do not often take into consideration the uniqueness of the individual child. Conflicting positions are often subdued for the maintenance of the unit, and adult authority still determines the decision process. (See Chapter 8 for a fuller treatment of this topic.)

Autonomous/integrated teachers and parents are sensitivie to the growth and change of the child and recognize that care for the young offers a chance for a completion of their own development. Rosalie Wahl, a mother, poet, and associate justice of the Minnesota Supreme Court, expresses this recognition:

A good many years ago, when my then four children were in school and I had gone with some trepidation to law school to prepare myself to help share the econmic burden of supporting those children, a poem came to me which expressed my feeling at that time of what it meant to be a woman:

> Foot in nest,
> Wing in sky;
> Bound by each
> Hover I.

Now I know it is not necessary to hover. Now I know it is possible to soar, to know the vastness of the sky and then come back, fully to the next, enriched by the vision of the whole and by the exercise.

Now I know it is possible to extend the next to include our children wherever they are—in the factories,

at the switchboards, in the mines, the shops, the halls
of finance and commerce and government—and nourish
there the values which were sprouted by the hearth—a
sense that every individual in the human family is a
unique and precious being, a sense of justice and fair
play, a sense of compassion where justice ends or
fails.

I pledge to you and ask your pledge that wherever
we are, we will never cease to work for these goals.
[Minneapolis Star 1977, p. 6]

TRANSCENDING SEX ROLE STEREOTYPES: PERSPECTIVES FOR PARENTS AND TEACHERS

Only when people develop appreciation for the uniqueness of self
and others can they encourage postconventional human qualities in
children and youth. A mature personal ego makes it possible for an
individual to cope with increasingly deeper problems—those of self-
ideal, proper care and guidance of the young, meaning in intimate
relationships, belief in the species, and being just in an unjust world.
But, how do we get there from here? Jack Mezirow (1978) writes:

A cardinal dimension of adult development and the learning most uniquely adult pertains to becoming more aware
that one is caught in one's own history and is reliving
it. This leads to a process of perspective transformation involving a structural change in the way we see
ourselves and our relationships. [P. 100]

He quotes the verse of Laing (1969) for a glimpse of this adult learning problem:

We have to help him realize that,
the fact that he does not think there is anything
the matter with him
is one of the things that is
the matter with him.

Just how do we adults rethink our belief systems? In particular,
how do we help other parents and teachers to guide the children of the
next generation toward a more complete conception of humanness?
The literature on developmental change points to unexpected break-
throughs in science, historical catastrophes, and major personal
tragedies as "disturbers of mankind's sleep" (Erickson 1977) and

resulted in a change in the "collective ego" (p. 28). But can we afford such a random, chaotic approach to human growth? The sameness, the absurdity of living our lives without challenging the roles we play, the loss to both men and women—is this not too great a price to pay? What can we do in a deliberate, educative way to help ourselves and others transcend sex role assignments?

Socrates has said that we should teach a person what he or she "almost knows." Research in ego and moral development advocates the use of pacers, guides, and constructive mismatches. To help ourselves, other parents, and teachers transcend sex role stereotypes, we can also learn from what has been discovered in developmental intervention research. We can better plan growth strategies if we understand that change in beliefs occurs slowly, is triggered by recognizing inconsistency, involves a rethinking of what is more adequate, involves perspective taking of consequences to others, is integrated through doing what we say we believe in, and is viewed as a continuing process. While there are no cookbook directions for learning to be a more mature person, here are some strategies for transcending sex role stereotypes:

1. Practice listening to your own beliefs on your own sex role expections. For example, I recently heard myself silently agreeing with a speaker that the great increase in "runaway mothers" most certainly reflected a "deep psychic disturbance in their attachment formation." Later, after a two-hour dinner with several other men and women who attended the seminar, I realized that of about one-third of adult males who are divorced, 98 percent of those who have children do not seek custody of their children. We do not, however, conclude that a deep psychic disturbance exists in these males' basic attachment. Thus, other interpretations for the disturbing figures need to be uncovered and understood for both men and women.

2. Practice listening to others on how they react to the everyday roles of males and females. This past winter I was driving with four colleagues across the state when it became apparent that we were in for Minnesota blizzard conditions. While returning to the car after a lunch stop, I heard a woman colleague say, "Well, one of you men had better take on the driving. It looks like the storm is right ahead of us." Her basic assumption, that men are better drivers under blizzard conditions, was not weighed against factors of experience, focusing ability, stress tolerance, and other related psychological variables. As we listened to her, some of us recognized that one of the women with us had been driving over 600 miles per week during the last year (in the Minnesota winter) to complete her doctorate training.

3. Take time to reflect upon and rethink your own experiences. If you felt embarrassed about an obvious statement of bias, if you sensed that other peoples' reactions to a statement of yours were negative, first of all, acknowledge that you are listening and you are self-aware enough to recognize the discomfort. But then decide to reflect and reprocess the exchange—what kind of assumptions did you make that were limited or biased? In a recent promotion review, I heard that a male faculty member dismissed a female faculty member's extensive research on women with the comment, "But, will she know how to do research when her interest in women peaks?" Many faculty members saw no problem with this question. Possible questions to stimulate reprocessing include: Is research on women not "real" research? Are women really not human subjects? Is research on women just a passing fad?

4. Actively do perspective-taking on the consequences of your beliefs and actions on others. In a workshop I taught recently to thirty state department curriculum directors, the group eventually shifted concerns from general male/female equality issues to actual differences they observed in how they themselves parented their daughters and sons. One man shared, "What it comes down to for me is that I have to protect her (his daughter) more . . . when a 200 pound guy crawls into the back seat of a car with her, there's not much she can do." The sex differences in physical strength and the misuse of this power will likely always be with us. In our discussion, however, we also tried to focus on the impact upon this young women of having her freedom, relationships, judgments questioned—almost to the point that she now expressed a "learned helplessness." The responsibility of parents to teach their sons about physical aggressiveness provided another badly needed perspective.

5. Act on your beliefs such that your thinking is integrated with your behavior and you then model this for others. A male social studies teacher in a local high school had taken fine leadership in teaching a unit on the Equal Rights Amendment. About six weeks later, five female athletes went to him hoping for his support to gain equal access to a gymnasium during practice time allotted disproportionately to male teams. The social studies teacher hesitated for two weeks, even though the logic and fairness were laid out by the female students in a careful, consistent fashion. He, of course, was faced with going against the expedient positions of the coaches and his fellow teachers and the long tradition of the supremacy of practice-time for the boys' winning basketball team. Furthermore, there were no clear "law and order" rules to support the fairness claim, so he continued to waver. However, when he did eventually take a stand, it was a strong one. He became an advocate for moving Title IX guidelines into the rules and spirit of the schools' athletics. His

actions resulted in both an inner confidence in himself and in needed modeling for others.

6. View growth as a continual process. In developmental psychology, <u>horizontal decalage</u> refers to the extending of a belief such that it is consistent across different experiences. For example, today, with the reestablishment of draft registration, we see dissonance over the issue of whether young females should also be drafted. In fact, some women and men who support the Equal Rights Amendment would not willingly extend these rights and the concomitant responsibilities to include women in the draft. The "filling in" of moral logic—the testing of fairness across issues and experience, the restructuring of our conceptions of fairness—occurs slowly and needs to be viewed as a continual recycling process extending over time. The human rights concerns involved in the basic draft questions—should any person be drafted, man or woman—will likely trigger another important period of social rethinking on this basic issue of justice. Because we each experience only one life at one time in history, collective changes in societal beliefs are only gradually cumulative; change comes slowly.

This chapter has put forward some theories for considering just what a human "ought to be" and so, I hope, begins to answer Socrates's question. It was my intent to stress that our work in applied developmental psychology and specifically in direct interventions for growth needs to move toward a life-span perspective (Witherell and Erickson 1978). My major point in this chapter is that sex role assignment in family and school systems limits human growth and is an issue of justice. I believe that the strategies suggested will increase the maturity of the average parent and teacher. Children have moral claims on us to guide them toward their potentials. We must do our best for them, for our own lives, and for the collective growth of the human condition.

12

THE MORAL EDUCATION OF
THE JUVENILE OFFENDER:
A SOCIAL DILEMMA

Peter Scharf

JUVENILE DELINQUENCY AS A MORAL ISSUE

Juvenile delinquency poses a difficult moral issue for society.
In recent years, juvenile offenders have increasingly threatened orderly and democratic society: they committed fully one-quarter of
all violent offenses, including some egregious and publicized maimings
or killings of innocent citizens. On the other hand, the juvenile justice
system represents a moral no man's land within the U.S. system of
justice. Juveniles are denied legal rights granted to adults and often
receive even sterner deprivations for acts than would adults had they
committed the same crimes. In the landmark Gault case (Gault, in
Re, 1967), for example, young Gault was remanded to the custody of
the state purportedly for having made an obscene call to a neighbor.

Statistically, crimes committed by juvenile offenders in the
United States represent a sizable proportion of offenses. In 1974 a
total of 1,444,632 arrests were made of juveniles. The total proportion of arrestable offenses committed by juveniles was 26 percent.
Demographic studies by Wolgang (1972), Farrington (1978), and others
indicate that delinquency is on the rise in the United States and the
United Kingdom. While part of this increase may be explained by the
rise in youthful populations (ages 16 to 21) from 1962 through 1980,
the rise in delinquency is far greater than what one might expect
from a simple increase in the relative size of the adolescent cohort
group.

Aspects of the moral dilemma of delinquency include: a conflict
between the welfare of citizens and that of the juvenile offender; the
problem of balancing the desire to ensure legal equity and procedural
justice with the commitment to have the juvenile justice system serve

the interests of the child; and the legal and moral difficulty of distinguishing acts committed by juveniles from adult criminal offenses.

This dilemma is difficult to resolve because the social and legal category of juvenile delinquency covers a broad spectrum of actions as shown by the following cases. The first shows that a child can be remanded to the custody of society for having committed a status offense (an action that would not be a legal offense were it committed by an adult).

> Jody, fifteen, was remanded to the custody of the state reformatory for her minority under the State's "obstinate" child act. She had run away repeatedly from her mother—a Baptist fundamentalist from a midwestern state. Her mother could not understand why Jody liked to "run with a rough crowd," when there were other places she could meet boys such as church socials and picnics. Jody was arrested in Reno, Nevada, as a "wayward child" and returned to her home and placed under a supervised probation. Three weeks later she ran away and was remanded to Juvenile Hall. After returning home to her mother, Jody and her mother fought continuously. Shortly after one fight her stepfather suffered a heart attack which her mother blamed on Jody's "obstinacy." After running away and living for a month in a trailer park with a Marine private, Jody was arrested for shoplifting and remanded to the court "'til she might reach the age of eighteen years of age."

Another case, reported in the New York Times (1974), represents a far more serious threat to society and its people, often those least able to deal with the viciousness that is unique to one type of juvenile offender.

> On the afternoon of Friday, Oct. 11, two 10-year-old boys left a private school in the Borough Hall section of Brooklyn and went shopping for hockey sticks on Fulton Street, where the big department stores are. Jim Jones was tall for his age, with long blond hair and mild blue eyes. He wore jeans and a football shirt. Bobby Ryan was shorter, quick-gestured, also blond, and wore jeans and a plaid wool shirt. Walking across the sports department of Korvettes, they noticed two black teenagers bouncing a basketball.

A floorwalker retrieved the basketball and ordered them off the floor.

When Jim and Bobby left the store, their new hockey sticks under their arms, the two black youths were waiting for them at the entrance. One pulled a knife and said, "Come around the corner." This was at 4 p.m., in broad daylight in the heart of downtown Brooklyn, on a street crowded with shoppers. Jim and Bobby were relieved of the $6 they had between them. "Get the refunds for the sticks and come back here," the boy who had the knife said. Jim and Bobby did as they were told.

They turned over the refund money and the two black youths took them across a parking lot behind Korvettes. The one with the knife, 15-year-old Ken Jordan, tall and lanky, neatly dressed with a pleasant face and a nice smile, climbed on top of a car. The attendant told him to get off. "These cars belong to everybody," Ken said, "They're not just yours."

"Call that man a nigger," Ken ordered Jim.

"I will not," Jim said.

The knife was at Jim's throat. "Call that man a nigger."

Jim did.

"Ain't these two the whitest kids you ever seen," Ken said to the other black youth, short, round-faced Bill Sherwin, who had just turned 14.

They boarded the No. 26 bus with the two 10-year-olds and got off at a construction site at Adelphi and Fulton Streets, on the edge of Bedford Stuyvesant. It was a 12-story building with cement stairs at each corner.

At the construction site, the two teenagers were "having some fun" with the 10-year-olds, as one of them later put it. They defecated on the floor and made the boys pick it up. They tied Jim to a ladder, applied lit matches to his body and set fire to his hair. They tied him upside down to a pulley and immersed him in a barrel of water for a minute at a time. They dangled Bobby, the smaller 10-year-old, out a window, and pretended they were going to drop him.

They broke pieces of plasterboard over their heads. They pounded wedges of wood into their knuckles with hammers. They beat them so badly in the face that a policeman later said, "I have never seen anyone, not

even a prizefighter, look like that." They then took
turns beating each 10-year-old.

Underlying these statistics and individual stories is a major
social problem requiring changes in education and law. Society badly
needs effective techniques to reform juvenile offenders who come into
the charge of delinquency prevention or rehabilitation programs. It
also requires a major overhall of the juvenile justice system—particularly in terms of the legal issues of fairness and equity.

In this chapter, I explore the impact of recent findings in developmental psychology and education for both understanding and acting upon
the problem of juvenile delinquency. To begin, I discuss some of the
research literature on the developmental characteristics of legal
reasoning. Then, I describe the moral and legal reasoning patterns
observed among juvenile offenders and use these findings to introduce
possible intervention strategies with juvenile offenders. I speculate
on some of the possible implications of developmental theory for the
reshaping of the legal institutions of the juvenile justice system.

PSYCHOLOGICAL THEORIES OF JUVENILE DELINQUENCY

Since the 1930s, substantial attempts have been made to explain
and, in some cases, predict the incidence of juvenile delinquency.
Sociological studies by Sutherland (1948), Cloward and Ohlin (1970),
and Matza (1964) have concerned themselves with prediction of delinquency. Sociological theories in the tradition of Durkheim (1908)
provide models to help explain changes in juvenile delinquency as a
collective social fact. Prediction of the overall rate of delinquency is
critical for such theories. What social conditions, these theorists
ask, might best explain an increase or decrease in the epidemiological
rate of juvenile delinquency?

Psychological theories of delinquency as found in the work of
Friedlander (1950), Aichorn (1938), and Warren (1974) attempt to explain delinquency as a psychological process. These theories address
the question of which persons within a particular group might become
delinquent. They also try to discover psychological differences between delinquent and nondelinquent groups and propose psychological
causes for delinquent behavior.

Such theories have analyzed the problem of delinquency from
both psychodynamic and behavioral points of view. Psychodynamic
approaches (see Friedlander [1950] or Aichorn [1938]) contend that
delinquency is rooted in the neurotic conflicts of early and middle
childhood. Repeated car theft might be interpreted as stealing in
order to get back at overly strict, lenient, or unloving parents. Behaviorist theories (see Platt 1977) focus upon delinquency as a learned

social behavior. The influence of peers, parents, or gang members (conceptualized in terms of rewarding deviant acts, attitudes, and life-styles) tends to be central.

As Schur (1973) and others have noted, these theories of delinquency frequently posit either implicit or explicit prescriptions for action. For example, psychodynamic theory has been used with delinquents in a variety of settings. These programs treat delinquency by making the delinquents aware of why they act the way they do. In the Girls Vocational High Study (1965), selected girls with potential problems received intensive psychotherapy. Many probation departments, especially those with professionally trained social workers, use an eclectic, but distinctly psychoanalytic, model of therapy. R. Warren's (1972) Center for Differential Treatment developed a psychotherapy based on "interpersonal differences among different delinquents." The California Youth Authority established the OH Close School, which developed a mode of treatment based on transactional analysis that is derived from Berne's (1964) interpretation of Freudian psychotherapy.

Behavior modification has also been implemented in a variety of settings to reward prosocial behavior and extinguish delinquent behaviors and attitudes. Schwitzgabel (1973) used behavior change techniques in both institutional and community settings. Platt (1977) developed innovative contingency management programs among juvenile offenders in several urban communities. Binder (1979) trained teams of crisis intervention workers to teach new behavior strategies to youths diverted from the juvenile court system. The California Youth Authority's Holton School and the John F. Kennedy School in Virginia both use "milieu therapy" based on social learning principles. In the Holton School, for example, prosocial behavior is rewarded in short-term (making Playboy magazine available) or long-term (points toward release) ways.

Existing psychological theories that have attempted to either explain delinquency or change juvenile offenders have suffered from an inability to develop a coherent predictive theoretical base. Also, the ideologies that have evolved from both psychodynamic theory and social behaviorism have been torn by serious moral contradictions (see Mitford 1973; Scharf 1977; Schur 1973; Szasz 1963). No psychodynamic study, for example, has demonstrated conclusively that specific parental child-rearing styles are associated with criminal juvenile delinquency; nor have there been efforts to compare the incidence of neurosis in delinquent and nondelinquent populations. Similarly, there have been few efforts to demonstrate that juvenile offenders have been exposed to different reward structures than nonoffenders in similar environments.

Moral concerns have also been expressed about some of the implications of adopting either psychodynamic or behavioral treatments for delinquency. The psychodynamic approach tends to view delinquent acts as pathological and strongly asserts the juvenile offender's need for treatment. Rather than looking at the moral nature of actions interpreted as delinquent, it tends to see all actions of people labeled as offenders in terms of the concept of psychological illness. Behaviorist psychologists view delinquent actions from the point of view of what is rewarded or "works" in a particular society at a particular point of time. This is a difficult moral position to defend in a society with widely conflicting standards, values, rules, and rewards. The question of who should define the behaviors to be rewarded is philosophically ambiguous.

THE COGNITIVE-DEVELOPMENTAL MODEL OF MORAL AND LEGAL REASONING

Since 1970, Joseph Hickey, Lawrence Kohlberg, and I have been applying cognitive-developmental theory to the problems of juveniles. In this effort, we sought to provide an alternative education ideology for interventions designed to control acts of delinquency. Our approach used the broad social epistemology reflected in the work of Cooley (1926), Mead (1934), Piaget (1960), and, most recently, Kohlberg, (1969, 1971, 1978). In Cooley and Mead, for example, there is an emphasis upon the child's increasing ability to role-take social perspectives. In Piagetian psychology, there is a similar assumption that the young child's conception of both natural and social events evolves through a sequence of stages. While experience may affect the rate of developmental change, the sequence itself is considered invariant. Consistent with his theory of intellectual development, Piaget postulates that the understanding of moral rules evolves in a similar sequence. Interviewing children from different cantons in Switzerland, Piaget posited three discrete stages of children's understanding of the rules of playing marbles: in the egocentric stage (ages three to six), rules are imitated but not internalized; in the moral heteronomy stage or morality of constraint (ages six to ten), any rule adopted by the children is presumed to be "right"—if a marble even touches a line, it is declared "out," even if this means that no one wins the game; in the final, moral autonomy stage, rules are intentional creations subject to change as players adapt to new conditions.

Building on Piaget's methodology and philosophic framework, which assumes a hierarchy of legal and moral ideas, Kohlberg (1969, 1971, 1978) has extended, refined, and elaborated Piaget's preliminary work on the process of moral reasoning. Kohlberg further proposes that as the child matures morally, there is a progressive reconsideration of what is morally right and the perceived relationship between law and society.

At Stage 1, law is conceived as the force of the powerful, to which the weaker must submit. At Stage 2, right action becomes that which satisfies one's own needs: law is thought of in terms of the rules of expedience or a naive rational hedonism ("In America, the law says everyone can get what he wants"). Stage 3 offers what is called the good boy/girl orientation: law becomes associated with collective opinion; one obeys the law because that is what others expect. At Stage 4, there is a shift toward fixed definitions of law and society: the law is justified by its order-maintaining function ("Without law, the entire fabric of society would crumble"). Stage 5 is a legalistic-contract orientation: law becomes the agreed-upon contract among social equals with duties of state and individual clearly defined and regulated. At Stage 6, Kohlberg argues that there is a universal basis for ethical decision making: the law is the repository for broader social principles and is subordinate where law and justice conflict.

The theory suggests the importance of social environment for stimulating moral reasoning. Social institutions help to determine both the rate of a person's moral growth and the final stage of moral reasoning achieved. Institutions that encourage open dialogue, moral conflict, and democratic interaction are associated with rapid sociolegal development (Kohlberg 1969). Individuals placed in positions where they are responsible for the maintenance of group and institutional norms develop more quickly than do others.

The empirical evidence for the validity of Kohlberg's stage sequence comes from two sources. First, he cites evidence from both cross-sectional and longitudinal studies suggesting that people do move through the stages in order. Cross-sectional data similarly indicate that in several cultures older children as a group were more mature in their moral reasoning than were younger children (Kohlberg 1971).

In addition to making an empirical claim for the validity of his six stages, Kohlberg argues that each higher stage offers a philosophically more adequate means of resolving moral conflict. This claim (which obviously is one of normative ethics rather than of science) is much more controversial. Using deductive ethical analysis, Kohlberg has attempted to demonstrate, at least through Stage 5, how each higher stage resolves ethical contradictions evident at earlier stages. He argues, for example, that the Stage 5 "legalistic" position offers an ethical perspective unavailable at the less mature Stage 4 law-and-order orientation (Kohlberg 1971).

COGNITIVE, MORAL, AND LEGAL REASONING

The relationship of cognitive, moral, and legal reasoning is complex. From Piaget's point of view, legal development might be considered in terms of horizontal decalage (or the spread of intellectual operations to new problems). Therefore, cognitive and moral concepts become applied to a new content area involving the realm of legal ideas and relationships.

Many of the published articles attempting to relate legal and cognitive reasoning have noted both the parallels between Piaget's description of intelligence and changes in legal reasoning. They have also remarked on the apparent qualitative difference between children's legal thinking and that of adults. Several studies in the area of political socialization focusing on legal development have consistently shown both logical and attitudinal differences in children's ideas of law and have related these differences conceptually to Piagetian stage development.*

Merelman (1969) was among the first political scientists to recognize the utility of Piaget's ideas for an understanding of the process of legal socialization. He argues that moral and cognitive development should be conceived of as a necessary but perhaps not sufficient condition for political thinking; without the ability to think causally, complex political and legal ideologies are impossible.

---

*Related research indicates that some important theoretical qualifications should be made in linking cognitive development with legal socialization. Jahoda (1964), in studying the relationship between cognitive development and ideas about law, found that developmental changes in children's ideas about nationality did not fully correspond to the child's conception of spatial constructs. Connell's (1971) research in legal and political development argues that the developmental interpretation of the growth of legal reasoning ignores the fact that few children have immediate contact with political and legal institutions. He doubts the developmental character of children's legal and political ideas, as the information the child receives about laws and politics is communicated and interpreted by adults. In Connell's view, legal ideas are less easy to explain in a structural framework than are ideas about physical phenomena. This view is consistent with the position stated by Turiel (1975) who argues that Piaget's notion of a stage as a "structured whole" is misleading when applied to complex social and political ideas (such as legal concepts).

Similarly, Adelson's (1972) empirical investigations lend support to the developmental perspective on the learning of legal ideas. Conducting more than 450 interviews with adolescents ranging from ages 11 to 18, Adelson argues that preadolescence forms a major watershed for changes in the evolution of the child's idea of law. Twelve-year-old children expressed the purpose of law simply as, "They do it like that in school so people won't get hurt" or "If we had no laws, people could go around killing people." Older adolescents understood the rationale for law more abstractly, explaining that law exists "to ensure the safety of government" or "to limit what people can do." Adelson and Merelman explicitly incorporate Piagetian insights relating the onset of a truly political ideology to the evolution of hypothetic-deductive thinking: being able to differentiate between social rights and prerogatives of the state requires a fully formally operative propositional mind.

Two additional researchers have related legal reasoning to developmental changes in moral reasoning. Lockwood (1973) found significant correlations between reasoning on Kohlberg's moral dilemmas and reasoning used on public policy cases. Leming (1974) found a high correlation between the content of a choice in a civil disobedience case and the moral stage of the respondent.

The most elaborate research program linking legal and moral reasoning is that undertaken by Tapp (1971) and her associates. They attempted to validate both the developmental progression of ideals of law as well as the relationship between legal and moral development. Using both cross-national and cross-sectional age comparisons, the authors administered an open-ended interview dealing with questions of law, justice, equity, compliance, and authority and coded responses using a typology related to the Kohlberg stages. For example, responses justifying laws in terms of physical harm were scored as preconventional (Stage 1 or 2), responses emphasizing the restraint of personal desires were scored as conventional, and responses emphasizing the guidance of self-regulating beings were scored as postconventional. Results from the interviews tended to support the hypothesis that legal reasoning follows a common developmental progression in both the United States and a variety of other societies. The researchers found an age trend in terms of the evolving idea of law moving from preconventional (Stage 1 and 2) to conventional (Stage 2 and 3) and finally postconventional (Stage 5 and above) stages. The study also suggested the dominance of conventional (Stage 3 or 4) legal reasoning in both the United States and other societies.

Other research has linked moral reasoning to responses to specific legal issues. Candee (1978) found that respondents' assessments of the moral issues of the Watergate incident were closely related to their stages of moral reasoning. Kohlberg and Elfenbein's

(1975) study of attitudes toward capital punishment finds a striking (considering the controversial nature of the subject matter) relationship between one's position on capital punishment and one's moral stage. Young children tend to defend the practice of capital punishment in terms of a Stage 1 theory of retaliation. Later development, according to this study, reveals a series of "flip-flops" in orientation closely related to moral stage. For example, most Stage 3 subjects favored leniency, Stage 4 individuals were supportive of the use of capital punishment, and principled subjects (those beyond Stage 4) were almost unanimously opposed to the use of the death penalty.

Scharf's (1978) study of police decision making has related police officers' moral reasoning to various types of situational legal decision making. Police officers grouped at Stages 2 to 3, 3 to 4, and 4 to 5 were asked to respond to moral dilemmas dealing with the use of deadly force in the line of duty. Scharf found differences in the willingness to use deadly force in a hypothetical shooting situation. Of the Stage 2 to 3 officers, 80 percent were willing to use deadly force in a similar situation. Studies of naturalistically observed shooting incidents indicated a close correspondence between officer moral reasoning used on hypothetical dilemmas and reasoning used to justify one's actions following the incident.

These studies suggest that there is an association between developmental moral reasoning and particular conceptions of law. The empirical evidence is strongest in the observed association of age trends with changes in legal ideas, and it shows that cognitive transformations parallel changes in legal and political ideas. Tentative evidence also exists that change in legal thinking follows a similar pattern in several societies. However, the assertion made by some developmental theorists that legal development follows an invariant sequence similar to cognitive development seems still at the hypothetical stage with no conclusive study clearly establishing or invalidating it.

JUVENILE DELINQUENCY AND LEGAL REASONING

Juvenile offenders think about legal obligations quite differently than mature adults: their reasoning seemingly approximates a premoral stage. An interview reported by Silberman (1978) of a fourteen-year-old "torpedo" (contract killer) displays a strikingly primitive moral conscience, considering the boy had killed his victim by setting her on fire:

Q. Did you have a good night's sleep?
A. Yeah.

Q. How did you feel? What was your mood? Did you feel upset after . . . she burned to a crisp?

A. She didn't burn to a crisp.

Q. Did you ever cry afterwards?

A. To tell you the truth, I had no feeling after I did it.

Q. No feelings at all?

A. No, I forgot about it until after they caught me.

Another juvenile offender, also convicted of murder, was asked by the author what he thought about what had happened. The boy declared that sometimes "it was like something tasted bad or a bad stomach ache, but it didn't matter." A young rapist similarly suggested that "the bitch deserved it. You know she was being real sassy and stuff."

Other offenders tend to be more sophisticated about their crimes. One convicted armed robber said: "I felt real bad about those old ladies. But I was sick. You know when you are sick, it's too bad for anyone. I think society should give heroin to addicts. Otherwise they got to expect what they get." Occasionally, some delinquents will justify their actions with more explicitly political rationales. One young black armed robber affiliated with a well-known black political group blamed his crime on capitalism: "White rich folks can go to a teller and get money. Poor people have to steal it."

Some of these differences in the reasoning among offenders and the typical legal ideology of juvenile offenders may be illuminated by an analysis from a developmental perspective. Chandler (1973) found that many of the offenders he interviewed in his study were extremely limited in their social reasoning ability and capacity for social role taking. Prentice (1971) used a Piagetian measure of moral judgment and found juvenile offenders markedly fixated relative to matched controls. Studies using Kohlberg's system of moral judgment by Franklyn (1979) and Kohlberg and Freudlich (1979) indicated that juvenile offenders on the whole tend to be less morally and legally mature than nonoffenders. A study by Kohlberg and Freudlich (1979) compared juvenile offenders of different ages with matched controls from comparative social environments: while only 16 percent of the offenders in the pooled sample were reasoning at conventional levels, over 70 percent of the controls had attained at least a Stage 3 level or moral thinking.

Kohlberg (1975) suggests that juvenile offenders ages 15 to 17 have a mean moral maturity much like that of 10 to 12-year-old middle-class children. To illustrate this "lag" in moral development, let us analyze the reasoning of a 16-year-old offender named Bill who had been incarcerated for stealing 32 cents worth of glue. In response to the Heinz dilemma,* Bill responded: "No he shouldn't. That's stealing. I wouldn't do no time for nobody, no matter what. I don't care if it was my wife. It doesn't matter. . . . He will get bagged if he does that." His reasoning here fails to differentiate even rational interests from fear of punishment. Similarly, when Bill was asked what a husband morally owes his wife, Bill responded: "Well, you get married and shit and make all these promises and stuff, like to obey and you put on a ring and promise to listen, but you are just saying it."

Revealingly, when Bill was asked if the judge "had a right" to sentence him for so much time for such a "small crime," Bill responded that "the judge could do what he wanted to do. He was the judge. He did it." Bill has seemingly no conception of the obligation of the judge to follow any specific laws, nor any conception that he has any legal rights. Neither does he know why laws exist: when the interviewer asked Bill why society has laws against stealing, Bill replied: "It's to save the 'average Joes' in society money, you know things they want." Similarly when he was asked if he did anything wrong in a later (more profitable) robbery, Bill responded: "Well, the judge wanted me in jail." For Bill (who scored a mix of Stage 1 and 2 reasoning) legal justice is a matter of specific persons' enacting specific sanctions against him. While Bill is lower in moral

---

*The Heinz dilemma:

In Europe, a woman was near death from a special kind of cancer. There was one drug that doctors thought might save her. It was a form of radium that a druggist in the same town had recently discovered. The drug was expensive to make, but the druggist was charging ten times what the drug cost him to make. He paid $200 for the radium and charged $2,000 for a small dose of the drug. The sick woman's husband, Heinz, went to everyone he knew to borrow the money, but he could only get together about $1,000, which is half of what it cost. He told the druggist that his wife was dying, and asked him to sell it cheaper or let him pay later. But the druggist said, "No, I discovered the drug and I'm going to make money from it." So Heinz gets desperate and considers breaking into the man's store to steal the drug for his wife. (Goslin, 1969, p. 379)

Question: Should Heinz steal the drug? Why or why not?

maturity than the average 16-year-old offender, his reasoning pattern illustrates how different many offenders' legal philosophies are, not only from non-offenders but also from what the law and justice system implicitly assumes to be required for any meaningful particpation in the legal institutions of society.

A typical delinquent's moral response to the Heinz dilemma corresponds closely to a pure Stage 2 moral ideology:

> Should he steal the drug?
>
> Yah. Because if my wife was dying I'd want to save her.
> She's with me. I would want to keep her around. I would
> care for her.
>
> What if she was sneaking around? They were about to be
> divorced?
>
> I'd say "later for her." You know what I mean? Why
> should he want her around then. I wouldn't be sticking my
> neck out for her.

This offender's Stage 2 hedonism is replaced by a morality of concern in a Stage 3 offender. Here the criterion of "rightness" becomes a matter of mutual expectations rather than simply a calculation of self-interest:

> Should he have done that?
>
> Yes, I think he should have done it because his wife was
> dying and he needed the drug, and if there was some sort
> of law, or some way he could have got the money besides,
> him and his friend couldn't raise the money, so I feel
> that he did the right thing that he had left to do. A good
> husband wouldn't let his wife die.

While roughly half of Kohlberg and Freudlich's sample of 16- to 20-year-old offenders manifested some Stage 3 thinking, a smaller proportion had developed what might be seen as a substantial Stage 4 thinking. An exception was found in an interview with a 17-year-old "safecracker":

> Do you think that Heinz should have done that? Was that
> wrong or right to break in?
>
> I think Heinz was wrong even though he was in a peculiar
> situation where it was actually a matter of life and death.
> He was still stealing from a man who had developed this

thing and it was his right to keep it because it was his
possession. Society cannot function if it allows theft.
Heinz violated the man's right by taking it. It's cut and
dried . . . it was wrong to take this drug.

The research on the moral reasoning of juvenile offenders indicates several axioms important for understanding the psychological
causes of juvenile delinquency:

1. Many offenders operate at relatively immature levels of
moral reasoning in which an adequate comprehension of the processes
and social meaning of the law becomes improbable and, in extreme
cases, logically impossible.
2. Offenses committed by these morally immature juvenile offenders may appear not as anomalies from a law-abiding adolescent
conscience but rather as extensions of what the offender believes to
be right and reasonable. For example, the act of theft might be an
extension of what the offender believes (at Stage 2) " a dumb store-
keeper" (dumb enough to allow himself to be robbed) deserves.
3. While juvenile offenders on the average tend to be less
mature than nonoffenders, it is also clear that offenders exhibit a
high degree of variation of moral judgment. The notion that all offenders are morally fixated is extremely misleading.

This research is important in the following major respects. First,
knowledge of the reasoning capacities of juvenile offenders is critical
to guiding educational efforts designed to narrow the gap between the
moral capacities of the individual offender and the cognitive demands
of a democratic society. And second, knowledge of the reasoning
abilities of juvenile offenders might be a useful consideration in reforming various aspects of the juvenile justice system, which makes
assumptions about the understanding of offenders regarding the law,
its procedures, and moral logic.
To explore these dimensions of developmental theory, I will
describe a few of the educational interventions used with juvenile offenders in school, court, and prison settings. These educational
interventions have used developmental psychology both to guide their
efforts and to evaluate their successes or failures. I then describe
some of the legal reforms flowing from these observations on legal
development and the sociolegal reasoning of delinquents.

MORAL EDUCATION AS A MEANS FOR BRIDGING THE GAP BE-
TWEEN THE JUVENILE OFFENDER AND SOCIAL ORDER

Our observations on the moral reasoning of juvenile offenders
infer a moral gap between the world view of the offender and that of

society. Many juvenile offenders have a moral outlook that is barely cognizant of the principles and logic underlying a democratic social order. This moral gap is evident in a variety of contexts.

In schools delinquent youths often fail to understand the reasons for school rules and order. In confrontations with the police, they often cannot understand "why police are bothering" them. A youth, who recently was found slumped in his car "stoned in the third lane of a highway," wondered "why the police hassled people just having a good time." Juvenile court is similarly a bewildering experience for delinquent youth who find judges' decisions to incarcerate or release them mysterious. Matza (1964) offers that this is especially the case when the judge uses psychological arguments (for example, the reformability of the offender) to justify either release or incarceration.

Obviously, bridging this moral gap forms a critical task for society and the social institutions charged with educating and coping with the problem of juvenile delinquency. Here I will look at some of the educational mechanisms proposed for coping with juvenile delinquency in the schools and criminal justice system. While the strategies I will describe focus on different settings, they share in common the goal of intensive developmental moral education as a means of stimulating the idea of the law as a central educational task.

Developmental moral education (Scharf 1978) assumes a quite different philosophic and psychological framework from other moral education strategies in use with both delinquent and nondelinquent populations. Most efforts at reforming juvenile offenders have advocated the inculcation of conventional moral conduct and standards. In "concept" or Synanon drug treatment programs, there is an intensive effort to "break down the old front" of the offender and indoctrinate him with new (that is, rehabilitated) forms of behavior. A few efforts have used a values clarification strategy to reform juvenile offenders. Fraser (1972), for example, has employed transactional analysis to "help delinquents make appropriate choices and eliminate antisocial conduct through their becoming aware of undesired emotions," Critical in these programs is the notion that education implies the conscious choice of values by the juvenile offender and that moral education for offenders implies primarily self-analysis.

The developmental strategies I will describe here assume an alternative set of assumptions about how moral education should proceed. Developmental moral education posits that (1) moral education should attempt to stimulate the reasoning processes of the juvenile offender through intensive social interaction and dialogue, (2) the goal of moral educators should be to lead the student toward more universal perspectives—such as those articulated in a constitutional body of law; and (3) the immediate goals of moral education should depend upon the moral stage of the student. For example, for a juvenile offender at Stage 2 an appropriate goal might be to raise him to Stage 3 in moral reasoning. Experiments with nondelinquent populations (see Kohlberg 1975; Mosher 1979; Rest 1973) indicate that it is possible through dilemma discussions or role-taking exercises to stimulate small gains in moral maturity (roughly one-third of a moral stage). These gains in moral maturity reflect consolidation of existing moral reasoning, as well as the generation of "new" moral ideas. Systematic developmental educational experiments have been conducted in social studies, English, women's studies, and other academic content areas (see Scharf 1978).

One new area of developmental education has focused on didactic instruction about the law and legal reasoning. During the past 20 years, a series of broadly disseminated curricula have been created that have attempted to instruct children systematically about the law (see, as examples, T. Clark 1977; Oliver and Shaver 1966; Quigley 1978). Oliver and Shaver's public policy series used a case method approach to legal and policy decision making, which trained students in legal analysis and problem solving. Quigley's "Law in a Free Society" program offers a more didactic approach to legal education, using legal content almost exclusively. These curricula offer intensive instruction about legal issues using cases relevant to adolescents. The Constitutional Rights Foundation (Clark 1977) has developed legal curricula especially for "at risk" inner-city students and incarcerated juvenile offenders (Ross 1978).

Another educational approach has been demonstrated in experiments guided by Kohlberg (1978), Wasserman (1978), Fenton (1978), Scharf (1977), and Mosher (1976; and in this volume) where students and faculty members have created and maintained school rules and discipline procedures democratically and collaboratively. During the past five years, these experiments have created frameworks that allow students to exercise a surprisingly high degree of control over decisions regarding student discipline and even staff hiring and curriculum. The schools involved have ranged from the affluent Brookline, Massachusetts, and Scarsdale, New York, public schools to an inner-city school in Cambridge, Massachusetts. In town meetings and disciplinary board hearings, students debate school policies and even such potentially divisive issues as teacher-student conflict and student drug use. These schools use participatory democracy to promote moral growth and to foster a greater understanding of legal and political processes in a democratic society. They also have used developmental measures of reasoning to monitor the outcomes of their programs.

Another means of bridging the gap between child and the law lies in the courts itself. Since it might be hypothesized (1) that few

juvenile offenders understand the motives underlying judicial sentencing and (2) that what the juvenile judge feels is useful and even just for
an offender appears to the child at once arbitrary and unfair, developmental psychologists have made a number of proposals to alleviate
this situation. Chandler (1973), for example, has suggested role-
playing exercises as part of the juvenile court experience. He recommends that the juvenile offender be asked to role-take the parts
of other people in the court process such as the victims, jurors,
prosecutors, and judges to help the offender comprehend the social
motives of those involved in the juvenile court experience. In informal judicial hearings, similar educational ends might be gained by
engaging paroled or probated juvenile offenders as an "advisory jury"
to give a peer perspective to the hearing judge and to offer an educational component to the offenders involved.

Developmental educational methods have also been created to
educate juvenile offenders incarcerated in medium and maximum
security prisons. An experiment conducted by the author and Joseph
Hickey at the Cheshire reformatory in Connecticut used moral discussions as a form of educational prison therapy. This program was
instituted by randomly establishing a 20-inmate experimental group,
which was divided into two equal sections. The sections met separately for 36 two-hour sessions (3 sessions per week) and, using a
Socratic technique developed by Blatt (1968), discussed both legal
issues and other topics introduced by the inmates. The pre- and
posttest evaluations indicated a mean change of 0.17 of a moral stage.
Six of the inmates in the experimental group progressed one stage of
moral reasoning, most moving from Stage 2 to Stage 3. The obser-
vers noted that the "changing" inmates were highly involved in the
discussions and participated more than did the average member.
However, while the program was successful in stimulating development in moral and legal thinking, it was obvious that the discussion
groups by themselves could not reform juvenile offenders either
within the prison or following release from prison.

To build upon this earlier approach to moral reeducation, we
designed a prison program to create a common community of inmates
and staff members and to stimulate moral affection among its members. This broader perspective relied on axioms in both Cooley's
(1926) and Mead's (1934) theories of social learning—that an individual's sense of morality derives directly from experiences in group
life. For Mead, the acquisition of conscience emerged from what he
calls the "generalized other," or the internalization of the perspective
of the group by the individual group member. When a person commits
an act that violates the norms of the group, according to Mead, a
part of the self views this action as the group might see it. For both
Mead and Cooley, an intensive community life is essential to the
development of an adult principled moral perspective.

　　　To demonstrate the possibility of a developmentally grounded prison reform program, we proposed the creation of what we called a "just community" prison program. We hypothesized that even within the prison context, it should be possible to create the conditions that encourage developmental interaction, create a positive sense of community, and allow for experiences in democratic governance. We undertook a democratic experiment from 1971 through 1977 in the Niantic, Connecticut, prison for women. Although mutual hostility between inmates and guards in this institution had almost caused a riot, both inmates and staff expressed some willingness to discuss the possibility of exploring new ways of coexisting. During the summer months, inmates, guards, and administrators met in what was called a "constitutional convention." Negotiations were difficult, but the convention agreed to experiment with a model cottage and to define limits for a proposed democratic framework. Inmates would control internal discipline, propose furloughs for members, and define the program objective and activities. In practice most prison offenses with the exception of major felonies were referred to a cottage community meeting. Any inmate member might call a community meeting at any time. When cottage-rules offenses were discovered, the community meeting acted as jury to determine guilt or innocence. If disciplinary action were in order, it was referred to a discipline board that included two inmates and one staff member chosen at random. Routine issues involving such matters as work assignments, love triangles, or interpersonal conflicts were dealt with through open dialogue and discussion. On rare occasions, the community dealt with such issues as contraband, escape, or even assault.

　　　Analysis of pre- and post-test moral judgment interviews indicated differences of 0.39 of a moral stage from pre- to post-test. This degree of change was seen as sizable since nearly one-third of the group shifted more than one-half a moral stage. Qualitative analysis of inmate interviews (specifically on legal issues) indicated that two-thirds of the inmates scored higher on legal issues than on their cumulative moral judgment.

　　　Since the Niantic experiment, several youth facilities have adopted this approach in work with a variety of juveniles. Studies by Jennings (1979) and Franklyn (1979) indicate that the approach is workable with young, serious offenders in both residential and institutional settings. Jennings reports a positively perceived moral atmosphere in a Florida just community home for juvenile offenders. Franklyn reports a substantial amount of moral change in a group that encouraged intensive moral dialogue as well as some degree of community democratic participation. She also found some evidence that participation in the program corresponded to changes in behavior by the "experimental" offenders in her study.

DELINQUENT MORAL JUDGMENT AND THE REFORM OF THE JUVENILE JUSTICE SYSTEM

What, therefore, are the implications of the existing research on juvenile offender moral judgment for the reform of the juvenile justice system? As I indicated in the beginning of this chapter, the juvenile justice system faces some severe moral choices. Two of the many disturbing issues that have aroused the greatest legal and political concern include the problem of differential sentencing of juvenile offenders of different psychological types and the problem of age in the legal definition of criminal responsibility. I will address both of these issues briefly, attempting to focus on the contributions of the developmental theory to the problem area involved. It should be noted that these issues involve considerations far broader than the reasoning processes of the juvenile offenders: They involve critical assumptions of value, politics, and law. Developmental observations on the reasoning processes of offenders may provide useful information to assist law making but should not in themselves determine legal policy.

DIFFERENTIAL SENTENCING AND THE JUVENILE JUSTICE SYSTEM

Judges have long indulged in differential sentencing of juvenile offenders based on both intuitive and more formal psychological assessments. One example of a more intuitive judgment is offered by Silberman (1978):

> A sixteen year old girl appears before the avuncular judge for a decision as to whether she might be released from the state training school. . . . Martha's probation officer recommends release telling the judge that plans have been made for Martha to attend an alternative school. . . . Peering into the record the judge responds, "Martha, I see you are not interested in cosmetology anymore; you told the court last time you wanted to be a beautician. . . . He tells the probation officer that if Martha returns to public school she won't be able to study cosmetology. . . . "Someday you will thank me for this," he tells the weeping youngster and her parents as he announces his decision to return Martha to the training school. [P. 316]

More formal methods of assessing risk in juvenile sentencing have been suggested by Warren (1974) and analyzed by

Morris (1974), Monahan (1976), and others. According to this approach, offenders in a high-risk psychological category might receive more restrictive custody than offenders found to be in lower-risk categories. For example, Warren has suggested that, as her "I4NX" (anxious neurotic) offenders have a higher recidivism rate than her "I4CI" (cultural identifiers), it is reasonable to prescribe more restrictive treatment for the neurotic group than the cultural identifiers. Similar proposals have been made using other psychological categories.

The contribution of developmental theory to this issue deals with the normative position of this psychological ideology. Given a conception of a Stage 5 or 6 legal philosophy (the higher stages of the system), certain types of actions become justifiable. In most other psychological systems, there is a separation between values and psychological processes: the psychologist's role is fact finding rather than moralizing. In developmental theory, the problem of values and psychological facts is far more complex. Values are inseparable from psychological processes in that each structural psychological unit (a stage) possesses its own value position. Also unique in the system is the preference of specific value positions over others.

Central to Kohlberg's conception of Stage 6 (see Kohlberg 1978) is a unique means of distributing welfare and liberty among persons. Given Stage 6 reasoning (as defined by Kohlberg 1971), differences in equality and liberty are restricted by the principle that such differences must be for the benefit of the least advantaged as well as the most advantaged person. Thus, losses in liberty or equality (relative to other persons) can be justified only if this could be agreed to by all persons were they not to know which social role they might occupy. Assuming this perspective, let us hypothesize punishment in the case of a juvenile offender who is given a greater punishment because he has been diagnosed as higher risk than another offender (for the same offense). For example, both 16-year-old boys might be armed robbers having committed their third known felony. One is diagnosed as high risk; the other is diagnosed as low risk. The question that emerges is whether we are justified in giving a more restrictive sentence to the high-risk offender compared with the low-risk offender.

Utilitarians might argue that the greatest good might be achieved by restricting the high-risk delinquent while releasing the low-risk offender. They might reason that the greatest good

requires the greater restriction of persons more likely to commit
social harm. Consider the facts illustrated below:

	High Risk (in percent)	Low Risk (in percent)
Delinquents who commit no future crimes	40	80
Delinquents who commit future crimes	60	20

The utilitarians would argue that society was justified in differentially
sentencing the two offenders as there would be a net savings of crime
as well as of penal resources given to offenders in need of them.
A Stage 6 position would disagree with this conclusion, arguing that
the mere reduction of crime does not justify the loss of the right to
equality suffered by the person who is diagnosed as high risk but who
in fact will commit no further crimes. This group it should be noted
is nearly 40 percent of the total.

This argument about the uses of psychology in sentencing transcends the issue of which psychological theory should be used to make
predictions. Even if moral stages were found to be nearly perfectly
predictive of future crimes (that is, if nearly all Stage 4's committed
no more crimes and all Stage 2's recidivated), such information would
not justify the differential sentencing of the Stage 2's from the Stage
4's. This would be true given our assumption that differences in
liberty and equality are only justifiable given that the differences
served both the most advantaged (low risk) as well as the high risk
person. This criterion is not met in the hypothetical situation discussed above.

THE AGE OF ADULT RESPONSIBILITY

Another troubling issue in the field of juvenile justice involves
the legal distinction between juvenile and adult criminal offenses.
For example, the state of Illinois has defined acts of juvenile delinquency as follows:

Those who are delinquent include (a) any boy who prior to
his 17th birthday or girl who prior to her 18th birthday
has violated or attempted to violate, regardless of where

the act occurred, any federal or state law or municipal
ordinance; and (b) any minor who has violated a lawful
court order under this Act.

Other states make the same distinction between adult and juvenile offenses; however, there is considerable variation on the precise age
of which a criminal offender might be considered old enough to be
tried as an adult felon. For seven states the age of criminal majority
is 16; for ten it is 17; for 31 it is 18; and for one it is 21.

Social conditions as well as legal criteria affect the legal definition of juvenile and adult offenses. In the 1950s and 60s there
was a tendency to raise the age delineating juvenile and adult offenses
predicated on the reformist notions that even older offenders might
be reformed. During the 1970s, the trend toward extending the
juvenile justice system has been reversed. Heinous publicized
crimes have been committed by younger offenders. For example, a
bored 16-year-old girl spent the afternooin in a San Diego home
shooting at children, teachers, and administrators in a crowded
school yard across the street. In Florida a 14-year-old replicated
in real life a horrendous murder he had seen on television. Courts
in the last decade have increasingly elected to try these offenses in
adult courts rather than process them in the juvenile justice system.

The question that has emerged from this reversal of the trend
is whether there exists any plausible justification for the legal definition of adult criminality. Intuitively, most of us would agree
that a murder committed by a 9-year-old child should be treated
differently from a similar offense committed by an adult; similarly,
most of us would agree that a 23-year-old offender should not be
classified as a wayward juvenile offender in need of help. The precise distinction between adult and juvenile offenses is quite elusive.
Should the age of legal criminal responsibility be set at 14, 15, 16,
17, 18, 19, 20, or 21?

Used cautiously, cognitive-developmental legal theory provides
a potentially useful tool to help define criminal responsibility. First,
we might suggest that such a theory be employed to measure what the
distinction between "juvenile" and "adult" offender seeks to differentiate. The law grants special immunities to the juvenile offender because it assumes that the juvenile is not fully able to comprehend his
or her adult responsibilites. The court, acting as legal parent to
the juvenile offender, tries to protect the offender from the full impact of the law and to protect society from the offender's actions.
The application of cognitive-developmental theory might provide an
intellectual test to see if the child in fact understands the basic legal
concepts involved in his or her offense.

I also suggest that cognitive-developmental theory might provide a tool to interpret to the young offender the reasoning of the courts in applying its sanctions or protections. As we noted earlier, there is substantial evidence that many juvenile offenders do not fully comprehend the reasoning underlying decisions made on their behalf by the courts. Part of the reason for this moral gulf between young offenders and the court is that few judges have the time or inclination to explain or justify their judgments to them. It is also apparent that few juvenile offenders possess the legal capacity to understand these justifications even if they were offered. A conceptual framework is badly needed to interpret the reasoning of the court in terms that are comprehensible to the young offender.

Much obviously needs to be done before this approach can be even partially implemented. An operational measure of legal reasoning needs to be developed in such a way that responses cannot be easily faked by the offender or the tester; it is also necessary to ensure that the measure avoids ethnocentric bias or does not rely too heavily on specific information. While at this time the idea of defining legal age by a cognitive rather than a chronological criterion is highly speculative, it seems to be more sensible than our present reliance on an arbitrary age established by statute and seems to follow reasonably from the empirical work on the cognitive aspects of law that I have described in this chapter.

CONCLUSION

This chapter has sought to describe a body of emerging work on a cognitive-developmental interpretation of juvenile delinquency. We have described what empirical knowledge exists in the field and have outlined a few of the action possibilities emerging from this interpretation. This approach to juvenile delinquency is a rather recent one and requires far greater elaboration before it can compete with alternative psychological interpretations of delinquent conduct. It is offered, however, as a new and unique interpretation of a major social problem badly in need of practical psychological and educational direction.

13

SEX EDUCATION AND VALUES: IS INDOCTRINATION AVOIDABLE?

Jean-Marc Samson

In a closed society, sex usually does not pose a problem. Fundamental sexual values and basic moral codes are transmitted through an implicit, almost osmotic-process, so explicit sex education is seldom needed. But the modern world has become—in Marshall McLuhan's phrase—a "global village"; rapid and easier communication has opened every society, every family, and every individual to an unprecedented range of different and often opposing sexual customs and values. Today everyone must face the challenge of deciding which sexual values to live by. Sex education—whether in the home, the school, or both—is now required to ensure healthy and harmonious individual development. This need is most pressing for the child at the onset of puberty. Since every child has the right to be well educated, sex education ought not to be left to the good will of parents or schools; rather, society has a duty to ensure that all children receive a sound education in sexual matters.

Questions about jurisdiction in sex education are hotly debated. To my mind, the home and school share this responsbility, though each has specific and different parts to play. Parents have a primary and irreplaceable role, but this should not be construed as conferring on them the exclusive right to influence children in these matters. Even when parental education is of a very high quality, the school retains a distinctive role. To complete the process begun in the family, the school, as an educational institution, should foster the sexual and moral autonomy of its students. Specifically, the school should extend students' information about sex and enlarge their field of sexual and moral references by introducing children to alternatives not likely to be encountered in the family context. This broadening of horizons is not an attempt to undermine the sexual and moral values of the family but is simply a necessary contribution to enhancing the autonomy of children.

Discussions about whether teachers or parents can do a "better job" are often based on questionable premises. The relationships between adult figures and the child are significantly different, making possible distinct but, hopefully, complementary contributions from each. In most cases, the parent–child relationship is more intense, more value laden, and more involved and longer than the one the child will have with the teacher. Because of the greater social distance in school interactions, the teacher is likely to be in a better position to facilitate certain developments important for sex and for education. For example, in a social situation where the child is less involved and with less at stake, it should be easier to judge the relative merits of different sexual values and customs. The second advantage of the school is that it can provoke systematic study and thought about human sexuality. By contrast, family life does not usually permit sustained attention to one particular question.

Since sex education in classrooms is both more explicit and more highly structured than it usually is in families, it is easier for me to make suggestions for teachers and schools. Because I believe that the theoretical and practical needs of teachers are relevant for parents, I invite parents to consider anew how they should attempt to influence the sexual values of their young. I will begin by considering four general approaches to the question of sexual values that merit attention: scientific, moralities, clarification, and developmental. Before turning to the last of these, I will consider the ticklish question of indoctrination. Because I believe that the developmentalist position provides a defensible theory for moral education, I devote the last half of this chapter, first, to demonstrating how it applies to sexual matters and, second, to drawing out its pedagogical implications.

THE SCIENTIFIC APPROACH

The scientific approach type of education is limited to presenting empirical facts by initiating students into the biological, psychological, and socilogical aspects of sexuality. For example, students would learn how conception occurs, how the embryo develops into a fetus, and how labor and birth take place. Teachers would present to adolescents the most exact data on the physiological mechanism producing erection, ejaculation, lubrication of the vagina, and menstruation. More recent programs may insist on knowledge of the different phases of orgasm as described by Masters and Johnston (1966), including a comparative analysis of the male and female experience. Teachers might note that erotic fantasies very often accompany masturbation and could report that "among [adolescent] boys raised on farms, as many as seventeen percent have had at least one orgasm through animal contact" (Katchadourian and Lunde 1972, p. 283). This approach might also offer advice on techniques so that students would learn how to choose a method of contraception or how to use a condom effectively.

So, this approach to sex education teaches the individual scientifically established facts about sexual behavior. With respect to sexual morality, the factual approach usually restricts itself to a historical presentation of moral conceptions. I do not, however, wish to be misunderstood. I believe that human sexuality constitutes an important area for scientific inquiry, and I favor providing students with as complete an account as possible of the facts of human sexuality to help them come to terms with their sexual being.

It is naive to believe, however, that this form of sex education does not transmit sexual values. Even if sexual values are not explicitly confronted, implicit transmission of sexual values begins even with the choice of subject matter. The educator who chooses to discuss orgasm, for example, indicates implicity that orgasm is an important element of human sexuality.

This approach also transmits values about sexuality when some studies are declared more scientific than others. As the presentation of all research is impossible, the practical problem is one of choosing what to present. When studying orgasm, for example, the educator may discreetly favor the observational method of Masters and Johnson (1966) rather than the more emotive account of Comfort (1972) or the technical approach of Kāma Sūtra of Vātsyāyana (Burton [1963]). By so doing, he makes it clear that one approach is of greater value than the other two.

Scientific sex education will, moreover, have to place the facts in a proper relationship, to construct interpretations, and to relate the facts back to the theories again. For instance, it is not enough to say that the young child at a certain age discovers his genitals: sex education attempts to interpret this event. Explicitly or implicitly, it will favor, for example, an interpretation given by a psychoanalytic theory of stages or, alternatively, one furnished by social learning theory—in either case transmitting sexual values. We can see the same process at work in the discussion of the facts of adolescent sexuality. Should we adopt Wojtyta's (1965) or Ellis's (1971) interpretation? Science does not simply observe and record acts or events; it is constantly engaged in interpreting them. In this sense, science is never perfectly neutral. Thus, the experienced sex educator will not be able to avoid the influence of sexual values even if he holds strictly to empirical facts, for these facts themselves are the results of studies and interpretations done by men and women who (unconsciously?) have allowed their own sexual values to pervade their studies.

Furthermore, scientific explanations themselves are subject to changing fashions within the scientific community. Gagnon (1977), a former member of the celebrated Kinsey Institute, writes:

> Scientific explanations also change over time. If a sex researcher subscribes to trait theory, he may study the relation of aggression or dominance to sexual behavior. But then the study of traits as explanations for behavior becomes less popular in psychology, so later interpretations of his findings change (Science, like clothing design, is sometimes the slave of fashion). He may have found that some subjects scored high on both a dominance scale and a scale of frequency of sexual activity. A later interpretation of his findings may conclude that a relationship between dominance and sexuality was found because dominant people are more likely to volunteer for experiments and more likely to violate social rules about sex. [P. 46]

Finally, sex education that is exclusively factual also transmits sexual values when it allows students to infer that biological rules and the generalizations of sociology constitute norms of conduct—that is to say, moral guidelines. Because we do not openly confront the question of sexual values, moral norms appear equivalent to factual norms. For example, if we study erection exclusively from the biological point of view, we can examine its steps and discover its "laws." But because we say no more, the individual is led to believe that erection is good in the moral order because it is normal in the biological order. The same things apply to masturbation. The individual who learns that masturbation is practiced by most adolescents and so constitutes a sociological norm can conclude that masturbation is morally good because it is socially normal. A quick survey of most manuals on sexuality is sufficient to uncover other examples of this subtle sliding from factual norms to moral values.

Sex educators (usually) do not openly propose to their students that they consider a sociological norm as a moral rule. They do not state explicitly that the sexual attitudes and practices engaged in most frequently in a society should constitute rules of conduct that ought to be adopted. Even, however, if they know very well that their students will make this inference, they will not (generally) take the time to prevent it, preferring to remain uninvolved in questions of value.

Once again, I recognize that studies of human sexuality have yielded valuable findings, but it is necessary to avoid confusion between factual norms and moral values. I do not mean to imply that moral discussion of human sexuality must not take into account prevailing cultural attitudes and conduct, but the difference between focusing on the phenomenon and elevating it to the level of a moral rule of conduct remains. Everyone acknowledges that there are sexual questions for which biology is relevant and others for which one would turn to psychology or sociology; but there are also questions that are the province of axiology or moral philosophy. Limiting the analysis of human sexuality solely to the verification of facts is tantamount to affirming that it is only by factual analysis that the individual is able to construct his moral and sexual values. In my judgment, sexual reality ought to be studied seriously in its biological, psychological, sociological, and anthropological aspects. But the scientific approach to sexual reality is, by itself, incomplete: the individual must be capable of giving it significance, and it is in this significance that moral sexual values reside.

Though we have spoken of teachers and students, the same is true for many parents and their children. Very often, parents limit what they say to the "facts of life." Having informed their children of anatomical sex differences and the physiological processes of birth and copulation, they often fail to carry discussions much further. They may have settled questions of sexual value for themselves but may be reluctant to talk openly of the value of different sexual gestures, attitudes, and practices. Their silence helps maintain their children's ignorance.

THE MORALITIES APPROACH

Another approach to the transmission of sexual values is to indicate those attitudes, gestures, behaviors, and customs considered desirable (in the light of some ideal of human nature). Euphemisms notwithstanding, this form of sex education seeks to promote a belief in a series of very precise sexual values. These sexual values may be organized in a coherent system where each value is hierarchically situated and justified by a superior value. In a coherent sexual morality, sexual values form a chain, each justified by the other until one reaches a key or ultimate value. This ultimate value is normally justified by psychological, sociological, philosophical, or political arguments.

The Traditional

In the traditional sexual morality, sexuality functions primarily in the service of the species and only secondarily in the service of the individual. Consequently, all valid sexual practice must be consistent with this procreation perspective. From this point of view, masturbation is disapproved of because it produces purely personal sexual satisfaction unrelated to procreation.

The New Moralities

The "new moralities" category could subsume all of the ways of considering sexuality where the primary benefit is to individuals themselves. According to these new moralities, sexuality does not function either primarily or exclusively in the service of the species through procreation but rather for the benefit of individuals in their pursuit of personal growth and pleasure. Some insist almost exclusively on the individual and his or her intrapersonal benefit; others, when concerned with sexual permissiveness, place some importance on affection, communication, or other dimensions of the interpersonal. In this way, the place and value of sexual growth and pleasure are relative to the importance of the interpersonal component.

The moral propositions characteristic of the new moralities are not organized as yet into a completely coherent system. For example, advocates will affirm that sexual pleasure constitutes a positive sexual value, placing this value very high in the hierarchy of sexual values. However, they hesitate somewhat to trace all the consequences of this assertion. They are reluctant to speak of masturbation as a value to pursue; it remains suspect. Certainly this sexual behavior is no longer considered a defect or a vice, but it still remains a behavior de passage, an act less desirable than a sexual relationship with a partner. The new morality rests in a logical hiatus tainted by attitudes inherited from the past. To be perfectly coherent, defenders of the new moralities would have to favor all acts that produce sexual growth and pleasure, particularly those that render it most intensely. However, even if they do not denounce masturbation when it happens, they never simply encourage it. But why?

Their responses are very evasive. They say that masturbation, while considered a normal means of expressing sexuality, risks turning the individual in on himself. Here again, one feels the pressure of the traditional morality imposing limits that the new sexual morality dares not exceed.

Prostitution and group sex present the same problems. If all sexual pleasure is valid, why not encourage all situations including these where one would have the chance to experience it? Principally, it seems, it is because these moralities have not succeeded in formulating a coherent theory of sexual morality. At the level of higher principles, these new moralities think of themselves as liberated from traditional morality; but when difficult questions arise, they show very quickly that they have not yet succeeded. By the front door, they stridently reject the dictates of traditional morality; but they return quickly by the back door when faced with conduct whose consequences are deleterious or unknown. What is missing from the new sexual moralities is precise understanding of the relations between the intrapersonal and interpersonal in the domain of human sexuality.

Social Sexual Standards

The morality of social sexual standards stands for nothing more than what is found in the conduct or attitudes adopted by a significant majority. This third position converts the modes and practices observed in the population into a sexual morality. In the name of sexual democracy, it establishes the dictatorship of that democracy.

For example, if it is established that group sexuality is practiced by a significant number of young people, as well as adults, all testifying to its benefits, one would expect to hear more or less immediately from advocates of this position that group sexuality constitutes a positive sexual value for modern man.

The criterion of significance used to justify sexual values presents problems because each sociomoralist will choose with care which group's opinion to consider. Second, this morality systematically eliminates the appeal to principles and substitutes statements of generalized practice. Not surprisingly, then, this morality inevitably proposes contradictory propositions. The contradictions are able to coexist easily because people do not always demand of themselves coherent patterns of sexual behavior. They can affirm, for example, that sexuality needs to be experienced in the context of a stable heterosexual relation while at the same time admitting that it is not bad for someone occasionally to have extramarital affairs. In the same way, one wishes both that the young would become responsible in the exercise of their sexuality but also that they not be able to experiment throughout the whole erotic universe in order to acquire mastery.

Let me point out that the morality of social standards has not always been the morality of the avant-garde, though for some years the appeal to democracy has been used by those who wanted to impose their "advanced" sexual values. For constrast, here is an example of a conservative appeal to prevailing social standards. As a result of a Saskatchewan teacher's discussing (with her ninth-grade students) a magazine article that described the first sexual experience of a young girl, a professional ethics committee was called to investigate. It concluded that there was no gross misconduct on the part of the teacher. Nevertheless, the minister of education declared:

> In my view, if the article in question was made available to students, it was a clear transgression of community standards. While it is the job of teachers to help students examine and challenge the world around them, there are bounds of good taste and there are limits to what material might be considered useful in the school settings. [Cited by Eisenberg and McQueen 1972, p 13]

Other examples of this kind are numerous. The reader will surely remember the bitter dispute about sex education in the schools during 1969 in the United States. The John Birch Society, the Christian Crusade, and various citizen action groups furiously opposed any form of school sex education. G. Drake (1969), spokesman of the Christian Crusade, asserted bluntly that "sex education is a new shame designed to demoralize our youth, all part of a giant conspiracy to rape the people, weaken their wills and make them sensuous, atheistic slaves". With evident McCarthyist accents, the John Birch Society Bulletin (1969) states that sex education is a "filthy Communist plot," designed to "subvert the morals of [American] youth" and to prepare the ultimate take-over of the U.S. by the Communists.

Under that right wing pressure, many state boards of education passed resolutions to ban sex education from the schools (ten years later, the majority of these resolutions had been rescinded or amended). For instance, on April 10, 1969, the California State Board of Education passed a resolution beginning:

> Whereas, the California Constitution prescribes "moral improvement" as one of the principal purposes of the public schools.

Item 5 of the resolution ruled that

> Harmful effects of premarital sex, etc., and a code of morals be emphasized with no derogatory instruction relative to religious beliefs and ethics, and to parents' beliefs and teachings. Emphasize family unit—and especially moral values. [SIECUS News Letter 1969 p. 5]

During 1973 France faced a similar controversy in the Mercier Case
(Doucet 1973). A philosophy teacher was asked by her twelfth-grade
students to comment on a short pamphlet entitled: "Apprenons à
faire l'amour" (Let's learn to make love). Well known by the students,
the pamphlet provided explicit sexual information emphasizing sexual
pleasure. All but one student expressly agreed to listen to the reading of the pamphlet by another student. The Saturday morning school
bell rang before the teacher made any comment.

The following Monday morning, the teacher was legally charged
with outraging public decency. The father of a student filed a legal
complaint, and the teacher was required to present herself that same
morning before the examining megistrate. During the following
months, individuals as well as teachers' unions, parents' associa-
tions, and educational and church leaders debated the issue in the
newspapers and from the pulpit. The magistrate threw out the bill of
indictment because no proof of intention was demonstrated against
the teacher. However, he referred the whole matter to the French
Department of National Education, which publicized this "pedagogical
notice" to the teacher:

> On pedagogical grounds, the Minister of National Educa-
> tion has determined that [the teacher] has committed a
> mistake in accepting that, during her course, in front
> of all students and by one of them, the integral lecture
> was made of a text that no newspaper was willing to
> publish in its entirety, and that no participant in a
> broadcast debate had judged acceptable to read on the
> air.
>   In effect, this pamphlet explicitly offers encour-
> agement to the practice to completely free sexual rela-
> tions, inciting to total irresponsibility.
>   According to the 1925 regulations on the teaching
> of philosophy, freedom of speech is guaranteed to the
> teacher. This freedom, however, carries with it
> restrictions that require the teacher to exercise tact
> and professional judgment, in short, to respect the
> freedom and nascent personality of the student. [P. 67,
> author's translation]

If this morality is incoherent and often contradictory in its
statements, it is because there is no wish or search for principles
with which to undertake a reflective and unifying analysis of experience. It elevates everyday experience to the level of principles,
where behaviors themselves serve as the rules of conduct. Appeals

are made to shifts in social norms, but their worth is not questioned nor are the factors that brought them about. This morality lies then at the mercy of powers and interests that are capable of creating these new modes. Luckey (1967) analyzes the situation this way:

> Insofar as morality is based on social consequences, when the consequences change, the moral values change. What is immoral in today's society may be moral in tomorrow's. And what is right for today's generation of young people may be wrong for the generation to come. One way to avoid getting hopelessly involved in dilemmas is to go beyond what is presently called "sexual morality" to a broader concept of morality. [Pp. 131-32]

To go beyond actual sexual contact, one reflects on sexuality—on its meaning and significance. This can be done only within the framework of certain principles. Simply denouncing the tenets of traditional sexual morality will not do the job. As I suggest later, there is a way for a new coherent statement of morality to emerge, and while the details must not be imposed on students, the framework of principles must be provided.

IMPACT ON SEX EDUCATION

There is, then, a transmission of sexual values as much in scientific sex education as through the moralities approach. The values will, however, be justified differently in each case. The moral authority for scientific sex education is science itself. The authority in the moralities approach varies according to the type. Both believe that their authority is grounded "in the nature of things," that "nature yields the evidence," and that "human reason grasps it." But they differ over what it is that reason discovers. Even among the moralities approaches the propositions are very different; in traditional morality the nature of things is related to procreation; in the new moralities it is related to the well-being or the pleasure of the agents.

Morality founded on social standards does not usually appeal to the nature of things, but one variant of it, which bases its justification on political authority, may do so. Thus, the sexual activity presented as natural by sex education (in such countries as China and the Soviet Union) is justified to the extent that it serves or contributes to societal needs. The proposition that sexual relations between adolescents are "unnatural" arises from the need of the state not to be burdened by the children born from these relationships. In the same way, affiriming, as in China, that it is unnatural for people to marry before they are 28 may result from a need to limit population growth. But it is not only in distant countries that we see reasons of state used to justify propositions about sexual morality. Economic arguments were invoked several years ago in Illinois by those who wished to justify the use of oral contraceptives. The costs to the state of unwanted children would have been greater than distributing contraceptives and educating the recipients in their use. It was politically expedient to "sweeten the pill," and this was achieved in part by a declaration that it was morally good.

Paraphrasing Adams (1918), one could say that today, with respect to sexual morality, mankind is situated between two possibilities: the one is dead (the traditional morality) and the other powerless to give birth (the new morality). This dilemma is the challenge that faces the theories of values clarification and cognitive moral development.

CLARIFICATION OF SEXUAL VALUES

Students generally are not satisfied with mere facts about sexuality but wish to find meaning in sexuality. While many sex educators are dissatisfied with simply factual programs of sex education, they are reluctant to embark on an explicit moralities approach. To escape from this dilemma, many favor the values clarification approach.

The clarification of values is ostensibly neutral. It has the advantage of not insisting on a content of values while still helping students become more conscious of their own sexual values. In the process, they may also become more conscious of similar or different sexual values among others in society. This form of sex education does not support a particular system of sexual values but insists only that students become clearer about what they believe. Critical scrutiny of the values discovered by this process is not encouraged.

For example, one might insist that students recognize their attitudes toward homosexuality and ask them to spell out in detail the content of their values as much to help themselves as their peers. The students might also be led to become more aware of the values and attitudes of other groups such as homosexuals themselves who might be part of their milieu. But in this method of questioning and describing, the teacher would never make an explicit judgment about these values. Here one applies with rigor the principle of de gustibus et coloribus non disputantibus! All allusions that could be perceived as a judgment are removed from the discussion as well as words like good, mistake, partial, and less desirable, because they, too, imply a judgment.

Whatever its benefits, this form of sex education tends to cut the individual off from others. It leaves the impression that reflection on personal sexuality is limited to the intrapersonal. The expression of feelings and values is also an important ingredient in such programs:

> "The goals for children and also adults are to develop ways of expressing feelings without too much delay and through manageable and acceptable behaviour" (Taylor 1970, p. 277). Furthermore, "when possible, feelings should be expressed at the time they are experienced, but if circumstances demand it, they can wait" (p. 278). How an individual makes these decisions is a matter for conscience, according to Taylor. He is incapable of indicating how such important decision-making skills can be developed because the construct he offers reduces education to developing the awareness of feelings and their acceptance.

Several of those who share Taylor's perspective preach the return to feelings as a moral panacea. Certainly, the traditional perspective held the expression of feelings suspect, particularly those connected with sexuality. The individual was to devote himself to controlling his feelings severely or, better still, preventing their birth. Taylor and others propose that modern man resume a relationship with his feelings by allowing the emotions to be experienced, particularly in the domain of sexuality.

The importance accorded to feelings ought not, however, to be made at the expense of the systematic neglect of other dimensions of the human being. The recognition and acceptance of personal feelings do not imply that being human is reduced henceforth to an emotional happening. Acceptance of feelings does not require rejection of thought.

In any case, the importance accorded to feelings and their unconditional expression is seriously questioned. A significant number of psychologists and psychiatrists, including May (1960), Farber (1966), and Arieti (1972), who agree that the individual should develop an awareness of his basic feelings and so acquire a well-integrated self-image, insist nonetheless that a human being cannot be reduced to a complex knot of feelings. They come close to suggesting that the individual will (la volonté) be admitted as the principal process by which an individual gives significance and direction to his being and his actions. According to them, the more individuals enlarge their conscience, the more they enlarge the area of their responsibility. Human liberty, though severely limited by both the individual's history

and culture, remains a reality. Certainly, as Arieti (1975) has indicated, "it would be absurd for [the individual] to think that his destiny
[is] entirely in his own hands," but on the other hand, he should be
made "aware that he, too, is a determining force in his own life"
(p. 41).

In sum, there are certain benefits in assisting the individual to
construct an accurate self-image. But it is necessary, at the same
time, for him to understand that his feelings, and so his sexual feelings, overwhelm him only to the extent that he allows them to do so.
And more, to express these feelings does not lead to a quasi-automatic
self-realization. To fulfill oneself is a legitimate aspiration, but what
this means for each individual is not predefined.

Let me return to the question of the alleged neutrality of values
clarification. I contend that it is more apparent than real. Let me
illustrate by presenting Morrison and Price's (1974) approach to sex
education:

> The teaching/learning designs presented here are primarily
> interaction exercises, with the purpose of increasing self-
> awareness, catalysing individual thought, critical self-
> assessment, and—through a confrontation with diversity—
> value clarification. There are no right or wrong responses
> to the problems posed. The only "examinations" are the
> continual self-examinations which occur in the process
> of group interaction. [Pp. 10-11, emphasis added]

These authors seem to slide away from this uncompromising position
when, in the following paragraph, they note that there are "qualitative
gains" that one can anticipate from their method: "Conscious awareness of the destructive potentialities inherent in some cultural and
interpersonal expressions of sexuality" (p. 11). It seems that some
values are considered better than others, and one can easily imagine
a morality of social sexual standards entering the scene. These
authors are, nevertheless, unwilling to push the relativism that they
propose to the extreme:

> While the approach in this book precludes endorsement
> or condemnation of any particular point of view with
> regard to sexual codes, there are certain assumptions
> underlying these teaching/learning approaches. They
> include the following:
> 1. Human sexuality is a function of the total
>   personality, and is not limited to genital or
>   reproductive processes.

2. Most people need a structure which permits them to explore and discuss sexual issues.
3. Interpersonal communication is a crucial component of healthy sexuality. Sex is not something men do to women nor is it a guessing game in which each partner tries to "psych out" the other, rather than indicate personal preferences and pleasures.
   [Pp. 11-12]

Hidden therefore, behind the curtain of neutraility is a philosophy of sexuality. These authors should be credited for having suggested, if very discretely, that all is not completely relative so that, for example, a healthy sexuality implies interpersonal communication. But they fail to expand on this critical dimension.

Further, many educators who favor values clarification do not seem to be aware that the insights gained may be nothing more than a subtle form of socialization. As Jung (1962) pointed out:

What is commonly called "self-awareness" is most often nothing but limited knowledge of what is occurring in the human psyche; and this knowledge, in its acuteness and dimensions, paradoxically depends less upon its object, than upon social factors and current ideas on the subject in society. [Pp. 13-4, author's translation]

Values clarification uses the peer group as a tool and as a context to help the individual examine his own sexual values in a non-threatening atmosphere. By definition, the peer group is declared neutral; that is to say, it is not to judge the attitudes nor the sexual values expressed by each member of the group. In practice, however, values clarification runs a strong risk of favoring social sameness. This is especially true for the adolescent who is much more sensitive to peer group pressure to conform than at other periods in life. The sex educator who uses values clarification, therefore, ought to be particularly sensitive to what Janis (1971) has called "group think."

Superficiality is another difficulty facing values clarification. Sexual self-knowledge is not synonymous with a simple overview of personal impressions. It is easy for someone to assert, for example, a belief in sexual pleasure; it is, however, much less easy to possess complete understanding of this personal belief; it is more difficult still to know with confidence the sequence of causes, events, and prior personal attitudes that led to the construction of this personal belief.

Depth of personal belief requires guidance by far surpassing that brought into play in group discussions or suggested by a personal checklist. The process of free introspection that is not limited to a superficial panning is a difficult and delicate operation that always runs the risk of provoking psychological storms. Here sex educators must take great care to know these limits: otherwise they risk disturbing their students more than assisting them.

Ironically, by refusing to engage in ethical discussions of the questions it raises, values clarification transmits to children and to adolescents very concrete values—that is to say, that personal and social sexuality are not subjects for moral scrutiny. It leaves the impression that sexuality and morality are incompatible. This is curious because in other areas of life the individual seeks to behave morally. But personal sexuality needs evaluation in order to become relevant for the individual. It is not a matter of transmitting a prefabricated moral code, for, "sexual meaning is an original human achievement which has to be re-invented, re-formulated, and relived by each generation and, to some extent, by each human person" (Guidon 1977, p. 36).

INDOCTRINATION

The preceding discussion might give the impression that sex education, however conducted, cannot avoid transmitting sexual values more or less explicitly. Is it therefore indoctrination? The word indoctrination normally carries negative connotations: it is perceived as an intention to reduce the individual to a machine externally programmed with "good sexual values." To many, indoctrination calls to mind the idea of some kind of mental cloning—of irresistible molding of the individual to a preestablished model, one corresponding to that of the indoctrinator himself.

Indoctrination is a little like pornography. All sex educators claim a little naively that they do not indoctrinate. A similar claim is made with respect to pornography: pornography is the eroticism of others, certainly not one's own eroticism. Analogously, indoctrination is the sex education of others. Indoctrination is always to be found in the neighboring family or in the nearby school but never in one's own home or classroom.

But what can be said about the concept of indoctrination? Here I concur with Schleifer's observation (1977) that "the recent debates about whether intentions, methods, or content determine indoctrination are somewhat sterile, since all three criteria are important in assessing whether teaching is adequate" (p. 3). In central cases, then, indoctrination occurs where teaching a false belief is done intentionally in such a way as to render present or future rational evaluation of this belief impossible or strongly improbable. The process can be assisted by fostering an inappropriate or partial approach to the question. If any of these conditions exist in the classroom or home, then indoctrination might occur. For example, to teach that masturbation makes one deaf or that it enfeebles the mind fulfills the first condition of transmitting a false opinion. To study masturbation only from a biological point of view, or exclusively from the point of view of sociology, might be indoctrination because of the limitations of this approach. Finally, to attempt to make our children prisoners of our or their actual beliefs, thus making reevaluation impossible or improbable, would be sufficient for us to claim that indoctrination has taken place.

Even for those committed to educating, it may not be possible to avoid elements of indoctrination completely. The truth of an opinion is always uncertain to some extent. No one, including experts in the field, is perfectly sure that intercourse during early or middle adolescence contributes to a person's present and future growth without any detrimental side effects. The same should be said of the method used with students. An educator-parent or teacher can never be sure that the method used will not render impossible or highly improbable the students' capacity to reevaluate what has been proposed. Finally, who is to say for sure that the approach used to evaluate any sexual proposition has not been partial in some possibly important respect?

As Hall and Davis (1975) have suggested, "the best approach to the problem, both theoretically and practically [would be to adopt] a criterion of non-indoctrination" (p. 35). One should be as determined as one can be to avoid as much indoctrination as possible, while remaining convinced that "education without indoctrination is possible, not as a definite attainment, but rather as an ideal toward which progress can be made, rather like love between individuals, or justice in society" (p. 42). With this view of indoctrination clearly in mind, we now examine the responsibility of the sex educator.

RESPONSIBILITY OF THE SEX EDUCATOR

Each of the different approaches to sex education transmits value about human sexuality either explicitly or implicitly. Each approach involves key or fundamental values relating to sexual phenomena in general but says little about individual instances of sexual behavior. We are, thus, some distance from moral codes specifying good and bad conduct for each situation. Katchadourian and Lunde (1972) provide an excellent illustration of such general orientations toward sexuality:

> Sexuality is not a wild horse that must be tamed and then exercised periodically. It is a potential with which we

> are born and which must be developed and nourished. It
> is every bit as important to be concerned about fulfilling
> our sexual capabilities as about fulfilling our intellectual
> or artistic capabilites. [P. 13]

Unfortunately, these general orientations are seldom justified, apparently because their rationale is self-evident. So these fundamental sexual values become the new dogmas, just as preemptive and indoctrinating as those of the past. Moving to questions of sexual behavior as quickly as possible, most authors use general assumptions without critical examination or defensible justification. By contrast, when addressing particular sexual attitudes, they cite as many studies as possible to support their proposals.

In this situation, the responsibility of the sex educator is to identify the fundamental sexual values underpinning the sex education program, to express these explicitly, and to justify them to students. In this way, the sex educator clarifies both the content and grounds of the program. The listener, then, is in some measure an evaluator. Making explicit general attitudes about sexuality could be viewed as a form of indoctrination. But the chances of indoctrination are even greater if one abstains from furnishing the rationale, because this discourages all evalatuion of these fundamental sexual values.

Such an approach views the sex educator as a practical philosopher having the courage to state explicitly and to justify the essential values in the sex education program. Kelly (1977) illustrates this process.

> I do not think it possible to write a book about sex without
> having many of my own values, opinions, and points of
> view showing through. . . .
>
> However, since many of my own values are going
> to be reflected in the pages ahead, I want you to know
> where I stand on many basic sexual issues. And I want
> you to understand that these are the values which have
> gradually come to have meaning and importance in my
> life. . . . This is not to say that they are the only "right"
> ways of thinking. You will have to sort through where
> you stand on these issues in your own way. I have hesi-
> tated to tell you about my sex-related values because I
> am afraid it might be too easy for you to adopt them for
> yourself. It is essential that you find your own. And
> yet, it would not be fair if I did not let you know where I
> am coming from so that you can better evaluate where
> you stand in relationship to this book. [Pp. 2-3]

In this citation, Kelly states his position clearly. Many sex educators have not been so open, not because they are afraid of indoctrinating but more probably because they do not wish to risk being judged by students, parents, or school administrators.

> The person engaged in teaching does not merely want to bring about belief, but to bring it about through the exercise of free rational judgment by the student. This is what distinguishes teaching from propaganda or debating, for example. In teaching, the teacher is revealing his reasons for the beliefs he wants to transmit and is thus, in effect, submitting his own judgment to the critical scrutiny and evaluation of the student; he is fully engaged in the dialogue by which he hopes to teach, and is thus risking his own beliefs, in lesser or greater degree, as he teaches. [Scheffler 1965, pp. 11-12]

While sex educators should not be required to relate their personal sexual practices, they should be capable of presenting a general view of human sexuality, including the importance of sexuality in the psychology of the human being, the place of sexuality in interpersonal relations, and the precise connection between individual sexuality and social life.

As sex educators, parents face a particularly difficult challenge. When asked to make explicit the reasons justifying their fundamental sexual values, they cannot hide behind the official doctrines of a sex education program nor behind the security of social customs; they know that they will have to justify their own fundamental sexual values and that their children are likely to look for coherence between these justifications and what they know of their parent's daily lives. Revealing the real grounds of personal sexual practice to immediate family members (inexorable judges) requires great courage. Will parents reveal, for instance, the true place of the quest for pleasure that was and perhaps still is present in their sexual lives (especially when this quest for pleasure may have played an important role in the decision to bring about the conception of their own children!)? Chances are that many parents would rather present to their children an idealistic facade of justifications to save their image.

People usually do not, moreover, live their sexual lives by conscious concrete decisions but rather by intuitive, global ones. They are often ill at ease when asked for justifications because they feel more than they can explain about sexual values. This difficulty in articulating coherently may mislead children to believe that in the field of sexuality, one really does not need to know or even that sexual values spring more from sexual impulse than reflection.

THE DEVELOPMENTAL APPROACH

Lawrence Kohlberg, a psychologist and educator at Harvard University, has postulated that a child's conception of social and moral rules is a precise and invariant sequence. He has attempted to demonstrate that his claim is not culturally bound; it is as true for children in Bogatá as New York, Edmonton, or Ankara. Kohlberg identifies six stages of moral judgment, each of which, he believes, is more philosophically adequate in that it is more coherent, more rational, more capable of resolving moral conflicts than the preceding stage. Thus, one aim of moral education might be to help students more through to the higher stages.

But what does it mean for a group of children to be at Stage 2, for example? It certainly does not mean that all such children hold the same views on a moral question, that is, make the same judgment. Kohlberg makes a sharp distinction between the content and the form of a moral judgment. Form refers to the kinds of reasons given to justify the judgment, and his stage theory is about the form of moral judgments. Children at the same stage will give the same kinds of reasons for holding a value position. Indeed, they might disagree among themselves about what position to take on a particular issue yet be giving each other the same sorts of reasons for the different views. This distinction between form and content in moral judgment is illustrated in the following example:

Opening inquiry:	What do you think of group sex?
Content of the moral judgment:	Oh, I'm not in favor of it.
Probing for the form of/or reasons for the content:	Really? Why not?

Possible answers categorized according to stage.

Stage 1   Because if my parents ever heard about it, they'd probably ostracize me.

Stage 2   Because, while it might be fun for awhile, people would soon tire of it and even turn against those who had been involved. Having sex would be more difficult for me then.

Stage 3   Because I would not be well thought of by my friends.

Stage 4   Because it would strike at the fabric of our
               whole social system and create social chaos.

Stage 5 and 6 Sex needs and creates profound interpersonal
               interactions between the partners. But,
               because no one can relate authentically to
               more than one person at a time, group sex
               runs the risk of diluting the sexual and effec-
               tive communication between partners and
               of increasing its superficiality. Clearly,
               this should be avoided because whenever
               possible, one should prize and foster
               <u>personhood</u> of the others and to oneself.

Stages are, in theory, independent of the value content. Thus, the person could be at any stage yet maintain a permissive attitude toward group sexual relations. In such circumstances, our dialogue would have gone something like this.

Opening inquiry: What do you think of
                                        "group" sex?

Content of the moral judgment: Oh, I approve of it.

Probing for the form of/or   Really? How do you
reasons for the content: justify your position?

Possible answers categorized
according to stage:

Stage 1   Because my partners believe that group
               sex is now an acceptable practice.

Stage 2   As no one sex partner is perfect, one needs
               several to experience a full range of sexual
               responses.

Stage 3   Nowadays, a really mature person should
               take advantage of the possibilities of group
               sex; a truly loving person should share
               with others these wonderful feelings.

Stage 4   Because group sex could be a good solution
               to the family disorder brought on by suc-
               cessive divorces.

Stage 5 and 6 Group sex is an excellent means of enhanc-
               ing interpersonal confidence and initiating
               the development of true, intimate relationships,
               promoting a new form of fidelity.

Let us apply the theory to one other example. Imagine if you asked, "Should we leave people alone rather than invite them—perhaps using a little force—to have some sexual pleasure?" The question might seem absurd to the sex educator: acts of coercion, including rape, are violations of personal liberty. But the answer will be far from self-evident for students, and responses will vary according to their stage of moral development. We can set out our dialogue in our familiar format:

Opening inquiry:	Should we leave people alone rather than to invite them—perhaps using a little force—to have some sexual pleasure?
Content of the moral judgment:	It certainly is right to leave people alone.
Probing for the form of/or reasons for the content:	What makes you think that?

Possible answers categorized according to stage:

	Answer	Commentary
Stage 1	Well, if you don't, they will complain to the police and then you would go to prison.	It is the fear of punishment that decides the morality of the act.
Stage 2	If you want to experience as much sexual pleasure as possible, it is probably best not to force people. Even if rape itself would be pleasurable— perhaps intensely so—trouble is likely to follow. There will be complaints and harassment; you may be ostracized socially for even	The agent calculates in a profit- and-loss manner to determine the rightness or wrongness of an action.

Answer	Commentary
being suspected. As long as there is this risk, rape is wrong because it does not pay. For those who can give you trouble, it is best to give the appearance that you believe that rape is unthinkable.	

Stage 3

| If a lad acted in that way, he would lose a great deal, particularly since no one on his street would think highly of him. | The argument may be similar at times to Stage 2 but with the added dimension of how others will see him—of his reputation. |

Stage 4

| Why pass laws about the rights of a person if they are not respected? If force is used to obtain pleasure for one's self, the consequences could be far-reaching. It could destroy our way of life, which though not perfect, is not bad overall. Chaos would be the result. Safeguarding the social order takes precedence over the reputation of the individual and personal benefit. | The ultimate moral criterion is respect for and preservation of a way of life, a social order. |

Stages 5 and 6

| One must leave people alone, above all with regard to their | The argument has gone beyond a concern for reputation |

Answer	Commentary
sexuality, because everyone has a right to be free from coercion. Using others as non-entities or as sexual outlets reduces them to the status of objects. We are free. And if someone forces us, we are no longer free. We are no longer treated as persons; we become packages of mere flesh.	or the preservation of the social order. Rape is immoral because it demeans what it is to be human.

This brief treatment is sufficient to illustrate Kohlberg's postulate that the sequence of structures is regular. The moral judgment of the child begins at Stage 1 and slowly progresses toward Stage 6. Thus, the educator has a responsibility to help students not only clarify their attitudes and opinions but advance their moral thinking until, hopefully, they arrive at the level of moral reasoning that makes appeals to moral principles—the postconventional level of moral thinking.

The Pedagogy of the Theory

The merit of the developmental approach is that is provides the sex educator with a framework to help students pass beyond the content of their value judgments and confront problems of justification. Discussions in response to questions such as, "Where do you stand on the issue of group sexuality?" are not restricted to sharing opinions and practices regarding group sex but examine the reasons purporting to justify these opinions and practices. In contrast to the values clarification approach, which is often satisfied with the immediate reasons offered, Kohlberg's theory invites us to inquire more deeply to seek the justification for these immediate reasons. So this approach is not satisfied with responses such as, "Many people do it and they are happy enough!"; the sex educator has a rationale for probing more deeply to establish why the student thinks that the fact that many people practice group sex constitutes a sufficient reason for doing likewise.

When one engages in dialogue in this way, the objective is not simply to afford an opportunity for honest expression but, more important, to develop structures of moral thought. Such development is not automatic but arises from interaction with the milieu. In a sense, it is individuals themselves who decide to modify their manner of moral thinking when confronted with questions and arguments from a more advanced stage.

To create the right kind of "cognitive dissonance," the sex educator must be able to raise questions for individuals at a particular Stage n, from the point of view of Stage $N + 1$. Imagine a discussion between two individuals, the one at Stage 2 and the other posing questions at Stage 3:

<u>Student:</u>	For my part, if petting gives me pleasure, that is a good enough reason for doing it.
<u>The sex educator, parent, or teacher</u>:	I don't deny that it is a pleasurable practice, but I think it would be better to say that it is all right because all the gang accept it. I mean they'd think you a little prudish if you didn't, wouldn't they?

The parent or the sex educator's reply is not designed to change the content of the student's belief or opinion. The reply invites the student to be open to another manner of moral evaluation, to enlarge moral perspectives, and to go beyond immediate self-benefit. While the response is pitched at Stage $N + 1$—in this case, Stage 3—it is unlikely to bring about a change in the student's egocentric perspective. Because they apparently agree on the content of the judgment, the student is unlikely to experience sufficient cognitive dissonance to feel the pressure of having to change the frame of reference. The student may well think, "The important thing is the value and we agree on that; if my reasons are different from my teacher's, that is insignificant." If this is likely to happen, the sex educator may deliberately choose content that is in conflict with that of the student's thought set at Stage $N + 1$. Thus, in our example, the teacher might initiate a discussion in this way:

I don't deny that petting is a pleasurable practice, but I don't think it is all right because a good ____ [fill in the name of some other group of which the student is a member—family, church, highly respected

classmates—and with whom the student identifies]
just wouldn't do it. I mean you do have your self-
respect to consider.

The sex educator, therefore, will have to adapt to the student's
developmental level just as the mathematics teacher does. The latter
knows very well that calculus is a very simple way of solving certain
complex problems but must adapt to students by first teaching them
the rudimentary formulas required for finding the areas of different,
regular figures and polygons. The teacher knows that the mathematical
mind develops gradually; thus the student needs to learn the fundamentals before attempting advanced mathematics. The same holds true in
moral education.

By putting themselves at the level of the child, adolescent, or
adult, sex educators avoid the risk of reinterpretation. So, for example, they may ask students at Stage 3 to reflect on the possibility
of tolerance toward a deviant or variant sexual practice. Instead of
invoking personal liberty as a fundamental right of the human being,
they advance arguments that are comprehensible by an individual who
is at Stage 3: thus they draw attention to the fact that tolerance permits greater harmony among people; that it smooths human relationships by avoiding conflicts; and that by tolerating these behaviors,
interpersonal relationships can be warmer and more amiable.

Sex educators need not, however, furnish all the arguments but
may support those presented by others in the group or the family. To
support does not mean to approve but rather to deem it worthy of consideration in the discussion. This limited act of affirmation leads to
discussion and questioning appropriate to the level of the class.

Parents and teachers often adapt quite intuitively with young
children. To a child who does not wish to share, we say, "Do you
think that you would be hurt if your friend did not lend you his game
of Lego?" We have used a Stage 2 argument that may or may not be
well adapted to the child. It is well-suited for the individual at, or
almost at, this stage but less suited for a child rooted in Stage 1.
Adults would only be shouting to the wind if they used a higher level
of argument such as, "What would your grandmother think of you if
you do not share the toys she gave you as a gift?" This Stage 3
argument surpasses the moral reasoning capacity of the child. The
words are heard, but they are reinterpreted to mean, "If I do not
lend them, grandmother will punish me in some way."

But must sex educators limit themselves to adapting to the level
of development actually attained by their students? Adaptation does
remove the risk of reinterpretation and ensures that discussion of
values really touches the individual. But to encourage students to
question their own opinions and judgments, it is necessary to provoke

a situation of conflict. For example, if all agree that sexual relations between adults are morally good, the discussion is reduced to going over the facts. It is here that sex educators intervene. Initially, they use counterarguments from the same level of moral thought as their students. Let us see how this might take place on the question of sexual relations between adolescents.

Imagine a group of adolescent boys and girls who support the view that sexual relations are good, even among adolescents. They reason that such relations are natural, that they encourage the development of attention to others, that they promote good cooperative relations between the sexes, and that they permit the adolescent to be authentic. Their arguments are correctly identified as Stage 3. If the sex educators play devil's advocate and propose that "sexual relations between adolescents are perhaps often morally blameworthy," they create a situation of conflict between two opposing viewpoints, both resting on Stage 3 justifications. They can, for example, support the view that sexual relations between adolescents may lower the esteem of adolescents in the eyes of the adult community or, again, that sexual relations can create bad relations between the adolescents' two families. Because the argument is pitched at a Stage 3 level, it will be understood as relevant to the problem without the danger of reinterpretation.

All adolescents experience dilemmas in which they must weight the value of apparently comparable reasons in that they are both grounded in the same stage of moral thought. Specifically, they have to choose between ensuring good relations between two families and promoting cooperation between the sexes. They must have recourse to another style of moral thinking to resolve the contradiction they perceive. To be sure, they could invoke Stage 2 arguments such as, "Everything considered, it is better to favor sexual relations between adolescents because they are pleasurable." The adolescent who is at Stage 3 knows that this argument has been transcended. He has forsaken this type of argument because he realized that it is too egocentric. Another type of moral thinking will enable him to decide the moral value of the reasons presented, one that introduces new elements or accords a different importance to the elements and motives already presented. Adolescents at Stage 3, however, are not yet capable of using this more developed type of moral thinking. It is here that the sex educator ceases to be simply a discussion leader and becomes an educator.

Educators know that adolescents must change their moral perspectives to resolve the dilemma. They also know that moral development proceeds according to a well-defined sequence of stages, the order of which is not problematic but determinant, and that the individuals cannot invent moral thought themselves and so must be furnished not with new content but with new moral perspectives—that is, a new means of evaluating the significance of reasons and consequently of appreciating and acknowledging the goodness or the badness of value judgments. Individuals do not memorize a solution but acquire new tools for thinking. Educators do not solve the conflict for individuals; on the contrary, having furnished them with new and better equipment, they encourage individuals to become more skillful with it by practicing on this and many other moral problems. To return to our analogy, is this not precisely what we recommend in mathematics?

The objective in proposing counterarugments is not to disturb student tranquility but to help them discover the limits of a type of moral thought. Educators, therefore, will indicate how moral thought at Stage 3 supports one or other of the values. For example, they could affirm, "There are people who support the view that sexual relations between adolescents are good because boys and girls must learn by experience to become responsible for their sexuality." According to these people, sexual irresponsibility results all too often in society's having to pay for the consequences. "It is not right to impose on everyone the financial burden of the social assistance needed by those incapable of having a stable sexual life." As for the opposing values, they could submit the following explanation:

> Other people support the view that sexual relations between adolescents are morally wrong because, they say, age plays an important role. They can accept petting but sexual relations demand maturity; if we agree that it is necessary to be 18 years old before being declared mature enough to vote in public elections, they say that it is necessary to be at least that age to have sufficient maturity to be sexually responsible.

Educators can present statistics showing a sharp increase in venereal disease among adolescents with repercussions affecting the whole society. They might also allude to the risk of pregnancy and its far-reaching consequences. Interestingly, the resulting birth could serve both as an argument for and against such relations. If students are capable of understanding Stage 4 moral reasoning, one could say:

> Yes, the child who is born of this union will be a new individual who, as much as others, will be permitted to be proud of his way of life in the society of tomorrow. At the outset, this baby may constitute a social burden but he will become a new citizen, capable of assuring the progress of our civilization. Further, if we do not maintain

a certain birthrate, an aging population will be the result and the progress of our society will be impeded.

As a counterargument, one could say that good citizens would delay
conception until they were capable of providing proper homes for their
children. The state has a right to protect itself against those who
are incapable of facing up to their responsibilities as parents.

Many readers may find these arguments too short, simplistic,
or faulty because they have passed beyond the type of moral thinking
characterized by Stage 4. They would prefer, perhaps, arguments
relying on higher-level ethical principles. According to the orthodox
theory, however, individuals at Stage 3 do not understand arguments
at the postconventional level, and they will probably reinterpret such
arguments in terms of Stage 3. When we present arguments from
Stage 4, we facilitate the passage of individuals toward Stage 4. It is
only when they reach Stage 4 that we will be able to present arguments
at Stage 5 or 6. Stage 4 arguments do not constitute the summit of
morality, but even if there are better arguments, sex educators ought
to respect the gradualism in the moral maturation of those they wish
to educate.

Parents may well have difficulty entering this counterargument
game. Usually, they are more concerned with the content of the sexual
values their children should acquire and less with the type of argument
they are using. Neighborhood and societal institutions hold parents
directly responsible for the shortcomings of their children's behavior.
Even beyond the age of majority, parents bear a moral responsibility
for their children's actions. How often do we assume—along with the
newspapers—that the rapist must himself have been the victim of a
"poor unbringing?"

For parents, open discussion with their own children might
seem like a risky business. When acceptable behavior and good
values are at stake, one might care less about the level of reasoning.
Momentarily at least, a child might accept the position in the counterargument and adopt it as a guide for action.

Because teachers are less responsible for wrong behavior and
less affectively involved with each child, they can engage in free discussions more easily than parents. Teachers may be in a better
position to develop a child's moral reasoning, though parents will
always remain an unforgettable moral point of reference for their
children.

Problems for the Theory and Its Pedagogy

Reflection on the developmental approach reveals several problems both for the theory and its pedagogy. These problems need to be

recognized and understood both by the sex educator implementing a sex education program in the school and the parent implementing a similar program in the home.

First, moral development is a slow process. Sex educators will be disappointed if they expect to see students pass quickly from a moral structure marked by instrumental hedonism (Stage 2) to post-conventional morality (Stage 5) centering on the principles of democratic equality. At the most, they might hope that their efforts and the slight gains achieved by their students are harbingers of better things to come. Some sex educators predictably object to this method's gradualism. They boast, just to be avant-garde, that they are not content to bring Stage N + 1 arguments but those from Stages 5 and 6. "I encourage them to reason right at the very top and the sooner the better," they say.

This reaction is quite normal for educators wishing to help students reach the higher levels of moral development as quickly as possible. Still, the studies of Rest (1973) have demonstrated that the majority of individuals do not understand arguments pitched more than one stage above their own. Let us consider the issue of tolerance of homosexuality, for example.

Imagine, a sex educator whose tolerances of sexuality rests on respect for the value of persons, whether homosexual or not, and the right of all persons to choose for themselves the objects of their erotic orientations. Individuals at each stage from 1 through 4 would be able to accept responsibility for a response such as, "I believe that it is good to be tolerant toward homosexuality because homosexuals are human persons." But the meaning attached to human persons will be very different at each stage. At Stage 1, human beings command respect because they are normally adults, powerful, and able to exact revenge if they are not respected. At Stage 2, individuals respect others as human beings because they want to be respected in their own choices. At Stage 3, one respects homosexuals as human beings because it is the fashion to do so. At Stage 4, the concept of the human being changes to that of the citizen. Here one would speak, for example, of homosexuals as being able to contribute to their city or country, their homosexuality notwithstanding.

Each stage thus recognizes the human being but in a different way. The full concept of the human being is too difficult for individuals at Stages 1 and 2 to understand. Individuals at Stage 3 can begin to perceive the idea, but there is little chance of their grasping it completely. Individuals at Stage 4 do understand that one can invoke this concept as part of a moral argument, but they will not know why it might be the key concept of a moral judgment.

It is the same for sexual pleasure. Individuals whose moral thinking is at Stage 2 will not fully understand arguments implying a reference to the rights of a person as a human being as a means of justifying the search for personal sexual pleasure. One may point out the fundamental right to obtain sexual pleasure, but that will not mean much. For them, what is good is what yields a return. The goodness or badness of a sexual act is evaluated not in terms of rights to be respected or safeguarded but in terms of personal interests. Consequently, when they hear appeals to the fundamental right of being human, they reinterpret them within the style of their own thinking. This they do because their moral thought does not have the structures needed to seize the full significance of postconventional arguments.

Second, the sex educator must recognize that the development of moral judgment is necessary but not a sufficient achievement in the overall task. Other factors needing attention include the development of logical operations and the capabilities for role taking. The studies of Kuhn et al. (1977) and Selman (1971) indicate clearly that moral development does not take place in a vacuum but is very much interconnected with varied forms of development. Thus, the individual who is not capable of formal abstract thought has very little chance of reaching a moral structure at the level of principles. Furthermore, the integration of personal sexuality is not completed simply through reaching principled postconventional morality. In addition to moral judgement, there exist dimensions of sexual experience that are not part of moral sexual education. One could have a "correct" sexual morality and yet be scarcely capable of experiencing a profound erotic relationship with a partner. So education about moral sexual values does not exclude the need for other forms of education, among them, education in eroticism.

Third, the character of postconventional sexual morality has not been well outlined. At present, the highest stage of sexual morality in Kohlberg's scheme is stage 4. Kohlberg (1972) himself notes the lack of necessary concepts to elaborate a strict postconventional morality.

> We haven't been given what we need to determine rightness or wrongness of choice from a moral point of view. We're not clear what the implications of this act [sex] are in terms of respect for persons, equity, or human welfare in these situations. As a result, we can't define clear obligations or rights or wrongs, though the situation isn't morally neutral. [P. 21]

As Baker and Elliston (1975) observe, major philosophers of the twentieth century have written very little on the philosophy of sexuality." The sexual revolution is in our midst and philosophers have only belatedly begun to contemplate it" (p. 27). Thus, it is not surprising that there are difficulties in developing a sexual morality at the postconventional level.

Fourth, there is a danger that judgments about stages will become judgments about persons and their worth. Imagine a group in which an individual at Stage 2 explains that personal sexual pleasure is the key value; another student always makes reference to conformity to the group as the key to interpreting and evaluating morality. According to the theory, Stage 3 thinking is more developed than the previous stages, but this does not imply that the person operating at Stage 3 is of great moral worth. In the same way, the individual who does not know trigonometry must be respected as a human being, just as the one who has a fine understanding of sines and cosines.

Fifth, there is a danger of accepting the first reason given as an accurate indicator of any child's moral stage. Thus, if someone says that sexual experience is good because it brings pleasure, one might conclude immediately that the individual is working from a Stage 2 moral structure. But the evidence of a single reply is an inadequate basis for judgment; those who are trained by Kohlberg to interview subjects and score the replies are expected to spend well over an hour with each person. Classrooms and living rooms do not often afford this luxury. The teacher and parent must be very cautious in classifying children's responses. To return to our example, the answer given is in no way inconsistent with a Stage 6 perspective; personal pleasure is one morally acceptable reason for pursuing sexual experience. It may not be an overriding principle, but when this level of consideration is satisfied, it may well be a reason. Teachers' or parents' interviews may not have been thorough enough to enable them to distinguish between a good reason for acting and a reason that accurately reflects the child's stage of moral reasoning.

Finally, an important reservation needs to be made about the examples used in this discussion; all of them assume that students are operating at the same stage of moral development. The world of real classrooms and real homes is likely to be much more varied than that, and so the sex educator faces the practical problem of meeting a range of developmental needs.

Practical Questions

Sex educators who wish to adjust their educational practices to accord with developmental theory will be confronted with several difficulties. The first is that of adapting to the students' stages and of furnishing convincing arguments exactly one stage above them. This demands of sex educators a degree of intellectual gymnastics that is very difficult to maintain day in and day out.

The second difficulty, a complication of the first, arises from the fact that in a group students normally are not all at the same developmental stage. In adjusting to some, educators risk being too advanced for others; should they lower the level of argument, they may be proposing arguments that are one stage below that which others have attained. Thus, in an attempt to assist the education of some, they risk bringing about a regression in others.

Finally, some studies have shown (Kuhn 1976; Samson 1978) that moral development does not appear to be absolutely sequential. It seems that between Stages 1 and 2 and Stages 3 and 4 there is a certain degree of oscillation. Williams and Williams (1970) have suggested that Stages 3 and 4 may represent two forms of conventional morality that are alternative or parallel rather than sequential. Nevertheless, what seems to be admitted—and until now has not been invalidated by scientific studies—is that moral thought proceeds by sequential levels from the preconventional level to the conventional, which in turn is followed by a postconventional level.

The insistence on moral argument should not make us forget the importance of other factors that are necessary, if not sufficient, conditions for the development of moral judgment—namely, the development of logical thought and the capacity for role taking. Several studies have demonstrated the importance of the developing of role-taking capacities as a condition for the development of moral judgment (Arbutnot 1975; Byrne 1974; Mosher and Sprinthall 1971; Selman 1971). Kohlberg (1971) affirms clearly that "the pre-condition for a moral conflict is a man's capacity for tole taking" (p. 192). Thus, the efforts designed to stimulate moral development must be accompanied by efforts to promote other forms of development.

Sex educators who wish to engage their students in sexual valuing do not need to wait for a definitive resolution of these difficulties. Further, they do not need to have a profound and detailed understanding of Kohlberg's developmental theory. In my judgment, they can act effectively if they attend to the following factors:

1. To begin with, they should insist that discussion not be limited to the content of values nor that it rest on a single exposition of the reasons justifying any particular content. More specifically, they must be able to confront students with an interaction of different forms of moral thought. To promote this, it is necessary that sex educators avoid playing the "law of the middle." Ultimately, they must support arguments derived from more advanced stages. In doing this, they encourage all students to take seriously arguments to which they would not have accorded much importance at first sight. Confrontations with arguments better formed than their own oblige

individuals to consider the possiblity of changing the stage or level of their moral thinking.

2. Sex educators must also support conflicts of opinion, not particularly because students should see both sides of the coin but because these conflicts over the content of value bring out the structures of moral thought. Conflict over content should encourage students to deepen the justifications for judgments.

3. As a pedagogical formula, sex educators must set to work promoting the capacity for role taking so that students will be more capable of taking the shoes of another and understanding the manner in which another thinks about and evaluates events morally. What is aimed at here is not the development of altruism, however desirable that might be on other grounds. When we think of the importance of role taking, we are concerned to develop a mental capacity or disposition to permit a decentering from one's own point of view, to develop, as it were, the capability of seeing through the eyes of another.

4. Finally, I believe that sex educators do not have to give inordinate attention to supporting those arguments from a stage immediately superior to those in which their students are found. Two reasons lead me to this conclusion,

First, as I have already remarked, it has not been demonstrated sufficiently that the two stages of each moral level are entirely sequential. The work of Rest, Turiel, and Kohlberg (1969), normally invoked to support the orthodox position, indicates clearly that 26 percent of the individuals questioned understood arguments two stages above their own (p. 239). Thus, exposing students to arguments from levels higher than their own is not necessarily a vain enterprise, even if one does believe that it is not the best tactic for all. Also, my own work (Samson 1978) indicates that a coming and going between the use of Stages 3 and 4 can occur. It is difficult then to know whether one must bring arguments from Stage 4 to an individual who has only temporarily regressed to Stage 3. Furthermore, the moral judgment of an individual is normally not situated 100 percent in the same stage. Most often it is otherwise. Each individual offers a profile of use from three neighboring stages around the one in which one is located. It is this that makes it difficult to use the plus-one stage technique with precision.

The second reason is a practical one. As indicated by Fraenkel (1976), it is difficult for educators always to adjust their interventions to the stage of each individual in a class. As well, discussion between pairs seems to contribute as much to moral development as the systematic

exposition of arguments exactly from the plus-one stage.
The studies of Colby et al. (1977) and the remarks of Kohlberg (1976) throw into doubt the necessity of holding strictly
to this method as the sole method of promoting the development of moral judgment.

This said, the sex educator need not regard the question of
stages as unimportant and so should feel free to bring any argument
to bear no matter what stage students are at. As a rule of thumb, the
educator ought to be occupied with plus-one level rather than plus-one
stage. More precisely, the educator ought to present or support
arguments from the first stage of the moral level immediately superior to the moral level where an individual is found. Thus, to individuals who are situated at Stages 1 or 2 (the preconventional moral
level), the educator insists on arguments at Stage 3 (the first stage
of the conventional moral level). In the same way, for individuals
who are situated in their moral development at Stages 3 or 4, the
educator will present or will support arguments from Stage 5—more
exactly from Stage 5a (the first stage of postconventional moral
thought).

This method of plus-one level makes the task of sex educators
easier because they need not constantly be changing the stages of their
arguments but will be able to offer a coherent or stable presentation.
There is also a greater probability that most of their students will
be situated at the same level of moral development. The one snag in
all of this is the requirement of presenting arguments at Stage 5a,
when, as we have already indicated, the sexual ethics of the postconventional level have not yet been satisfactorily elaborated. At
this level, it will be necessary for sex educators to innovate. However, this method of plus-one level should be considered provisional,
at least as long as new data have not confirmed its value over the
plus-one stage method. Thus, educators capable of presenting plus-
one stage arguments should not stop doing so, for they run less risk
of being reinterpreted and thus have a greater chance of promoting
the development of moral reasoning.

CONCLUSION

During the last 50 years, the Western world has experienced a
sexual revolution. Much sexual behavior, yesterday considered antisocial, is now socially acceptable. Homosexuality and group sex,
for example, are no longer illegal. Recently, the Law Reform Commission of Canada (1978) suggested that "incest between consenting
adults should not be the object of criminal prohibition" (p. 43). One

can safely conclude that the old sexual code as enshrined in law is in steady retreat.

Today many individuals, free from the burden of the old code, lack a personal value system: they live in a "value vacuum" (Cox 1976), a general sexual anomie. Individuals of the 1980s seem as yet unable to grasp the idea that their sexuality is a manifestation of their selfhood. Liberated from the burden of a sexual-social orthodoxy, they have accepted uncritically new sexual dogmas; they are re-modeled "bran' new" and become slaves to the most recent postures and techniques invented by the "sexo-specialists." Changing modes and fashions, celebrated as new totems by the mass media, fill the void caused by their lack of any sense of personal sexual direction and value.

Sex education in this social context has as its main objective to help individuals accept fully the responsibility for the content of their own sexual values and the actions that flow from them. Sex education has, thus, a threefold task: (1) to help individuals become aware that they can and ought to establish their own sexual values, taking into account their own developmental process and at the same time respecting the societal context within which they are living; (2) to support individuals in their quest for factual information about sex so as to ensure that their moral decisions are as well grounded as possible; and (3) most important, to assist individuals to become skilled in using the best tools available for the tasks of moral evaluation and judgment. Postconventional morality seems to offer the best set of tools for doing the job, but to master these tools, according to the theory, is a long, slow developmental process.

This does not mean that the content of the sexual values processed through a postconventional moral mind will necessarily be better, but the justifications of these sexual values will have been made using a structure of moral thought that is discriminating, perspicacious, and well equipped to face new and difficult situations. One should also not infer that the other criteria such as personal benefit, social harmony, and the stability of the social system are rejected as invalid criteria for judgment in the sexual domain; rather they remain present, but they do not occupy—as it were—"the first row."

Many argue against developmental theory on the grounds that the content of sexual values is more important than the moral stage furnishing the reasons. They ask, "Given the demands of social living, should not the content of students' moral judgment be a matter of greater educational concern than the type of moral structure they are capable of using?" This challenge is not easily answered.

I have argued that we live at a time when the sexual values and habits of the traditional morality need reevaluation and when we face new sexual questions for which answers are not yet clear. In both cases, a high level of moral analysis is required, something that is more possible for those operating at the postconventional level of moral thinking than at the two preceding levels. We know, however, that not all individuals will become habitués of postconventional morality; most will establish their sexual values on the basis of Stage 2 or 3 moral reasoning. Some of these people might conclude that it would be moral to engage in rape, oral sex, and incest. Could such persons be the perfect products of developmental moral theory? The problem is to determine what minimum content is required to ensure that human, social life is preserved.

Which elements make up that minimum is undoubtedly a delicate question. According to most if not all morally refined minds, rape would threaten that minimum; thus, all students in a sex education program must come to the conclusion that rape is wrong no matter what level or stage of moral thinking is being used. But while moral content is justifiably transmitted, the time-and-place characteristic of this value content should always be stressed so as to leave open the possibility of the future reevaluation of that question.

Compare the case of rape to those of oral sex and incest. Oral sex is no longer considered to be an absolutely inhuman practice, though it was thought to be so for many centuries. One can no longer inscribe that sexual moral content into the "minimum." As for incest, the process of rethinking has not yet been completed. New distinctions are being put forward, and there is a feeling that not all forms of incest should be seen as threatening the minimum required for human, social life.

The question of the minimum, and so of content, has to be taken seriously by developmentalists. In my view, the minimum should be defined on the lean side. Its contents ought not to be decided on the basis of which arguments are most often repeated nor on the basis of what the average, "well-thinking" middle-class person might be expected to believe. New marginal sexual practices, though still habitually judged immoral, have to be reevaluated constantly, for the human being defines himself through his decisions and actions, not by predetermined, conceptual definitions. This is in concert with Ricoeur's view (1973) that "freedom only posits itself by trans-valuing what has already been evaluated" (p. 165).

Finally, we must confront the question of indoctrination. Is the developmental approach to sex education any less indoctrinating than the scientific, moralities, and clarification approaches? The answer, to me, is yes because the emphasis is not placed on the content of values. Second, the individual is slowly led to enlarge the range of concerns he will consider as important in a moral question. Finally, to me it is surely not indoctrination to assist individuals to cross the stages of moral development that lead them toward a more defensible morality, one not bound by conformity to the group nor committed to safeguarding a particular set of societal attitudes, norms, and practices—but one where the key is the worth of the human beings as sexual beings, capable of creating their own objectives in the domain of sexual morality.

14
MORAL PERSPECTIVES IN
THE INTERRACIAL CLASSROOM

Don C. Locke

Yvonne V. Hardaway

In the years since the <u>Brown</u> v. <u>Board of Education of Topeka</u> decision (1954), the administrative, legislative, and judicial branches of the U.S. government have mandated a wholesale dismantling of the institution of racism. Discriminatory practices in voting, public accommodations, job selection, and educational opportunities have all been declared illegal. However, it has become apparent that the impact of administrative policies, court orders, and legislated statutes on racial attitudes and race relations have been, to say the least, disappointing. Cross burnings and Klu Klux Klan rallies continue; "reverse discrimination" suits have appeared; funding for private schools has become a political bandwagon; white flight has increased; and the relative socioeconomic status of black Americans has declined. Regarding public education, at least one major school system has made national headlines for racial disturbances following court-ordered desegregation in each of the 25 years since the landmark Supreme Court decision.* Though the tensions in desegregated schools appear to subside as interracial contact continues over time, rarely do they totally disappear. Even in interracial settings void of overt racial conflicts, students tend to form isolated, racially

---

*For a discussion of desegregation litigation and community reactions from 1954 through 1974, see Kluger (1976). Since 1974, the following cities have experienced racial disturbances in reaction to court-ordered desegregation: Boston (1974); Chicago, Dallas, St. Louis, and Louisville (1975); Omaha, Milwaukee, and Dayton (1976); Philadelphia, Detroit, and Washington (1978); and Chicago and Boston (1979).

identified subgroups. Clearly, proximity and forced desegregation have done little to alleviate prejudice between the races.

Against this backdrop of racial unrest, and in response to several other social situations, a growing number of parents, teachers, school administrators, and educational psychologists have embraced the position that public schools must assume some responsibility for actively promoting prosocial attitudes and behaviors among students. They also believe that the socialization function of public education can be greatly facilitated by expanding the curricula of elementary and secondary schools to include moral education. To be sure, the increasingly popular challenge to educational institutions to participate in the moral development of students has given rise to considerable controversy. In fact, some critics argue that moral education is not within the purview of educators. Others insist that moral education cannot be operationally distinguished from indoctrination. Even among supporters of moral education, there is disagreement about goals, objectives, strategies, and evaluation. These issues are beyond the scope of this chapter and have been discussed in detail elsewhere in this volume (see Chapters 1 through 3). What follows is a statement of our position on moral education and its implementation in interracial classrooms.

First, our conception of moral education involves the formal or informal teaching of rules of conduct and the development of values underlying these rules. Second, we believe that the classroom can be both appropriate for and conducive to moral education; that is, teachers can greatly facilitiate the process by which students are brought to understand moral problems in our world. Finally, it is our position that racism is morally wrong and must be confronted as such in any program that purports to promote moral education. Consequently, teachers in interracial classrooms must be prepared to transform many instances of day-to-day activities into learning situations by using the students' experiences as topics for discussions of racial prejudice and discrimination as moral issues.

On balance, we contend that the continuing conflicts in interracial schools constitute a moral crisis for educators. Further, we propose that moral education is both a legitimate function of public schools and a plausible vehicle for the resolution of racial strife. The issues confronting moral educators in interracial settings are many. How can race and race relations serve as useful topics in classroom discussions of moral issues? How do we determine which techniques are most educationally productive in interracial classrooms? How is it that groups of eminent educators can differ sharply on the efficacy of specific techniques? How can school systems gauge the public's willingness to accept certain practices? Why is it that some children adjust well to interracial settings while others do not? Toward the end of addressing these issues, we will explore the current status of racism, describe the conditions under which moral education can be more effective in interracial classrooms, and present practical strategies for facilitating classroom discussions of race relations. But first, a more detailed discussion of the interracial situation in schools is necessary.

NEED FOR A PERSPECTIVE

While one of us worked as a school counselor in a northern high school, a large fight (described by the media as a riot) erupted between black and white students during the first week of school. Black students had been bused to this suburban school after the predominantly black school was closed.

In discussing that fracas, blacks made such statements as, "We don't want to be bused into their part of town"; "They don't want us out here"; and "We wanted to keep our own school." Whites frequently remarked, "We don't want them out here" and "They should have kept their own school." In spite of the imagined vast differences between them, both racial groups discovered that their feelings toward one another were mutual. Teachers were encouraged that common ground had been established and proceeded to use the situation as a learning opportunity for students. Both black and white teachers reported that the most significant factor in the resolution of the conflict was the constructive communication between the two groups despite their initial unhappiness with one another.

This experience illustrates how situations of racial conflict and hostility can become learning experiences for all participants when teachers utilize proper interventions and approach incidents with calm perspective. Unfortunately, the positive outcome in this situation is not the norm; more frequently, open racial conflicts among high school students result in mass suspensions, greater racial polarization, physical injuries, and/or community uprisings.

One convenient interpretation of racial difficulties in multiracial schools involves assumed cultural differences between the two groups. It has become popular to attribute a weak, lowerclass value structure to blacks who experience difficulty "assimilating." Such a value structure is presumed to characterize black cultural heritage. Aside from our suspicion that this conceptualization is more firmly rooted in racism than in anthropology, it is far too superficial to explain the complex social system that results when children from monocultural backgrounds are abruptly integrated. To the extent that a culture represents a historically developed form through which members of a group relate to those within the group and to those outside

the group, the contribution of cultural differences to interracial interactions is undeniably significant. However, it does not follow that the
outcome of interracial interactions is necessarily conflict ridden; nor
does it follow that conflicts between persons of different races can be
accounted for always and completely by cultural differences. Above
all, surely the characteristics of black culture cannot single-handedly
explain the behaviors of blacks and whites and their respective reactions in interracial settings. Rather, it would appear that a proper
perspective on interracial interactions must consider the extent to
which the characteristics of both cultural groups contribute to any
conflicts that might arise.

However, there is some controversy regarding the existence of
a unique black culture that can account for some of the differences in
beliefs, opinions, attitudes, and values between blacks and whites in
interracial encounters. Sociologists and anthropologists disagree on
the issue of a uniqe black culture even when they examine identical
data. For example, Myrdal (1944), Frazier (1949), Glazer and
Moynihan (1963), and M. Gordon (1964) all discount the existence of
an authentic cultural heritage among black Americans. Their arguments suggest that the process of enslavement stripped blacks of the
identity necessary for maintaining a cultural heritage. In support of
their argument, these writers refer to the numerous villages from
which slaves were originally taken as evidence of the lack of a single
African culture. S. Drake (1965), Keil (1966), Suttles (1968), and
Szwed (1969) are among the many scholars who used their observations to offer support for some form of cultural uniqueness among
black Americans. While the former group tends to focus on black-
white relations, the latter group emphasizes black-black relations and
the development of a culture through suffering as the source for justifying a unique culture.

Nevertheless, both parties agree on the extremely important
role that slavery and the subsequent prejudice and discrimination has
played in the lives of black people. Numerous encounters with racism
pervade the lives of all black Americans regardless of social class or
status. Malcolm X is often quoted as having said that a black person
who earns a Ph. D. is still a "nigger with a Ph. D." Though the
academic argument regarding the qualification of black Americans as
a cultural group continues, it cannot be denied that the black experience
is a unique one. Further, those mechanisms traditionally considered
representative of culture (that is, music, language, art, and literature) have certainly evolved as distinctive forms in black Americans.
And, inasmuch as these historical and expressive differences have
proved sufficient for the identification of black Americans as an entity and as distinct, we consider that they have a functionally unique
culture.

Our purpose in this chapter is not to describe a unique morality associated with black culture. Rather, we seek to present our view of a unique black culture that is largely the product of racism. Thus, it is necessary to examine racism and its possible manifestations in interracial classrooms closely.

RACISM

Although most social institutions have been established for reasons totally unrelated to race, some of these institutions have become perpetuators of racism. To illuminate this process, we turn to a treatment of racism at both the individual and institutional levels. While individual racism is more easily identified and explored, institutional racism is the framework through which individuals express racial attitudes. Don Locke, a coauthor of this chapter, has developed a conceptual model that views the expression of racism along two dimensions: overt versus covert and intentional versus unintentional. The "racism matrix" yields four types of racism: overt intentional, overt unintentional, covert intentional, and covert unintentional. Figure 14.1 presents examples at the individual and institutional levels for each of the four quadrants. The matrix is useful for understanding the problem of racism and may also serve as a teaching device in helping students understand how racism operates. This list can be expanded by asking students to provide specific instances based on their experience. It is important to promote an atmosphere of openness so that students will actively discuss these examples rather than passively accept them. Strategies for facilitating these sessions will be presented later in the chapter.

Black students are likely to be so pleased with the opportunity to discuss racism in class that they may dominate the discussion in its early stages. It may be seen as an open invitation to "dump" all frustrations on the listeners. Black students are also likely to confront the listeners as if they were personally and individually responsible for the state of affairs in a particular school. Frequently, teachers report that black students begin describing white students in rather harsh language, often using black jargon, and ridiculing whites in general when discussions of racism begin. This behavior frequently encourages whites to resort to such a defensive position that meaningful dialogue becomes impossible. The resulting impasse serves to reinforce the belief systems that many black youngsters hold toward whites: all whites are alike; they cannot be trusted; they are unwilling to deal with racism; and they are not serious about discussing issues that are important to blacks. Teachers need to remember that for many black children these issues are so very critical

FIGURE 14.1

A Racism Matrix

Overt Intentional

Openly espousing the doctrine of innate inferiority among blacks

Significantly lower per pupil expenditures for students in predominantly black school districts

Building new schools only in suburban areas—ostensibly in support of the "neighborhood school" concept

One-way busing of students from black neighborhoods to white neighborhoods

Failure to recognize black students in class discussions and refusal to acknowledge their correct responses

Overt Unintentional

Counseling black students toward curricula that will limit them to career options that are low in socioeconomic status

Grouping students in classes as a result of subjective evaluations of ability

Using culturally biased textbooks and ones that deny the contributions of blacks

Designing bulletin board displays that only include white people

Expressing negative attitudes toward the clothing and hairstyles of black students

Covert Intentional

Discounting high achievements of black students by designating them as atypical and/or exceptions to the rule

Failure to provide adequate in-school time for participation in extracurricular activities so as to preclude the involvement of students who are bused long distances

Celebration of traditional white holidays only

Neglecting to publicize school activities in black communities

Avoiding eye contact with black students

Covert Unintentional

Failure to provide adequate role models for black students in invited speakers and school personnel

Lack of responsiveness to the unique interests of black students with regard to clubs, assembly programs, and special events

Avoidance of racially sensitive issues as classroom discussion topics

Introducing only those conversation topics with blacks that reflect stereotypic racial perceptions (that is, soul food, dancing, ghetto backgrounds)

Explicitly identifying the race of blacks when inappropriate behaviors are discussed while omitting racial identifiers in other instances

Source: Constructed by Don Locke.

274

to their whole way of life that they cannot easily be debated at an intellectual level.

The positions of white students in such discussions are often presented as reactions to the attitudes and behaviors of black students. Frequently, the white students claim that race is unimportant in their interactions; black students are the ones who always focus on race; the use of quotas and affirmative action gives advantages to blacks to the disadvantage of whites; blacks are too sensitive; and blacks should focus on the tremendous progress already made in race relations. Other whites may respond to the black students out of guilt either because they recognize that some of their own actions have been motivated by racist attitudes or because they acknowledge the evils of their ancestors. Making amends can take many forms. In extreme cases, white students may try to become black in their attitudes and behaviors and/or support suggestions made by black students in an attempt to win their approval. Aside from the frequently observed consequence of disfavor from both blacks and whites, such compelling guilt is not conducive to moral growth and autonomy.

The introduction of the issue of racism should be an open opportunity for all to learn in the classroom. In the fighting incident mentioned earlier, it was necessary for school officials to negotiate some of the rules that had previously been considered absolute. For example, name calling—particularly of a racial nature (nigger or honkey)—had been forbidden by school rules. We found that these students who had been involved in the fight used name calling to release their pent-up anger before they were able to talk with each other about means of resolving their differences. Small groups of eight to ten required about two hours each to accomplish this task. The school officials thought these sessions were important enough to allow these behaviors so that students could express some of their general anger and frustration.

To this point in our paper, we have addressed prejudice and racism primarily as they are used against black children. We recognize that there are also instances of black prejudice against white children.

With busing widespread across the United States, more white children are finding themselves in classrooms where they are in the minority. Many black children come from homes where hostility toward whites is openly discussed and encouraged. Teachers enrolled in our classes frequently report that even kindergarten children have said that they do not like white people. Though these children are probably only repeating what they have overheard their parents, neighbors, and others say, still it is probably safe to believe that these attitudes begin very early in life and continue as long as they are reinforced. For many black children who grow up in an environment where open violence is practiced against blacks, it is difficult for them to develop healthy attitudes toward their white classmates. Discussions of racism, then, can result in growth and attitude change for black students.

Also, it is our position that black students' self- and racial images have suffered from racism. The identity confusion that often results may be expressed in erratic and inappropriate classroom behavior. Many black children have learned that if they are to survive in a world dominated by whites, they must either be unassertive or become openly hostile and aggressive. It is important, therefore, for teachers to respond to children in a confident and relaxed manner. Black children—as do all young people—need guidance and support in order to learn to control their impulses and to channel their aggressive energies into constructive actions. We believe this task is best accomplished when teachers set good examples. Black children need to learn that constructive change does not occur as a result of hostile threats against white children but rather from deliberate discussions and organized, cooperative actions. The goals of education for black children must include (1) helping them become aware of racial prejudice, its origins, and consequences; (2) helping them learn to neutralize prejudice; (3) helping them develop a positive racial identity without rejecting those whites who are committed to the equality of all peoples; and (4) helping them develop a sense of control over their lives and their destinies.* These goals seem consistent with what most teachers wish to accomplish without regard to the race or ethnic origin of their students.

SETTING THE STAGE

Desirable outcomes of racism discussions can only be achieved if the proper classroom environment is provided. The classroom is best viewed as a laboratory for moral learning in which the teacher guides and facilitates experiences for students. What follows is a

---

*Of course, for this sense of control to be realistic, it may be necessary to reform the social-authority structure of many classrooms. Clearly, a great many students have little or no such control, and to promote merely the sense in these circumstances would be to promote an illusion. For a report on one attempt to reform the social authority of a school, see Chapter 6.

discussion of those conditions necessary for a climate of cooperation in interracial settings.* The four conditions listed here are not exhaustive; nor are they unique to interracial encounters. They are presented as guidelines for teachers in hopes that from them they might develop effective coping strategies to achieve interracial understanding.

Condition 1: Respect for Students as Persons

It is important for teachers to remember that all students who come into a class are unique and capable of becoming more than what they are when they enter the class. This awareness and acceptance of the individuality of each person should help deemphasize the importance of race as a determiner of behavior. The teacher who demonstrates this condition educates for "empathy, compassion, trust, non-exploitiveness, nonmanipulativeness, self-growth and self-esteem, tolerance of ambiguity, acknowledgement of error, patience, and suffering" (Michael 1968, p. 218). These conditions in a classroom are capable of providing the proper atmosphere in which children can grow individually and learn both the subject matter involved as well as more about themselves and others. (See Chapter 5 for an extended discussion of respect for persons.)

Condition 2: Encourage the Expression of Feelings

When college students are asked to describe their most memorable elementary-school teacher, quite frequently the teacher recalled is one who allowed, if not encouraged, the student to express painful feelings. Too often, teachers focus most of their attention on the subject matter with little or no attention to how the student is feeling. As a result of experiences where cognitions became the central focus in early schooling, adults are unable to express feelings. There are many packaged programs available for elementary school classroom guidance that focus on the affective domain. Notable among these are Developing Understanding of Self and Others (DUSO)[†] and The Human

---

*Developing Understanding of Self and Others (DUSO) is available through the American Guidance Service of Circle Plains, Minnesota.
[†]For an extended discussion of facilitating a classroom environment that promotes moral growth, see Chapter 7.

Development Program (commonly called _The Magic Circle_).[*] Materials are also available for junior high and high school that focus on feelings, life skills, humanistic education, or values clarification.

Perhaps the most effective means by which teachers can encourage the expression of feelings is to respond reflectively. Reflective responses are those that are nonjudgmental and accurate and that convey a caring for the other. They are responses that seem to suggest that the teacher believes in the potential of the student while encouraging the student to explore the feelings more deeply.

Another way in which teachers may facilitate the expression of feelings is by refusing to label the student negatively. A child is not likely to express feelings to a person who refers to his or her behavior as being lazy, stubborn, careless, or clumsy. There is considerable evidence to show that children respond to labels by behaving as they believe they are expected to behave (for studies on the signifiance of the self-fulfilling prophecy in educational experiences, see K. Clark [1963]; Katz [1964]; Rist [1970]).

Finally, the teacher is likely to learn much about the feelings of students by observing their behavior. The old saying that "Actions speak louder than words" is probably as accurate for feelings as many other areas of experience. One word of caution is necessary. When responding to behaviors, be careful to respond in a tentative manner, for body language is not even as precise as verbal language. Saying, "You _seem_ upset" is tentative, while asking, "Why _are_ you angry?" presumes much more.

Condition 3: Establish Reasonable Limits and Expectations

Limits are simply those boundaries established for behavior in the classroom. Expectations are perceptions held by the teacher about the potential behavior of students. It is imporatnt that norms be established based on individual needs and abilities and not on the whims of the teacher or the racial identity of the students. Stories abound that suggest that teachers expect black children to be underachievers. These ideas are so persistent that many black children themselves believe they cannot achieve in the regular classroom. A prevalent myth is that black students are allowed to live under different rules from whites. These practices can do no more than create ill feelings among students in a class. If teachers should err

---

[*]_The Human Development Program_ (The Magic Circle) is available through the Human Development Training Institute in La Mesa, California.

in establishing reasonable limits and expectations, it is better that they err on the side of having limits too strictly imposed and expectations too high.

Condition 4: Recognize Limitations as Teacher

The preceding conditions may seem to some to be very difficult to achieve. They are. The teacher must recognize that it is possible to provide the necessary environment for good interpersonal relations but that environment may not be sufficient for the elimination of all hostility and racial strife. A teacher must remain aware that the influences of the home, community, and peers may have an equal effect on—and so an equal responsibility for—the behavior of students in a classroom.

Having set the stage with these conditions, we would like to turn now to some specific strategies for classroom use. These activities, when used in an atmosphere of acceptance, respect, and honesty, have the potential for fostering effective moral education.

Strategy 1: Use of Moral Dilemmas

The literature on moral education is filled with research on moral dilemmas. Much of the work of Lawrence Kohlberg at the Center for Moral Education, Harvard University, is of this kind. Moral dilemmas appear to be an ideal means for studying values in interracial settings. We recommend that students work with non-racial dilemmas before being introduced to those with racial dimensions. In some instances, dilemmas might be rewritten to include racial identities. In others, it will be necessary to write original dilemmas that focus on prejudice or racism as the principal issue. The following black-white moral dilemma is appropriate for students in grades 6 through 12.

> Beulah and Amy are two 12-year-olds who grew up together and were best friends since childhood. Though Beulah was black and Amy was white, their racial difference had seemed unimportant in the past.
> However, Beulah's father was recently fired from his job at the local industry after having worked there for 22 years. He has filed charges of discrimination against the company for what he described as "racist" treatment. His firing has put the community in a turmoil with blacks marching in protest of his firing and the local Ku Klux Klan marching to protect the community from violence. The local police were trying to maintain

order in a community that had considered itself a model
of racial cooperation. Most recently, the company was
fire bombed and more violence was expected.

Amy's parents insisted that Amy avoid any further
contacts with Beulah because Amy's father was also an
employee of the company and he did not wish to arouse
suspicion.

One night, Amy heard a knock at the door and when
she opened it she found Beulah standing there crying and
out of breath. Beulah told Amy that when she had returned
home from playing with another friend, she had found
her house in flames and surrounded by lots of people in
sheets. Not knowing what to do, she ran to Amy's house.

The following questions identify relevant dimensions of the
dilemma and serve to stimulate discussions: What should Amy do?
Should she turn Beulah away? Should she invite her inside? From
Beulah's point of view, what should Amy do? From the point of view
of Amy's parents, what should Amy do? Suppose they were only
classmates and did not know each other well, would that make any
difference? What would be Amy's responsibility if Beulah were
white? What would be Amy's responsibility if Amy were black?
What is the obligation of a friend to another? Should a friend risk
scorn for the welfare of another? Should a friend risk life or limb
for the welfare of another? Is the obligation of a friend altered if
the friend is of a different race? What is Amy's responsibility in
keeping her promise to her parents and being obedient?

Strategy 2: Use of the Value Inquiry Model

The "Value Inquiry Model" developed by Banks (1979) can serve
as a useful guide in translating racially sensitive material into useful moral education topics. In fact, Banks presents illustrations of
his model in discussing value problems related to race and ethnicity.
The stages of the process are:

1. Defining and recognizing value problems: Observation-
   discrimination
2. Describing value-relevant behavior: Description-
   discrimination

3. Naming values exemplified by behavior described: Identification-description, hypothesizing
4. Determining conflicting values in behavior described: Identification-analysis
5. Hypothesizing about sources of values analyzed: Hypothesizing (citing data to support hypothesis)
6. Naming alternative values to those exemplified by behavior observed: Recalling
7. Hypothesizing about the possible consequences of the values analyzed: Predicting, comparing, contrasting
8. Declaring value preference: Choosing
9. Stating reasons, sources, and possible consequences of valued choice: Justifying, hypothesizing, predicting [P. 110]

The classroom teacher may use this model to analyze situations from newspapers or magazines that report racial incidents such as affirmative action decisions, open-housing disputes, and school integration disruptions. One such news item (Jet 1979) reported that a black high school football player had been paralyzed after having been shot by two white students as he huddled during a football game in Boston.

The following questions parallel the stages of the Value Inquiry Model and can be used to discuss the Jet news item with grades 6 through 12:

1. What happened in this incident?
2. What problem is presented in this incident?
3. What does the behavior of the attackers tell you about what is important to them? Why do you think they feel the way they do?
4. How are the values and beliefs of the attackers different from the boy who was attacked?
5. What values do the statements made by the school system after the boy was shot reveal? Why do you think they feel the way they do? What values were revealed by the mayor of Boston? Why do you think he responded as he did?
6. What values are revealed by reactions of the black community in Boston? Why do you think they feel the way they do? Have persons in the community overreacted to the situation?
7. What are some things community leaders might do to quell the anger on both sides? What do you think will be the results of their actions?
8. What would you do if you were the black boy? What would you do if you were one of the white attackers?

9. Why would you do this? What might happen as a result of your decisions?

Strategy 3: Teaching Cultural Diversity

The concept of the "melting pot" has come under increasing attack during the last two decades. What was once thought to be a single cultural identity in the United States has come to be an identity with many different and unique manifestations.* Blacks, Native Americans, Spanish Americans, and other ethnic groups have contended that the survival of their culture and identity is a basic human right. This trend has caused many to reappraise the educational system's ability to teach persons of such diverse backgrounds. One result is much research that seems to support the idea that difference does not imply inferiority (Sedlacek and Brooks 1976; Triandis 1972; Valentine 1971). Much of what was once called "disadvantaged" is now called "different." Teacher education institutions are being evaluated on their efforts to equip their graduates with skills to work with students from a variety of cultural settings. School systems are seeking teachers, counselors, and administrators who can be responsive to the needs of students from diverse backgrounds. It is critical to the development of all students that the environment of the classroom is one in which cultural differences are respected and in which students are not asked to reject their own culture for another. The following questions are designed to help students in grades 7 through 12 evaluate parts of a culture different from their own:

1. What are some values, beliefs, and attitudes typically identified with black Americans? White Americans?
2. In what ways might these values conflict with each other? In what ways might they complement each other?
3. What contemporary problems do you think have developed as a result of these differing belief systems?

(Teachers should be prepared to answer students who may argue that there is only one value system operating in the United States.)

---

*In Canada where awareness of cultural diversity is an older phenomenon, the common metaphor for this concept of many cultures in one nation is "the Canadian mosaic."

4. Do you think it is possible for a black person to hold "value X" and function effectively in the general society? Why or why not? How might the conflict be resolved?

(Examples of values might include: "All whites are racists" or "All whites are deceptive.")

5. Are there values of blacks (or whites) that you personally endorse? Why? Which do you reject? Why?

Strategy 4: Valuing African Heritage or What Is in a Name?

If an interracial classroom is to foster and develop an appreciation for cultural diversity among students, one means is to focus on the origins of some parts of another student's culture. This serves to help students become familiar with the origins of values, religious beliefs, family structures, roles, and behaviors of another cultural group. The goal of this particular strategy is to foster intercultural acceptance among all groups included in a classroom.

Receiving and taking names appear to serve significant functions in all cultures. The activity that follows is designed to help students, both black and white, develop an appreciation for a culture through an examination of the use of some names of "famous" black persons. The activity may be used in grades 4 through 12. The first three questions are based on the novel, Roots, by Haley (1976):

1. Why do you think Toby preferred the name Kunta Kinte?
2. Why was Kunta hostile to the name Toby?
3. Why did Mr. Waller find it difficult to accept Toby's African name?
4. Why did Malcolm Little adopt the name Malcolm X?
5. Why was he ashamed of the name "Little"?
6. Why did many people resent Little's name change?
7. Why did LeRoi Jones adopt the name Imamu Amiri Baraka?
8. Should individuals be allowed to change their names if they wish? Why or why not? Under what circumstances?
9. As a follow-up learning activity, have students research the origin and meaning of their given names and surnames and write a personal reaction to them. For another activity, have students research the original names of movie stars and immigrants and determine why they changed their names.

Strategy 5: Use of Persons and Models of Moral Behavior

A teacher may being a discussion of morality and moral behavior by asking the students to identify "moral" persons. The exercise requires students to focus on the behavior of individuals in situations demanding moral reasoning. Teachers should encourage students to think of familiar community figures as well as the usual heroic figures. One person who frequently is named is the late Martin Luther King, Jr. He receives this recognition as a result of his doctrine of nonviolence and his leadership in the civil rights activities during the 1960s. An ideal means of introducing the life of Martin Luther King, Jr., as exemplary of moral behavior would be to show the class a film of filmstrip on his life and times. The students need to know the basic chronology of events in his life as background for the discussion. The questions that follow are designed to elicit a discussion of behaviors related to moral issues. Some questions may be used with children in grades 2 through 12. Other questions are best used with advanced students:

1. What behaviors exhibited by Martin Luther King, Jr., suggest that he was a moral person? Why are these behaviors suggestive of moral behavior?

2. What childhood and early life experiences do you see as contributing forces in the development of his nonviolent philosophy?

3. From what sources did King borrow in developing his nonviolent philosophy?

4. Why do you believe King organized the bus boycott in Montgomery?

5. Which civil rights events best illustrate King's beliefs in nonviolence?

6. What do you think of King's religious faith as a foundation for his philosophy of nonviolence?

7. Why did some blacks (or whites) reject King and the nonvilent philosophy?

8. Why do you think that King came to a violent death?

9. From a present perspective, what do you think King and the nonviolent movement contributed to the United States and its people?

These strategies, when combined with the conditions for a climate of cooperation discussed earlier, can make significant contributions to resolutions of racial conflicts in the classroom. Each community and each classroom has unique features that are best evaluated by members of the community and individual teachers. Teachers are encouraged to employ their experience and judgment with regard to selecting and implementing strategies. Some strategies may be more successful than others in some groups. Some will lead to stimulating discussion while others will be greeted by lack of interest. However, participation of students has long been thought to be significantly facilitated by teachers' modeling. Teachers might introduce activities with relevant anecdotes from personal experience and/or video tapes of previous discussions.

CONCLUSIONS

Moral education means something completely different from indoctrinating students with socially accepted rules for getting along with others. Moral education at least entails fostering healthy attitudes in students through interactions with persons who are culturally different and through problem solving in both hypothetical and actual interracial dilemmas. Attitudes toward persons of a different race are influenced by past involvements, anticipated interactions, and the present needs of the participants. Some events that affect racial attitudes may seem unrelated to race at the time of their occurrence. However, when an event is perceived as unrelated to race, the participants may need to examine the event further after the suggestion by nonparticipants that racial overtones are present. This requires an evaluation of the incident in the present as well as in terms of historical background and possible future impact.

The use of classroom discussions of racial issues can serve as useful source material in moral education. Because teachers are usually important role models, they can foster healthy racial attitudes by treating students from culturally different backgrounds fairly and can greatly reduce the discomfort experienced by many youngsters in discussing race by initiating open dialogue on the subject.

The role of the teacher is a very important one in our society. Along with parents, teachers are responsible for preparing our youth for adult living. Therefore, moral guidance in the area of race relations cannot be excluded from their responsibility. Teachers may have a great impact on the difference between a society of ignorance and fear in race relations and a society in which the "New World" dream remains a real possibility for all North Americans.

EPILOGUE:
A DISCUSSION AMONG COCHRANE,
LICKONA, SAMSON, SCHARF, AND WILSON

HOW IS MORAL DEVELOPMENT PROPERLY CONCEPTULAIZED?

LICKONA: In our earlier discussions, I have tried to establish, John, whether there are phenomena that we both recognize as having some reality and that we both are trying to explain. If we grant that moral understanding, mathematical understanding, esthetic appreciation, or whatever "develops," then our problem becomes how to conceptualize this process. Is there some sort of predictable, sequential, and universal progression to levels of complexity or confidence, just as we learn to crawl, then to walk, to babble, and then to speak? You puzzle me: On the one hand, you sometimes seem to say that a student needs to learn arithmetic before he learns calculus, in which case there is no dispute between us; at other times, you seem to say that you could teach a five-year-old calculus if you only went about it correctly. So I'm not really sure where we agree and disagree.

WILSON: Let me say first that I wouldn't want to quarrel with the data about what kids tend to say at various ages. There is no doubt that there is a phenomenon there. I don't think the whole thing is a kind of a giant hoax, nor would I want to quarrel particularly with whether one could call that development. I don't object to the word stages. And if children characteristically move from one stage to another in certain cultures at various ages, I wouldn't quarrel with that either. That, I think, is sort of common ground in a way.

LICKONA: That's important, I wasn't sure there was common ground.

WILSON: Well, I think thereaare two problems. One is, just how does one describe this? Is it a question of the development of understanding reasons, being able to give reasons, or wanting and willing to use the reasons? Connected with that, I think, is the question of whether this is something you can do anything about. If you did engage in teaching children certain kinds of things, or put them under different sorts of regimes, would the picture look very different? How far can a child's understanding or use of reason be affected by stringent teaching? It's not that I disagree with Larry Kohlberg—it's just that I just don't think he has answered some of these questions, that's all!

WHAT ARE STAGES?

SCHARF: Myself, I'm inclined to back off the orthodox version of the stage theory. I have been much influenced by an article by Vandervale (1970) where he distinguishes three types of relationships between stages. The first type is characterized by axioms that are "logically derivable." Let's say you have Stage A and Stage B: B is in some sense logically derived from A. I think that certain kinds of mathematical development have that quality. He calls the second "non-derivable type stages" similar to Maslow's, let's say. These are like a layer cake: one stage follows another, but there's no logical reason to move from security, for example, to self-actualization. And the third is what he calls—somewhat similar to Turiel's typology— "partially derivable axioms."* Now if you look at Damon's (1977) critique of Stage 1, or Gibb's (1977) analysis of Stage 5, it becomes apparent that Kohlberg's stages are really collections or clusters of ideas. Further, the characterizations are very skewed. Damon's critique of Stage 1 is absolutely right: it's not quite clear that what Kohlberg is calling Stage 1 actually happens.

LICKONA: I'm not sure Damon says that. In his stage sequence, he has equivalents of "Kohlberg's 1" but he says that it is only one of about eight stages that characterize reasoning in childhood.

SCHARF: Right. But I mean Stage 1 is a collection of a series of things of varying structural dimensions, characteristic contents, and everything else. So I assume that it's partially derivable. In Stage 5, for example, you have a social contract theory, a natural rights theory, and a utilitarian theory all lumped together. I assume that's the status of it.

---

*For a critical discussion of this issue, see Nicolayer and Phillips (1979).

Stages as a Function of Different "Regimes"

WILSON: I think that what the stage hypothesis purports to prove remains obscure. One explanation of stage theory would be that it is unsurprisingly a matter of empirical fact that children start off by acting on impulse, then have to obey parental commands, then get a few general rules like keeping promises, and then meet their peers. There are, as it were, different regimes, and, if that is so, and inevitably so, given the fact that children have to grow up and survive, it's unsurprising that at different ages when they are under their regimes, they produce the kinds of reasons appropriate to the regimes. That's nothing to do with being _able_ to understand reasons. The kid has his orders from his parents and unsurprisingly will given as a reason "cuz Mommy says so." That's just one possible explanation that we might describe as the preference style of dishing out reasons. This empirical account provides one explanation of what the stages are stages of.

LICKONA: What if you found that all people, regardless of the regimes that they grew up under, went through a phase of identifying what is moral with what is conventional? Then your explanation wouldn't quite work.

WILSON: I don't think the phrase "regardless of what regimes they grew up under" makes any sense. I mean it's a point of necessity, not of contingent fact. If the child starts by being impulsive, then its first experience of a rule is its parents telling it to do something. . . . I mean, that's inevitable, I think.

COCHRANE: Why's that?

WILSON: Well, I think that you would have to work that out from the concept of what it is to be a child. How could it be different?

COCHRANE: Could one have the concept of a rule prior to the notion of a command? It seems to me that a rule is a command that exists across time and across space for reasonably similar circumstances. If one were to work out this line of reasoning, stages might be logically, not simply empirically, related.

WILSON: Yes. Certainly that would be true for Piagetian stages whereby the child is egocentric, then accepts commands, and then has peer groups. That seems to be unavoidable.

SCHARF: It seems to me that stages could, in some sense, be mathematical and truly invariant. For example, I have had a conversation with my three-year-old son Sage about what he would be when he grew up and he said, "I want to be a woman." He also wanted to change his name. He was going to do that by putting on a Wonder Woman costume! There is something about conservation of one's form or conservation of identity that presents a structural problem at this age. There are things you can't teach a child unless he has the appropriate structure. Now the problem is that Kohlberg has called this thing a stage and lists its Piagetian characteristics—psychological wholeness, hierarchical integration, and adequacy. But I think that the details of his characterization are controversial. If you look at how Kohlberg describes any of the stages, it's not quite clear where or even whether all of the elements could fit. Do they have that some kind of structural quality as the Piagetian stage? It is fair, as you say, to ask, "What is a stage?"

But then we move to the realm of moral development where it's not quite clear that the things any of us have been talking about are stages of moral development, having those same structural properties. Looking at your work, Tom, and that of Bill Damon, I would suspect that some of the A-B alterations are very much products of regime. It's not quite clear what parts of an A-B shift are genuinely structural. The critical empirical test, it seems to me, would be to look at variations of regimes to determine whether there is a reciprocal variation in order. All we have now is that limited study of Kohlberg's—it's about males living in Chicago in one 26-year period of history. It seems to me that until we have much stronger longitudinal and cross-historical studies, I, for one, would not be willing to assert what parts of it are, in fact, structural.

WILSON: By structural you mean that they are invariant?

SCHARF: Logically invariant.

LICKONA: I don't think that there is any real quarrel. Kohlberg was the first to say that he'd confused content in structure in some of the stage descriptions, and he sees part of the process of improving the the theory as sorting out what is content and what is structure. I think the more basic question is this: Does a content-structure distinction have any psychological reality? Now, if I understand some of the things John said, he's suggesting that it doesn't. If you say that what the child says, or how the child reasons, is simply a product of the social regime, then we are just talking about content. And we could put any content into the child's head and have a five-year-old reasoning like Martin Luther King if we just get the content into his head in the right way. So the question becomes, Are there any structural limitations? Structure has to do with, in a sense, how capable the child could be in reasoning about the subject matter. If I understand John, he is saying it's really all subject matter, and we're saying that the subject matter is there, but that's only half of it. The other half of it is the child's capacity to reason about the subject matter.

Stages as the Limits of Understanding

COCHRANE: Let me attempt to make John's point more forcefully. His challenge is an attempt to compel the developmentalists to clarify what a child who is seven years old and "on schedule" can't understand. Tom, for his part, would say that there are limits: "Here I am with my son who will reason only at Stage 3, and I'm battering his head trying to get him to understand a Stage 4 dimension to his situation. He just can't get it. I try a new tack and back he comes with solid Stage 3 stuff." Now that's the phenomenon that John refuses to try to explain. John replies: "Look, it's not enough just to say that you tried different tacks and your son doesn't understand. What is it that your son doesn't understand?" He offers the didactic model as an alternative. It goes something like this: Look, there's a concept of a person, right? It's pretty elementary. It doesn't matter whether it is a descriptive or prescriptive notion; that's an issue for another day. By and large, there is a rough and ready concept of a person. We know how it's different from tables. Furthermore, we kick tables, but we don't tear people apart. There are some rules that we associate with "proper conduct towards persons"—not slugging them, not insulting them. We can draw up a list of quite striaghtforward rules. What seven-year-old child can't understand that? He knows the range of objects to which the rules pertain and he understands the rules. Now we have to work on his motivation. Why all this puzzling about stages?

SCHARF: Can I give you a glib answer? By choosing your range of problems (Stage 1 dilemmas), there is no really complicated issue. Why shouldn't I kick Tom? That's a simple problem. But if I tell you that your Jewish friend is running by your house, should you turn him in to the Gestapo? Situations like this are more complicated. You make an easy case because you take easy examples. Any seven-year-old ought to be able to answer them. It's quite consistent with the theory. He understands because there is a very simple reason. Sure, you can teach that, but let me give you a hard dilemma. That's where it falls down. That's where children don't understand.

WILSON: Why do you think that the seven-year-old doesn't understand the reason rather than that he prefers to use another one? That's the point.

LICKONA: Well, you can't keep coming back to that because there comes a point where you could simply say, "Well, the child prefers not to use his Stage 6 reasoning," and how would we ever prove you to be wrong? The burden of proof really rests upon you to find a case where that seven-year-old really does reason like John Rawls. If you are saying that he really has it but we haven't given him the situation that taps it, then you would have to find a situation that brings out his preferred judgments, since all the ones that I've given obviously don't.

WILSON: That's a fair challenge. Taking the example of older people who are quite intelligent but occasionally go mad and obey their <u>Führer</u>, how would one test that out? Well, there would be three ways. One would be to see if they use that kind of reasoning in the course of their everyday lives; and the second would be to see if they understood it after you taught it to them. A third one, which I think would be quite adequate, would be to say that if he has the concept of a person and a concept of what's nice for them, then how could it be the case that he doesn't understand the reasoning? That's what we mean by understanding the reasons. I should be very surprised if the kids couldn't learn that. I should be very surprised also if kids didn't have a clear idea of what sorts of things are nice and what sort of things are nasty for people. Now, what else is there to understand?

AN ANALOG WITH HISTORICAL UNDERSTANDING

SCHARF: Let me give you an analogy with history to show you where I think we are misunderstanding each other. When you are talking about history, you are talking about what Collingwood refers to as scissors-and-paste history, additive history: battles, facts, kings, institutions, and so forth. What we're talking about in this analogue is historiography—systems of history, ways of conceptualizing history. The parallel would be if we were to ask an eight-year-old to compare the views of Marx and Spengler. He might be able to tell you what happened in 1066, but our position contends that he would be unable to order or conceptualize such facts into any systemic or ideological position. What Kohlberg is picking up on is how we think about facts, not the facts themselves.

WILSON: I think the analogy with history would go rather differently. If you had a society, and I suppose there are some, where when people were asked why some people in the past did certain things, and they replied with things like, "Angels did it" or "Perhaps they just felt like it," then there would be a question of whether it would be possible to teach a child to look at a piece of evidence like what the person wrote in his diary instead of bringing in angels to explain events. Or, in mathematics, could you show a student what sort of reasons he was to use in a general way in order to arrive at the right answers? It seems to me that you could teach a child at an early age to do history—at least in this sense. When you are trying to find out why someone did something you would say to the child "Dont't talk about angels, or the Will of God."

FORM AND CONTENT IN MORAL DEVELOPMENT

COCHRANE: Is John stuck on content? Of course, there is the concept of a person and there are rules such as "Don't kill persons," but for Lawrence Kohlberg that's not form at all—that is content. And surely Kohlberg would agree that the content of most rules could be taught to most seven-year-olds. But then if you asked such a student, "Why not kill?", he would respond in a Stage 1 manner, "Well, I would be severely punished"; or if he was at Stage 2, he would answer something like, "Well, if I could engage in that kind of behavior, others could too," and so on prudential grounds he would develop a limited kind of loyalty to fellow beings: "I won't engage in threatening behavior to others with the expectation that they will do likewise to me." And so on through the stages.

WILSON: I wouldn't want to teach them particular rules. What I would want to do is shake them until their teeth rattle and say, "Look, whenever you need to decide what you ought to do, you must learn the following principle: You must decide what to do on the basis of what's nice for other people. You may often find it difficult to know what's nice for other people; you may have to ask around, but you are not to decide it on the basis of any other principle."

SAMSON: Do you give children any instruction on why this should be the basis for morality?

WILSON: Well, there you start getting into moral philosophy. Then I guess I would get them to read Professor Hare and all that. But that's another matter.

SAMSON: But we have found that people can understand the words of an argument but not its rationale, or the force of the rationale. Are you saying that they are unable to understand or simply that they don't want to?

WILSON: If you want to explain to a child the "why" of the rules, which is after all a different issue, the characteristic move with children is to say, "Well how would you like it if you were the recipient of that action?" They can understand the basic kind of reasoning behind rules. It's one thing to claim that they don't understand the rules—it's another thing to claim that they don't understand the reasons behind them. But who does understand them fully, unless they are intimate with the mind of Dick Hare or whoever the philosopher is that's preferred?

LICKONA: Yes, but what Jim Rest (1973) has done systematically in his research is to ask people to paraphrase an argument pitched at a different stage, and he finds that in paraphrasing it that they bring it down to their stage. So you give them a Stage 5 response and they run it through their mill and it comes out at their Stage 3. And if you find that consistently, why say that they are doing it because they are stubborn or because they have a particular vested interest? They are being asked their responses on various moral problems that have nothing to do with their own personal self-interest. And yet they consistently do this sort of distortion, bringing it down to their stage.

SCHARF: Let's decide on a hypothetical experiment to disconfirm either position. Let's say we followed children under ten discrete regimes. We would include one regime with the kind of direct instruction you advocate. Then we would have to have something to measure their capacity to reason with. What if we found that independent of regimes that there was the same invariant sequence?

WILSON: Well, one thing that might show is that there is something like what you chaps call the developmental structure in the human flow or unconscious that proceeds independent of regime. But that would show only what they were driven to do or preferred to do—not what they understood. If you wanted to find out what they understood, you would have to do quite different things.

LICKONA: Well, what would you do? Rest asked people to paraphase arguments. What would you do in order to find out what a chap understood?

WILSON: Well, what do teachers mainly do? They'd get hold of kids and they'd ask what are the characteristics of persons in this room. Do you have any idea of what's nice or nasty for people? You might take one case and give different sorts of reasons.

LICKONA: We would agree that you can get a seven-year-old to have a concept of a person as you're describing it. And that the student should base moral decisions on the basis of other peoples' interests. Those things young children can grasp. But what we say changes is the way that the concept of a person is applied to moral problems, so that children at different developmental stages apply the concept of person in moral situations in different ways. So it isn't that they don't have a concept of a person but how that is translated into the making of moral decisions. And the intervening variable would be the moral stage.

WILSON: Well, I half sort of want to go along with that. It would seem to me that the better description of that would be to say that although they are capable of understanding that you must do what's nice for people, part of understanding that they've got to use that role would be understanding that they didn't have to use other rules like simply what they've agreed to do, what the contract is, and what they feel like doing when all their friends want to. I wouldn't count a child as properly understanding that anything important they do must be governed by peoples' interests, unless they understood that they weren't simply to follow rules their parents laid down for them. Of course, under the pressure of events, regimes, or temptations, they may lapse and do something else. When it comes to dilemmas, if they've got the concept of a person and that they must act in a persons' interests rather than p, q, and r, that's as much as any of use can do. They will acquire a more sophisticated view of what constitutes a person's interest as they grow older.

LICKONA: Well, that's exactly what we're talking about. I think you can look at stages as answers to the question, What are the interests of other people that you should consider? or How are other peoples' interests to be defined?

SCHARF: I think one of the problems we're having here—and it's a very common one—is that, as partisan theoreticians, we tend to focus on our favorite phenomena. In our case, we use dilemmas with legitimate conflicting claims; so for us, it's not a question of whether to respect someone's interests but what happens when interests come into conflict.

WILSON: Then, what you're testing is something quite different. You're testing their informational sophistication.

SCHARF: Well, our assumption is that it's quite different from that, because what we are attempting to measure is not simply additive but qualitatively different.

SEEKING MORAL ADVICE FROM AUTHORITIES

WILSON: Suppose that somebody actually believed that God or some ideal psychiatrist or my mother was much better than I was at deciding what was in people's interests. I don't think that you could possibly mark him down for saying that in terms of what kinds of reasons he uses. "Yes," he says, "I'm not concerned with just obeying anyone, but I happen to think that my quickest inroad into just what is in people's interests—and after all those are the only reasons I'm concerned about, having learned Wilson's rules—is to do what the Bible says." Fine.

LICKONA: No, no, no, not at all, because, you see, the argument can be turned around. If I granted you the right to go by what authority A says, then I'd have to grant someone else the right to go with what authority B says. And authority B might be Richard Nixon or Adolph Hitler. You see, I couldn't concede it to you and deny it to others.

WILSON: Well, it's not exactly an appeal to authority. It's rather like saying this is what's in people's interests because this is what the doctor at the hospital said. He asked, "What would make most people well?"

ASSUMPTIONS UNDERLYING THEORIES OF MORAL EDUCATION

SCHARF: When we're doing what we call educational theory, we recognize that we make both psychological as well as philosophical assumptions—assumptions about what there is to learn, about what children can and ought to learn, and about what can and cannot be taught. I think that you're oversimplifying matters when you say, "Look, let's just get down to it and let's advance in the field—let's just go out there and do it." I think that you're working from some very clear assumptions also. You can almost trace them back to John Locke. You assume that there is "moral information" that is additive. You assume there is a "substance" called reason. Then there are "emotions" that can interfere with the proper exercise of reasons. In addition, there is a theory of social contract. It seems to me that there are very real tensions between this and other positions; so I don't think that it's quite intellectually fair for you to say, "Let's just forget all this dispute and just get on with it," because you want to get on with it quite differently from how we want to get on with it. Let's be straight, we just disagree on what's right and how children learn. Let's be honest about that. There really are some issues here!

WILSON: Well, there are two things. First, there are what we could call philosophical assumptions. Presumably, one must have some clear idea about where these children should end up ideally if they are to be morally educated at all. These views we probably share. Stage 6, so far as I'm able to understand it, seems to represent a set of philosophical truths that are okay. That I don't think we would quarrel on. Second, if I, as a philosopher, make any psychological assumptions, that would be wrong. I would just say, that if psychologists can tell us what we can and cannot do, that's fine.

All my queries about Kohlberg, or at least the form they were supposed to have taken, are about just what his studies do show. Is he talking about understanding, or is it preferences, or what? Of course, there must be psychological truths about people; for example, when children become adolescents, they just tend to rebel. These are important. How much of it is common sense is another matter.

FROM THEORY TO PRACTICE: SOME PROBLEMS

SCHARF: As a result of our discussions, I'm inclined to back off a lot on the Kohlberg business. I think we agree that there are these interesting psychological questions and that most of the data isn't in. We don't really understand very much. Further, there are some phenomena here that John is picking up on that our system doesn't deal with. The assessment of facts, the prediction of consequences, the capacity to experience empathy—all sorts of things that go through the sieve of our theory. For example, there is considerable, quite fascinating variation among those in Stage 4.

It seems to me that there are three kinds of issues: psychological, philosophical, and educational utility. I've decided that proposals concerning educational utility don't necessarily follow from either of the first two. In other words, Wilson's contention about what children can learn could be correct, and his theory of morality could be proved through deductive argument or whatever, but they could be absolutely useless as a pedagogical approach. Now as for the Kohlberg position, I am less and less convinced that his position is very useful for teachers. It seems to me that there are any number of restrictions in Kohlberg, and I think that you escape some of them in your approach, Tom, with you emphasis on the distinction between justice and cooperative moral education. If you believe Kohlberg, all you do is have moral discussions, and the kids get bored. A theory can become a self-fulfilling pedagogical prophecy.

WILSON: I think that's not quite as open as you imply. If it's the case, as I certainly think, that the nature of what you want them to learn to some extent determines what the methods are—and that is probably a logical or a philosophical matter—then there is at least that much to be said for what methods must be used. Of course, there is still a great deal of free play, because students and teachers vary. I mean, even in something like the education of the emotions, or the developing of "EMP,"* there are certain things, because of what it is to understand an emotion, that they've more or less got to do. Now, you may ask whether you do it at ten o'clock on Tuesdays or what the order of different styles is. Though quite a lot of that is given, some of it is open.

CAN A STRICT DEVELOPMENTALIST USE A DIDACTIC APPROACH?

LICKONA: I think Peter makes an excellent point when he says that the developmental theory doesn't address a lot of the things that

---

*"EMP" stands for the ability to feel concern for other people and to know what oneself and other people are feeling, or would feel, or have felt in particular situations. For a full discussion of this and other components, see Wilson (1970, 1973).

John's approach does. For example, in the intellectual domain someone has reported that Inhelder, Piaget's colleague, has shown that
children all testing the same on the concrete operation task of conservation and inclusion turn out to have very different problem-
solving capacities, so that if you give them a maze problem, or some
sort of puzzle, some kids go at it in more effective ways. They're
more systematic or they check themselves. So there is something
there that is dropping through the structural sieve if you simply take
a developmental approach. You could take two Stage 3 kids and train
them to anticipate consequences, to systematically take different
points of view, to try to keep all of this in mind, to attempt to identify the moral principle, or to do any number of things that wouldn't
necessarily show up if you gave them each the same moral dilemma.
They both might reason at Stage 3. You could say of one, though,
that he was a better Stage 3 reasoner—more systematic, more
thorough going, more thoughtful, more reflective, or more of a lot
of things that might comprise rationality. That kind of thing is being
missed in our system. One question that is wide open in my mind is,
What are the limits of the effectiveness of didactic teaching? I think
the Kohlbergian model, taking its cue from Piagetian constructivism,
is saying that the person constructs morality. That is, you don't
open the kid's head and put it in, but the kid works it out as a way of
looking at the world. A rational morality comes through experience
and an active struggle with the world. Unfortunately, we have gone
on to develop a systematic bias against telling the child anything.
It's as if the child has to discover all moral truths on his own. Well,
that may be absurd educationally, for parents as well as teachers.
And it may make a lot of sense at opportune points in development
to be very didactic.

My dissertation (1971) attempted to explore four different
ways of advancing a child's grasp of intentionality. I started out with
kids who said that John was naughtier because he broke eight cups
and other kids who said Henry was naughtier because he was trying
to swipe the jam, even though he only broke one cup. I took the kids
who were at a low level in the Piagetian sequence, who didn't count
intentions as being important, and who counted only concrete damage,
and I tried four different approaches to training or developing what
Piaget calls their subjective conception of responsibility, which
counts motives and intentions more than consequences. In one
method, I had the kids look at pictures. In the first, they would see
John carrying the eight cups with a nice smile on his face and Henry
reaching up sneaking the jam, and then, in the second, they would
see the eight broken cups on the floor and in the other case, the one
broken cup. This process—where I tried to get the children to focus
and refocus from one aspect to the other and, as it were, to hold it

all in their cognitive field—I called decentering. One of the problems is that the kids focus on the concrete damage as salient, and they don't hold the other things in mind because they are less salient. In another approach, I attempted to use peer interaction. I brought a child in who was focusing on the intentions in the pretest, introduced him to another child who was focusing on damage, and had them engage in a little argument. I said to them, "You're the parents. You are going to have to decide who you are going to punish more. What do you think?" Another condition, which I called the "adult conflict condition," utilized tapes of adults arguing. So one adult would say, "I think that kid who broke all the cups"—that sort of thing. The other parent points out that one child was trying to help and so on. This was adult conflict, and the attempt was to pry the child loose from adult constraint. And then the fourth condition, presented as a counter-Piagetian foil, was one in which I, the experimeter, simply sat the child down and said, "Don't you realize that what is important is to consider the intentions of the child?" I just laid it right out. It was the pure Wilsonian approach! What was most effective? The Wilsonian approach was most effective in getting the kids to move on the posttest two weeks later from ignoring intentions to considering them!

WILSON: Now he tells me!

LICKONA: Not only was it effective on the types of items that I used in the training, but it was the only training condition that produced significant generalization across to lying and other intention items that were unlike those used in the training. What I concluded as a Piagetian was that didactic instruction can be quite powerful in stimulating the advance. There could be various counterarguments to this, but it could be that there are times in development where a child's structural thinking or developmental stage is at a point where didactic instruction can be extremely effective in developing or consolidating the new mode of thought. Maybe we shouldn't fool around but be very clean, incisive, and straightforward at those points. I think that parents inevitably do this because it's difficult to be the moral manager in a home without doing it. That isn't all you should do from my position. And if it were all that you had to do, kids would soon turn you off—they'd become very passive; they would spit it back but not really incorporate it into their thinking patterns.

WILSON: I agree with all that.

FORM, CONTENT, AND PRACTICE REVISITED

SCHARF: Let me sum it up this way. In this game of moral education, there are only two kinds of acts. One we could call "horizontal education," and the developmentalists may have underemphasized what the child can understand about the concept of a person and the relevant rules. We haven't played that out: how far can you go with the notion of a person and a rule? What Wilson has been talking about is this horizontal type of education. This is what we have ignored. The other is what we could call "vertical education." This requires doubt; you question the system itself. What have we learned? I think Tom, Jean-Marc and I have been convinced of the importance of that horizontal education—the role and variety of didacticism. The question that we could leave with you, John, is, What didacticism? Are there certain kinds of didactic practice that are relevant in certain periods? That would be interesting to explore.

LICKONA. There's a great danger in perpetuating in schools what Piaget calls "false accommodation," which is just regurgitating what authorities want students to regurgitate. Often what we hear at the elementary level is that teachers should simply be engaged in inculcation. Tell students what's right and reinforce them. John, I'm not reducing your approach to this, but it could be easily assimilated into it. It would be easy for people to see your approach as another does of an authoritarian message to the kids about what's right and wrong.

SAMSON: I might argue with you on this. If you take the point of view of the Kohlberg theory, what would be wrong with presenting the students with a teacher who is the voice of Stage 4 authority? Students would then be able to develop the sense that authority is at least a good reference, and such a view is quite consistent with Stage 4. The trouble would be to go from Stage 4 to 5.

LICKONA: I would say that the trouble is the same at every transition. If I have students who are misbehaving and if I think that they are going to respond better to Stage 4 arguments—like "Do it because I say so," or "I'm the authority," or whatever—than they would to Stage 5 arguments, then as a practical measure I might use Stage 4 arguments. That is not to say that I will be more effective in using those arguments in helping them develop a Stage 4 rationale themselves. I think there are two different goals here: the first is getting them to accommodate to my regime; the second is helping them advance the complexity of their thinking. For me, the most basic principle in Piagetian psychology is constructivism. Now the active construction of that knowledge may involve some quite didactic input at various points. We can go to a great lecture and take a great deal away from it. I point out to Peter that he was arguing that we ought to raise doubts to promote conflict dilemma, and he made this point at our Summer Institute through a very didactic lecture! That is, you can use a very straightforward didactic mode in some cases. But, on the whole, I don't think that's optimal for stimulating development, because it doesn't really engage people in making ideas their own. Piaget says we have only what we conquer ourselves. I don't think that you simply write on the blank slate. I think you have to force people to work out the thing so that they can now see it through role play, a great lecture, or a moral dilemma discussion or by going out and marching in the streets—these are a different sort of pedagogical issues that are very important, and I don't think we know much about them at all.

WILSON: It may not be an empirical question at all, as a matter of fact. I agree with what you say absolutely, but not because I agree with constructivism or anything of that kind. It's like saying, "Why not give the children the answers to the sums in the book instead of making them do the working out of the answers?" I mean, some of one's aims are precisely that the kids should be able to think for themselves, and you couldn't, in principle, achieve this by telling them.

SCHARF: My idea of an educational theory is something like this. It's a unity of ends and a plurality of means. Let me explain what I mean by that. One of the problems of Kohlberg is his attraction to the plus-one approach. He has followed Mose Blatt (1968) who, on the basis of studying ten Jewish kids in Hebrew school, said that you should argue one stage above your students So that has become reified as a cardinal principle of moral education. That doesn't make any sense at all. I admit that we know next to nothing about how kids change. Who's kidding who? We just don't know. What I think is so attractive about Tom's work in his distinction between cooperation and the justice ethic as an end or as ends in moral education. But in the pursuit of these ends, let's not fall in love with any of our means. More experiment should be conducted at the level of developing strategies. We should assume that that is very much up for grabs. There is no mathematics teacher in his right mind who would continue to give the same problem or kind of problems time and time again. Those of us who are developmentalists have not been imaginative enough. . . . I think your work, Tom, has done something to get us out of our lock step. I mean, what the hell do you do after moral dilemmas?

APPENDIX:
THINKING ABOUT THINKING—
SOME EXERCISES

Barry Walker

INTRODUCTION

People use all sorts of methods to help them arrive at decisions and form opinions. Unfortunately, many of these have little to
do with thinking—certainly not good thinking. Surprisingly, some of
these methods have achieved a degree of respectability in some social
circles. If your neighbor decided where to take his vacation based on
how the leaves settled in his morning teacup, you would be unlikely to
consider the decision as being well thought out. Still, most of us know
people who determine how to live good portions of their lives by con-
sulting horoscopes and reading their charts, following advice columns,
playing I Ching, relying uncritically on "authorities" and public figures, and so on. So widespread are these substitutes for thinking
that these people can usually count on considerable community support. The exercises that follow are designed particularly for young
people to counter the hold that these practices can have. They should
be treated not as instructions to be followed rigidly but as suggestive
examples to be modified and updated as the circumstances require.
The purpose of these exercises is essentially to "clear the decks"
by exposing the limitations—and, in some cases, the plain irrationality—of these substitutes for thinking. What should replace these
practices is worked out in other chapters of this book.

Exercise 1

A.   Provide examples of substitutes for thinking that people can call
      upon to help them make up their minds in our society without
      fear of scorn from others. In other words, what are some of
      the respectable substitutes for thinking in our society?

301

302

B.   Provide examples (using the library if necessary) of substitutes for thinking considered respectable in other societies.

C.   Given an example of a situation where relying on one of the substitutes for thinking (that you identified in A above) might lead to problems. Describe the situation and point out why problems could arise.

D.   Compare the substitutes for thinking in our society with those of another society. Are some substitutes more valid than others? What makes them so?

Exercise 2

A.   Given an example of a situation where people often use one of the following substitutes for thinking (describe fully, one situation for each example below):
1. "It just felt right, so I did it."
2. "That's what everyone does these days, so I felt that I should."
3. "All decent people feel this way, and this is how I feel about it, too."
4. "That's what (name of influential person) would do under these circumstances, and if it's fine for him or her, it's fine for me."
5. "My conscience told me so."
6. "Human beings were meant to behave in this sort of way."

B.   For each situation that you have described above, what could the person have done or found out to ensure that his or her decision or belief was correct?

Exercise 3

A.   A teacher plays a contemporary ballad about a teenage, pride-inspired "drag race" that ends in disaster: "Race Ballad" by Humpty & the Dump-Trucks (Sunflower Records, Box 3028, Saskatoon, Saskatchewan) in the album Cruel Tears. The teacher identifies or prompts the students to identify the three factors that led to the catastrophe—whiskey, jealousy, and pride. The teacher cites these things as being or relating to, in this case at least, substitutes for thought. With this in mind, students were asked to comment upon:
1. The degree to which the decision to race might have been affected by the manner in which the racers responded to the bystanders around them.
2. The common belief that "pride is always a good thing, without which you're nowhere.

3. What, besides displaying the speed and power of their cars, were the racers attempting to express? What other ways might they have used to express themselves?

B. The students are asked to describe other sets of circumstances (either real or hypothetical) in which pride and/or jealousy could be identified as getting in the way of reasonable decisions or actions.

Exercise 4

A. The students are asked to gather their courage, take their built-in camera, and, for a specified period, play back parts of their past to see what they sometimes do and say. They are asked to consider, for their own information, whether actions and thoughts were well reasoned out or based on substitutes for thinking. The students could be encouraged to record in diary form anything they find out about themselves. This exercise could be repeated on a regular basis (perhaps at the end of each week) so that students could measure changes in themselves and their ability to use reason in various circumstances.

B. Thinking for oneself saves one from allowing other people or groups of people (possibly the wrong people) to do one's own thinking. In your opinion, who are some of the people or groups of people (for example, organizations, clubs, and political groups) who have done others' thinking for them to the detriment of these followers? Select one of these people or groups and speculate about what methods were employed in order to influence their followers.

Exercise 5

A teacher presents a quotation from Wilson's Moral Thinking: A Guide for Students (1970):

It should be plain that the business of thinking is best done in public, that is to say, in the process of discussion, cross-questioning, arguing, giving reasons, and so forth. This is because being reasonable, or thinking correctly, is a public matter and not a private one: it must stand up to public inspection (p. 12).

A. Comment upon the often-heard statement: "Well I have my own ideas and feelings about this and they suit me fine." What do you think are some of the things that cause people to resort to this type of method for selecting answers rather than bothering to find out new things that might bring understanding to the matter?

B.   Often, discussions collapse as people try to discover an answer to a question or sort out the correctness of certain facts or opinions. What sorts of things do you think a participant in a discussion should or should not do so that the discussion proves valuable to the participants?

Exercise 6

The teacher presents a number of ideas (see below) and requests that students list the various ways, valid or invalid, by which one might come to entertain each idea. Students should first use the brainstorming method, and when this is exhausted, students should be given an opportunity to go outside the classroom in their quest for supporting arguments for the listed ideas. Initially, students will be interested in recording all arguments regardless of their apparent strengths or weaknesses. Students might be encouraged to use library resources and question informed persons (for example, parents, senior students, teachers, and persons within the community at large who concern themselves with the particular matters in question). Subsequently, the validity of each of the collected arguments is to be analyzed in terms of the degree to which it results from clear thinking.

Ideas such as these might be presented for scrutiny.

The earth is round.
Women have more patience than men.
The world's energy sources will run out by the year 2000 A.D.
Developing poor nations ought to receive very generous aid from
    developed countries.

Exercise 7

A.   The teacher selects a video-taped, filmed, or audio-taped discussion featuring a range of common escapes from thinking and asks students to identify and record instances of resorting to substitutes for thinking. For recording purposes, each student is supplied with a tallying sheet listing categories of substitute thinking beside which to mark instances of various types of escapes. Categories should be discussed in advance of the sessions so that each student becomes familiar with them. Selected categories might follow Wilson's guide (1970) and include reliance upon:
      1. Authority—(a) obeying: (b) rebelling
      2. Ideal people

3. Divine purpose and meaning
4. Special experiences
5. Faith
6. A matter of taste
7. How one has been brought up
8. Other people

If, then, a student were to hear, "Respectable people in our area just don't go for that sort of thing," he would cite this as an example of category 8 (other people). It would be worthwhile, also, to review the tape and allow students to signal when the instances they recorded arise. Each instance could be discussed at this time. If access to a recording device were possible, teachers might find it valuable to tape class discussions for future analysis.

B. Students are asked to decide what sorts of information speakers lacked and/or failed to call upon in order to clarify any particular matter prior to forming an opinion or deciding upon a course of action.

C. Did speakers give any indication of their need for additional information before forming an opinion or deciding upon a course of action?

D. Did speakers ever actually request or seek out additional information?

Exercise 8

This exercise is designed to reveal the extent to which the acceptance of a particular statement can be a function of the prior regard one has for the presenter.

The class is divided into three groups. Each group is isolated and exposed to the same piece of art such as a drawing, a painting, or a written work. Each group is given either positive, negative, or no bibliographical information about the artist before being asked to record evaluative opinions of the work. The class is reunited for a comparison of results.

Exercise 9

Often, the kinds of worries that people have influence their ability to think and to talk rationally. One example of an obstacle to clear, rational thinking is a fear that others might think one's beliefs or actions wrong if they are in any way unconventional.

Give an example of an act or opinion that although it might be quite appropriate, would likely be disapproved of by the people you chum with. Identify other common worries that tend to get in the way of people's thinking out their own course of actions or their ideas.

Exercise 10

If opinions are to be considered reasonable, they must:

1. Stick to the laws of logic,
2. Use language correctly, and
3. Attend to the facts.

Moral opinions must follow these rules and satisfy these others as well. They must:

4. Lay down a principle of behavior, not just for one particular person or occasion but for all people on all similar occasions;

5. Prescribe that the principle should be acted on, not just observed, stated and left; and

6. Be overriding (that is, they must take precedence over other opinions). (For further discussion of what makes an opinion moral, see Wilson's Moral Thinking [1970, pp. 39-44].

Give an example of a moral opinion that you think meets the above requirements. Note: Teacher might devise a system whereby students' work, distributed anonymously, is exchanged and evaluated by classmates in terms of the above criteria.

RULES AND THE ABILITY TO THINK

If an individual acts compulsively either to conform to or to rebel against rules, we may assume that the time spent actually thinking about the pros and cons of particular rules is relatively diminished. It seems reasonable to conjecture further that the extent to which emotional reaction to rules is curbed affects one's ability to get down to the matter of thinking.

The presentation of a particular set of rules can have a negative or positive influence on a person's ability to think objectively about practical or moral issues. Granting that rule setters must be able to think clearly before effective rules can be decided upon, it becomes clear that teachers must concern themselves with both the rules that govern their classrooms and the process of selecting the rules. If rules are to be imposed upon the class by the teacher and/or the school administration, it must be certain that the ground rules of the institution (and the classroom) are based on the right criteria. If students are considered to be capable enough to be given some degree of self-government, then this decision must be based upon a careful estimation of the students' ability to reason. (Use of the exercises here proposed should not only enhance this ability but should also assist the teacher in estimating student readiness for some degree of self-government.)

The idea of self-government, characterized by communication in rule making and rule following, represents a desirable means to curbing blind conformity to and/or unreasonable rebellion against the rules of the classroom. Furthermore, the ongoing process of teacher/student rule selection and refinement not only requires a certain level of thinking ability but also provides students (and the teacher) with ongoing practice in the skills of thinking.

BIBLIOGRAPHY

Adams, H. 1918. The Education of Henry Adams. Boston: Houghton Mifflin.

Adelson, J. 1972. "The Political Importance of the Young Adolescent." Daedalus 100:1013-50.

Aichorn, A. 1938. Wayward Youth. New York: Viking Press.

Aldous, J. 1978. Family Careers: Developmental Change in Families. New York: John Wiley & Sons.

Anyon, J. 1979. "Ideology and United States History Textbooks." Harvard Educational Review 49:361-86.

Arbutnot, J. 1975. "Modification of Moral Judgment through Role Playing." Developmental Psychology 11:319-24.

Archambault, R., ed. 1964. John Dewey on Education. New York: Random House.

Arieti, S. 1975. "Psychiatric Controversy: Man's Ethical Dimension." American Journal of Psychiatry 132: 39-42

———. 1972. The Will to Be Human. New York: Quadrangle/New York Times.

Armentrout, J. A., and G. K. Burger. 1972. "Children's Reports of Parental Child-Rearing at Five Grade Levels." Developmental Psychology 7:44-48.

Bailey, S. K. 1971. Disruption in Urban Public Secondary Schools. Washington: National Association of Secondary School Principals.

Bakan, D. 1966. The Duality of Human Existence. Chicago: Rand McNally.

Baker, R., and F. Elliston, eds. 1975. Introduction in Philosophy and Sex. Buffalo, N.Y.: Prometheus Books.

Banks, J. A. 1979. Teaching Strategies for Ethnic Studies. 2d ed. Boston: Allyn and Bacon.

Barnard, C. 1974. "One Life." In Childhood Revisited, edited by J. Milgram and D. J. Sciarra. New York: Macmillan.

Barrett, D. 1977. "The Just Community School Intervention Program, The School-within-a-School, Brookline High School." Unpublished paper. Boston University.

Baumrind, D. 1971. "Current Patterns of Parental Authority." Developmental Psychology (Monograph) 4(pt. 2):1-103.

Becker, J. A. 1963. "An Exploratory Factor Analytic Study of Interests, Intelligence, and Personality." Psychological Reports 13:847-51.

Berne, E. 1964. Games People Play. New York: Grove Press.

Bidwell, C. 1965. "The School as a Formal Organization." In Handbook of Organizations, edited by J. G. March, pp. 972-1022. Chicago: Rand McNally.

Binder, A. 1979. "Pretrial Diversion: Project no. 1426." Mimeographed. Costa Mesa, Calif.: State of California.

Blatt, M. 1968. "Effects of Classroom Moral Discussion upon Children's Moral Development." Ph.D. dissertation, University of Chicago.

Block, J. 1976. "Issues, Problems, and Pitfalls in Assessing Sex Differences: A Critical Review of the Psychology of Sex Differences." Merrill-Palmer Quarterly 22:282-308.

———. 1973. "Conceptions of Sex Role: Some Cross-Cultural and Longitudinal Perspectives." American Psychologist, June, pp. 512-26.

Block, J., and N. Haan. 1969. "Socialization Correlates of Student Activism." Journal of Social Issues 25:143-78.

Boslooper, T., and M. Hayes. 1973. The Femininity Game. New York: Stein and Day.

310

Bristin, A. 1975. "A Developmental Model of Self-Awareness." Counseling and Values 18:79-85.

Bronfenbrenner, U. 1961. "Some Familial Antecedents of Responsibility and Leadership in Adolescents." In Leadership and Interpersonal Behavior, edited by L. Petrullo and R. Bass, pp. 239-72. New York: Holt, Rinehart and Winston.

Burger, G. K., R. E. Lamp, and D. Rogers. 1975. "Developmental Trends in Children's Perceptions of Parental Child-Rearing." Developmental Psychology 11:391.

Burton, R. 1976. "Honesty and Dishonesty." In Moral Development and Behavior, edited by T. Lickona, pp. 173-97. New York: Holt, Rinehart and Winston.

Burton, R., ed. 1963. Kāma Sūtra of Vātsyāyana. Translated by F. F. Arbuthnot. Edison, N.J.: Allen and Unwin.

Byrne, D. F. 1974. "The Development of Role Taking in Adolescence." Unpublished manuscript. Harvard Graduate School of Education.

Candee, D. 1978. "The Moral Psychology of Watergate." Journal of Social Issues 31:56-62.

Carlson, R. 1964. "Environmental Constraints and Organizational Consequences: The Public School and Its Clients." In Behavioral Science and Educational Administration, edited by D. E. Griffiths, pp. 262-76. Chicago: University of Chicago Press.

Chandler, M. 1973. "Roletaking in Juvenile Delinquents." Developmental Psychology, Vol. 9, No. 3, 326-332.

Clark, K. B. 1963. "Educational Stimulation of Racially Disadvantaged Children." In Education in Depressed Areas, edited by A. H. Passow. New York: Columbia University Press.

Clark, T. 1977. Report. Los Angeles, Calif.: Constitutional Rights Foundation.

Cloward, R., and L. Ohlin. 1970. Delinquency and Opportunity. New York: Free Press.

Cochrane, D. B. 1977. "Recent Developments in Moral Education in California." Montclair Education Review 6:12-24.

———. 1975. "Moral Education—A Prolegomenon." Theory into Practice 14:236-46.

Cochrane, D. B., C. M. Hamm, and A. C. Kazepides, eds. 1979. The Domain of Moral Education. New York: Paulist Press.

Cochrane, D. B., and D. Williams. 1978. "The Stances of Provincial Ministries of Education towards Values/Moral Education in Public Schools." Canadian Journal of Education 3:1-14.

Colby, A. L., L. Kohlberg, E. Fenton, B. Speicher-Lubin, and M. Lieberman. 1977. "Secondary School Moral Discussion Programmes Led by Social Science Teachers." Journal of Moral Education 6:90-111.

Comfort, A. 1972. The Joy of Sex: A Gourmet Guide to Love-Making. New York: Crown.

Connell, R. 1971. A Child's Construction of Politics. Victoria, Australia: Melbourne University Press.

Cooley, C. 1926. Social Organization. New York: Schocken.

Coopersmith, S. 1967. The Antecedents of Self-Esteem. San Francisco: W. H. Freeman.

Cowan, A. 1955. Delinquent Boys. New York: Free Press.

Cox, H. 1976. The Secular City. New York: Macmillan.

Cross, D. W., M. A. Long, and A. Ziajka. 1978. "Minority Cultures and Education in the United States." Education and Urban Society 10:263-76.

Cusick, P. 1973. Inside High School. New York: Holt, Rinehart and Winston.

Damon, W. 1977. The Social World of the Child. San Francisco: Jossey-Bass.

Darley, J., and C. Batson. 1973. "From Jerusalem to Jericho: A Study of Situational and Dispositional Variables in Helping Behavior." Journal of Personality and Social Psychology 27:100-8.

Darley, J., and B. Latane. 1968. "When Will People Help in a Crisis." In Readings in Psychology Today, 428-33. Del Mar, Calif.: CRM Books.

De Risi, W. J., and G. Butz. 1975. Writing Behavioral Contracts: A Case of Simulation Practice Manual. Champaign, Ill.: Research Press.

Dewey, J. 1968a. Democracy and Education. New York: Free Press.

———. 1968b. Problems of Men. New York: Greenwood Press.

———. 1964. "The Need for a Philosophy of Education." In John Dewey on Education, edited by R. D. Archambault, pp. 3-14. 1934. Reprint. New York: Random House.

DiStephano, A. 1976. "School-within-a-School, Parents' Night." Unpublished memorandum. Brookline, Mass.

Doucet, L. 1973. Qu'est-ce que l'information sexuelle en classe? Paris: Pierre Horay.

Drake, G. 1969. Blackboard Power. Tulsa, Okla. Christian Crusaders.

Drake, S. C. 1965. "The Social and Economic Status of the Negro in the United States." Daedalus, Vol. 96:771-814.

Dreikurs, R., S. Gould, and R. Corsini. 1974. The Family Council. Chicago: Henry Regnery.

Duke, D. 1978. "Looking at the School as a Rule-Governed Organization." Journal of Research and Development in Education 11:116-31.

Durkheim, E. 1908. Moral Education. New York: Free Press.

Duvall, E. M. 1971. Family Development. Philadelphia, Pa. J. P. Lippincott.

Eisenberg, J., and G. McQueen. 1972. Don't Teach That! Don Mills, Ontario: Paperjacks.

Elder, G. H. 1963. "Parental Power Legitimation and Its Effect on the Adolescent." Sociometry 26:50-65.

Ellis, A. 1971. "A Rational Sexual Morality." In The New Sexual Revolution, edited by L. A. Kirkendall and R. N. Whitehurst, pp. 47-61. New York: D. W. Brown.

Erickson, V. L. 1977. "Deliberate Psychological Education for Women." Developmental Counseling Psychology 6:25-29.

————. 1975. "Deliverate Psychological Education for Women: From Iphigenia to Antigone." Counselor Education and Supervision, June, pp. 297-309.

————. 1974. "Psychological Growth for Women: A Cognitive-Developmental Curriculum Intervention." Counseling and Values 18(Winter):102-16.

Erikson, E. 1974. Dimensions of a New Identity. New York: W. W. Norton.

————. 1963. Childhood and Society. New York: W. W. Norton.

Farber, L. 1966. The Ways of the Will; Essays toward a Psychology and Psychopathology of the Will. New York: Basic Books.

Farrington, D. 1978. "Social Functions of the Juvenile Delinquent." Unpublished address. University of California at Irvine.

Fenton, E. 1978. "Moral Education: Research Findings." In Readings on Moral Education, edited by P. Scharf. Minneapolis, Minn.: Winston Press.

————. 1977. "The Pittsburgh Area Civic Education Project: A Report to the Danforth Foundation for the 1976-1977 Fiscal Year." Pittsburgh: Carnegie-Mellon University.

Ferber, A., M. Mendelshon, and A. Napier. 1973. The Book of Family Therapy. Boston: Houghton Mifflin.

Finegold, J. 1977. "Town Meeting: Is It Necessary?" Brookline, Mass.: S.W.S. Newsletter 3:2.

Fraenkel, J. R. 1976. "The Kohlberg Bandwagon: Some Reservations." Social Education 40:216-22.

Franklyn, M. 1979. "Moral Reasoning among Juvenile Delinquents." Ph.D. dissertation, University of California at Los Angeles.

Fraser, T. 1972. Transactional Therapy with Delinquent Youth. Stockton: California Youth Authority.

Frazier, E. F. 1949. The Negro in the United States. New York: Macmillan.

Friedlander, K. 1950. Psychoanalytic Approach to Juvenile Delinquency. New York: International Universities Press.

Friere, P. 1972. Pedagogy of the Oppressed. New York: Harder and Harder.

Fromkin, H. L., and Sherwood, J. J., eds. 1976. Intergroup and Minority Relations: An Experiential Handbook. La Jolla, Calif.: University Associates.

Fitzgerald, F. S. 1925. The Great Gatsby. New York: Scribner's.

Gagnon, J. 1979. "Parents' Messages about Sexuality to Pre-Adolescent Children." Paper presented at the International Symposium on Childhood and Sexuality, University of Quebec, Montreal.

———. 1977. Human Sexualities. Glenview, Ill.: Scott Foresman.

Gartner, A., M. Kohler, and F. Reissman. 1971. Children Teach Children. New York: Harper & Row.

Gault, in Re. 1967. 87 Supreme Court, p. 1428.

Gert, B. 1966. The Moral Rule. New York: Harper & Row.

Gibbs, J. C. 1977. "Kohlberg's Stages of Moral Judgment: A Construction Critique." Harvard Educational Review 47:143-61.

Gibran, K. 1964. The Prophet. London: Heinemann.

Gillespie, J. A., and J. J. Patrick. 1974. Comparing Political Experiences. Washington, D.C.: American Political Science Association.

Gilligan, C. 1977. "In a Different Voice: Women's Conception of the Self and of Morality." Harvard Educational Review 47:481-517.

Glasser, W. 1969. Schools without Failure. New York: Harper & Row.

Glazer, N., and D. P. Moynihan. 1963. Beyond the Melting Pot. Cambridge: Massachusetts Institute of Technology Press.

Gordon, M. 1964. Assimilation in American Life. New York: Oxford University Press.

Gordon, R., J. Short, D. Cartwright, and F. Strodtbeck. 1963. "Values and Gang Delinquency." American Journal of Sociology 60:109-28.

Gordon, T. 1970. Parent Effectiveness Training. New York: Peter Wyden.

Goslin, D. A. 1969. Handbook of Socialization: Theory and Research. Chicago: Rand McNally.

Gou-Zeh, Y. 1979. "Moral Education in Korea." Journal of Moral Education 8:75-80.

Grimes, P. 1974. "Teaching Moral Reasoning to 11-Year-Olds and Their Mothers." Ph.D. dissertation, Boston University School of Education.

Guidon, A. 1977. The Sexual Language: An Essay in Moral Theology. Ottawa: University of Ottawa Press.

Haan, N. 1975. "Hypothetical and Actual Moral Reasoning in a Situation of Civil Disobedience." Journal of Personality and Social Psychology 32:255-70.

———. 1971. "Moral Redefinition in Families as the Critical Aspect of the Generation Gap." Youth and Society 2:259-83.

Haan, N., M. B. Smith, and J. Block. 1968. "Moral Reasoning of Young Adults: Political-Social Behavior, Family Background and Personality Correlates." Journal of Personality and Social Psychology 10:183-201.

Hakkarainen, P. 1978. "On Moral Education in the Finnish Comprehensive School Curriculum." Journal of Moral Education 8: 23-31.

Halberstam, D. 1969. The Best and the Brightest. New York: Random House.

Haley, A. 1976. Roots. Garden City, N.Y.: Doubleday.

Hall, R. T., and J. U. Davis. 1975. Moral Education in Theory and Practice. Buffalo, N.Y.: Prometheus Books.

Heilbroner, R. 1974. "The Human Prospect." New York Review of Books 21:21-34.

Henry, J. 1955. "Docility: Or Giving Teacher What She Wants." Journal of Social Issues 11:33-41.

Hersh, R. H., D. P. Paolitto, and J. Reimer. 1979. Promoting Moral Growth. New York: Longman.

Hill, R., and D. Hansen. 1969. "The Identification of Conceptual Frameworks Utilized in Family Study." Marriage and Family Living 22:299-311.

Hoffman, M. 1970. "Moral Development." In Carmichael's Manual of Child Psychology, edited by P. H. Mussen, pp. 261-359, Vol. 2. New York: John Wiley & Sons.

———. 1963. "Child-Rearing Practices and Moral Development: Generalizations from Empirical Research." Child Development 34:295-318.

———. 1960. "Power Assertion by the Parent and Its Impact on the Child." Child Development 31:129-43.

Hoffman, M., and H. Saltzstein. 1967. "Parent Discipline and the Child's Moral Development." Journal of Personality and Social Psychology 5:45-57.

Hogan, R. 1975. "Theoretical Egocentrism and the Problem of Compliance." American Psychologist 30:533-40.

———. 1973. "Moral Conduct and Moral Character: A Psychological Perspective." Psychological Bulletin 79:217-32.

Hollenburg, E., and M. Sperry. 1951. "Some Antecedents of Aggression and Effects of Frustration in Doll Play." Journal of Personality 1:32-43.

Holstein, C. 1972. "The Relation of Children's Moral Judgment Level to That of Their Parents and to Communication Patterns in the Family." In Readings in Child Development and Relationships, edited by R. C. Smart and M. S. Smart, pp. 484-94. New York: Macmillan.

——. 1968. "Parental Concensus and Interaction in Relation to the Child's Moral Judgment." Ph.D. dissertation, University of California, Berkeley.

Hower, J. T. 1976. "The Effects of Parent-Child Relationships on the Development of Moral Character." Ph.D. dissertation, Rosemead Graduate School of Psychology, Rosemead, Calif.

Hower, J. T., and K. J. Edwards. 1979. "The Relationship between Moral Character and Adolescents' Perception of Parental Behavior." Journal of Genetic Psychology 135:22-32.

——. 1978. "Interparent Factor Analysis of Children's Perception of Parent Child-Rearing Behaviors." Journal of Genetic Psychology 132:261-66.

Hutchins, R. M. 1976. "The Unfinished Revolution. Is Democracy Possible?" Boston Globe, February 16, 1976.

Illich, I. 1971. Deschooling Society. New York: Harper & Row.

Jackson, P. 1968. Life in Classrooms. New York: Holt, Rinehart and Winston.

Jahoda, C. 1964. "Development of Scottish Children's Ideas and Attitudes about Other Countries." Journal of Law 58:91-103.

Janis, I. L. 1971. "Group Think." Psychology Today 5(6):43-46.

Jennings, W. 1979. "Moral Atmosphere in Three Therapeutic Programs." Ph.D. dissertation, Harvard Graduate School of Education.

Jensen, L., and K. Buhanan. 1974. "Resistance to Temptation Following Three Types of Motivational Instructions among

Four-, Six-, and Eight-Year-Old Female Children." Journal of Genetic Psychology 125:51-59.

John Birch Society Bulletin. 1969. January 1969.

Johnson, D., and R. Johnson. 1975. Learning Together and Alone. Englewood Cliffs, N.J.: Prentice-Hall.

Jung, C. 1962. Present et avenir (1957). Translated by Roland Cahen. Paris: Buchet/Chastel.

Karrby, G. 1978. "Moral Education in Sweden." Journal of Moral Education 8:14-22.

Katchadourian, H. A., and D. T. Lunde. 1972. Fundamentals of Human Sexuality. New York: Holt, Rinehart and Winston.

Katz, I. 1964. "Review of Evidence Relating to Effects of Desegregation on Intellectual Performance of Negroes." American Psychologist 19:381-99.

Kaufman, A. S. 1973. "Comments on Frankena's 'The Concept of Education Today.'" In Educational Judgments edited by J. F. Doyle. London: Routledge and Kegan Paul.

Keil, C. 1966. Urban Blues. Chicago: University of Chicago Press.

Kelly, G. F. 1977. Learning about Sex: The Contemporary Guide for Young Adults. rev. ed. Woodbury, N.Y.: Barron's Educational Series.

Keniston, K. 1970. "Students' Activism, Moral Development and Morality." American Journal of Orthopsychiatry 40:577-92.

Kluger, R. 1976. Simple Justice: The History of Brown v Board of Education and Black America's Struggle for Equality. New York: Alfred Knopf.

Kohlberg, L. 1978. Introduction to Readings in Moral Education, edited by P. Scharf. Minneapolis, Minn.: Winston Press.

———. 1976. "Moral Stages and Moralization." In Moral Development and Behavior, edited by T. Lickona, pp. 31-53. New York: Holt, Rinehart and Winston.

———. 1975. "The Cognitive-Developmental Approach to Moral Education." Phi Delta Kappan 56:670-76.

———. 1973. "Stages and Aging in Moral Development—Some Speculations." Gerontologist 13(Winter).

———. 1972. "The Implications of Moral Stages for Problems of Sex Education." Unpublished manuscript. Harvard University.

———. 1971. "From Is to Ought: How to Commit the Naturalistic Fallacy and Get Away with It in the Study of Moral Development." In Cognitive Development and Epistemology, edited by T. Mischel, pp. 151-235. New York: Academic Press.

———. 1969. "Stage and Sequence: The Cognitive-Developmental Approach to Socialization." In Handbook of Socialization Theory and Research, edited by D. A. Goslin, pp. 347-480. Chicago: University of Chicago Press.

———. 1966. "A Cognitive-Developmental Analysis of Children's Sex-Role Concepts and Attitudes." In The Development of Sex Differences, edited by E. E. Maccoby. Stanford, Calif.: Stanford University Press.

Kohlberg, L., and Elfenbein. 1975. "Development of Moral Judgments Concerning Capital Punishment." American Journal of Orthopsychiatry 45(July).

Kohlberg, L., and Freudlich, D. 1979. "Moral Reasoning of Juvenile Delinquents." In Recent Research in Moral Education, edited by L. Kohlberg and A. Colby. Cambridge, Mass.: Harvard University Press.

Kohlberg, L., K. Kauffman, P. Scharf, and J. Hickey. 1975. "The Just Community Approach to Corrections: A Theory." Journal of Moral Education 4:243-60.

Kohlberg, L., and R. Mosher. 1976. "Brookline-Cambridge Moral Education Project: A Report of the Second Year, 1976-77." St. Louis, Mo.: Report to the Danforth Foundation.

Kozol, J. 1975. The Night Is Dark and I Am Far from Home. Toronto: Bantam Books.

Kuhn, D. 1976. "Short Term Longitudinal Evidence of the Sequentiality of Kohlberg's Early Stages of Moral Development." Developmental Psychology 12:162-66.

Kuhn, D., J. Langer, L. Kohlberg, and N. S. Haan. 1977. "The Development of Formal Operations in Logical and Moral Thought." Genetic Psychology Monograph 95:97-188.

Kur, J. 1977. "Love Is Working Together." In Minibook on Fostering Moral Development in the Classroom, edited by T. Lickona. Cortland, N.Y.: Project Change, State University of New York.

Laing, R. D. 1969. Knots. New York: Random Vintage Press.

Law Reform Commission of Canada. 1978. Report on Sexual Offences. Ottawa: Minister of Supply and Services of Canada.

Leming, J. 1974. "Moral Reasoning and Sense of Control in Social and Political Activism of Students." Adolescence 9:507-28.

Leonard, R., and D. C. Locke. 1979. "Teaching Interracial Communication Skills: A Model." Guidance Clinic 11:10-12.

Lickona, T. 1978. "Creating the Just Community with Children." In Readings in Moral Education, edited by P. Scharf, pp. 174-85. Minneapolis, Minn.: Winston Press.

————. 1977. "Creating the Just Community with Children." Theory into Practice 16(April).

————. 1976. Moral Development and Behavior: Theory, Research and Social Issues. New York: Holt, Rinehart and Winston.

————. 1971. "The Acceleration of Children's Judgments about Responsibility: An Experimental Test of Piaget's Hypotheses about the Causes of Moral Judgmental Change." Ph.D. dissertation, State University of New York at Albany.

Liebert, R. M., J. Neale, and E. Davidson. 1973. The Early Window: Effects of Television on Children and Youth. New York: Pergamon.

Liebert, R., and R. Poulos. 1976. "Television as a Moral Teacher." In Moral Development and Behavior, edited by T. Lickona, pp. 284-98. New York: Holt, Rinehart and Winston.

Lindner, R. 1956. Must You Conform? New York: Rinehart.

Lipset, S. M., and W. Schneider. 1977. "America's Schizophrenia on Achieving Equality." Los Angeles Times, July 31, 1977.

Locke, J. 1956. Two Treatises of Government. New York: Hafner.

Lockwood, A. 1973. "The Effects of Values Clarification and Moral Development Curricula on School-Age Subjects: A Critical Review of Recent Research." Review of Educational Research 48:325-64.

Loevinger, J. 1976. Ego Development. San Francisco: Jossey-Bass.

London, P. 1970. "The Rescuers: Motivational Hypotheses about Christians Who Saved Jews from the Nazis." In Altruism and Helping Behavior, edited by J. Macaulay and L. Berkowitz, pp. 241-50. New York: Academic Press.

Luckey, E. B. 1967. "Helping Children Grow Up Sexually." Children 14:130-35.

Maccoby, E., and C. Jacklin. 1974. The Psychology of Sex Differences. Stanford, Calif.: Stanford University Press.

Manley-Casimir, M. 1978. "The Supreme Court, Students' Rights and School Discipline." Journal of Research and Development in Education 11:101-15.

Mantell, D. M. 1974. "Doves vs. Hawks: Guess Who Had the Authoritarian Parents?" Psychology Today, September, pp. 56-62.

Masters, W. H., and V. S. Johnson. 1966. Human Sexual Response. Boston: Little, Brown.

Matza, P. 1964. Delinquency and Drift. New York: John Wiley & Sons.

May, R. 1960. Love and Will. New York: W. W. Norton.

McCord, J., and W. McCord. 1958. "The Effect of Parental Role Model on Criminality." Journal of Social Issues 14, 66-75.

Mead, G. H. 1934. Mind, Self, Society. Chicago: University of Chicago Press.

Merelman, R. 1969. "The Development of Political Ideas." American Political Science Review 63:548-61.

Mezirow, J. 1978. "Perspective Transformation." Adult Education 28(Winter):100-10.

Michael, D. N. 1968. The Unprepared Society. New York: Basic Books.

Minneapolis Star. 1977. June 7, p. 6.

Mitchell, M. 1936. Gone with The Wind. New York: Macmillan.

Mitford, J. 1973. Kind and Usual Punishment. New York: Knopf.

Monahan, J. 1976. Community Mental Health and the Criminal Justice System. New York: Pergamon.

Morris, N. 1974. The Future of Imprisonment. Chicago: University of Chicago Press.

Morrison, E. S., and M. U. Price. 1974. Values in Sexuality: A New Approach to Sex Education. New York: Hart.

Mosher, R. L. 1979. Adolescents' Development and Education: A Janus Knot. Berkeley, Calif.: McCutchan.

———. 1976. "A Three-Year Democratic School Intervention Project." Unpublished proposal to the Danforth Foundation. Boston University.

Mosher, R. L., and N. A. Sprinthall. 1978. Value Development as an Aim of Education. Schenectady, N.Y.: Character Research Press.

———. 1971. "Psychological Education: A Means to Promote Personal Development during Adolescence." Counseling Psychologist 2:3-83.

Myrdal, G. 1944. An American Dilemma. New York: McGraw-Hill.

Newmann, F. M. 1972. Education for Citizen Action: Challenge for Secondary Schools. Berkeley, Calif.: McCutchan.

Nicolayev, J., and D. C. Phillips. 1979. "On Assessing Kohlberg's Stage Theory of Moral Development." In The Domain of Moral Education, edited by D. B. Cochrane, C. M. Hamm, and A. C. Kazepides. New York: Paulist Press; Toronto: Ontario Institute for Studies in Education.

Oakeshott, M. 1967. "Learning and Teaching." In The Concept of Education, edited by R. S. Peters. London: Routledge and Kegan Paul; New York: Humanities Press.

Oliver, D., and J. Shaver. 1966. Teaching Social Studies in Secondary School. Boston: Houghton Mifflin.

Parke, R. D., and R. H. Walters. 1967. "Some Factors Influencing the Efficacy of Punishment Training for Inducing Response Inhibition." Monograph of Social Research in Child Development 32.

Patterson, G. R. 1971. Families. Champaign, Ill.: Research Press.

Peck, R. F. 1958. "Family Patterns Correlated with Adolescent Personality Structure." Journal of Abnormal Social Psychology 57:347-50.

Peck, R. F., and R. J. Havighurst. 1960. The Psychology of Character Development. New York: John Wiley & Sons.

Peters, R. 1966. Ethics and Education. London: Allen & Unwin.

Peterson, G. B. 1978. "Moral Development and Parenting: Raising Some Issues." Counseling and Values 22:108-14.

———. 1976. "Adolescent Moral Development as Related to Family Power, Family Support and Parental Moral Development." Ph.D. dissertation, University of Minnesota, Minneapolis.

Peterson, G. B., R. N. Hey, and L. R. Peterson. 1979. "Intersection of Family Development and Moral Stage Frameworks: Implications for Theory and Research." Journal of Marriage and the Family 41:229-35.

Peterson, L. R. 1977. "Ignatius Donnelly: A Psychohistorical Study in Moral Development Psychology." Ph.D. dissertation, University of Minnesota, Minneapolis.

Piaget, J. 1965. The Moral Judgment of the Child. 1932. Reprint. New York: Free Press.

———. 1960. "The General Problem of the Psychobiological Development of the Child." In Discussion on Child Development, edited by J. M. Tanner and B. Inhelder, pp. 3-27. Vol. 4. New York: International Universities Press.

Pikas, A. 1961. "Children's Attitudes toward Rational versus Inhibiting Parental Authority." Journal of Abnormal and Social Psychology 62:315-21.

Plato. 1914. The Apology of Socrates, edited by A. M. Adam. Cambridge: Cambridge University Press.

Platt, J. 1977. "Reinforcement of Delinquent Conduct." Paper presented at the colloquium on April 6, University of California at Irvine.

Pratt, D., and G. McDiarmid. 1971. Teaching Prejudice. Curriculum Series no. 12. Toronto: Ontario Institute for Studies in Education.

Prentice, N. 1971. Moral Reasoning of Juvenile Delinquents. Washington, D.C.: American Psychological Association.

Quigley, C. 1978. Law in a Free Society: A Curriculum. Santa Monica, Calif.: Law in a Free Society Foundation.

Reimer, E. 1971. School Is Dead. New York: Doubleday.

Rest, J. 1979. Development in Judging Moral Issues. Minneapolis: University of Minnesota Press.

———. 1973. "Hierarchical Nature of Moral Judgment: A Study of Patterns of Comprehension and Preference of Moral Stages." Journal of Personality 41:86-109.

Rest, J., E. Turiel, and L. Kohlberg. 1969. "Level of Moral Development as a Determinant of Preference and Comprehension

of Moral Judgment Made by Others." Journal of Personality 37:
225-52.

Ricoeur, P. 1973. "Ethics and Culture." Philosophy Today 17:
153-65.

Rist, R. C. 1970. "Student Social Class and Teacher Expectations:
A Self-Fulfilling Prophecy in Ghetto Education." Harvard Educational Review 40:411-51.

Robert, H. M. 1973. Robert's Rules of Order. New York: Pyra-
mid Books.

Rode, A. 1971. "Perceptions of Parental Behavior among Alienated
Adolescents." Adolescents 6:19-38.

Rosenhan, D. L. 1969. "Some Origins of Concern for Others." In
Trends and Issues in Developmental Psychology, edited by P. Mus-
sen, J. Langer, and M. Corington, pp. 132-53. New York: Holt,
Rinehart and Winston.

Rosenstock, J., and D. Adair. 1976. Multiracialism in the Classroom—A Survey of Interracial Attitudes in Ontario Schools.
Ottawa: Department of Manpower and Immigration.

Ross, B. 1978. Evaluation of Legal Learning: Three Law Curricula. Los Angeles: California School of Professional Psychiatry.

Rundle, L. 1977. "Moral Development in the Fifth Grade Classroom." Ph.D. dissertation, Boston University.

Russell, M., R. Hey, E. Jolly, and G. Thoen. 1975. Personal
communication.

Ryan, D. 1976. "A Good Marriage." In At School at Brookline.
Brookline, Mass.: School Committee, Summer.

Samson, J. M. 1978. "L'efficicité a long terme d'une intervention
structurée d'éducation sexuelle à l'adolescence, conduite selon
la pédagogie du +1 stade de la théorie de L. Kohlberg." Mimeographed. Montreal: Université du Québec, Départment de
Sexologie.

———. 1974. L'éducation sexuelle à l'école? Montreal: Editions
Guerin.

Sanders, N. M., and M. Klafter. 1975. "The Importance and Desired Characteristics of Moral/Ethical Education in the Public Schools of the U.S.A.: A System Analysis of Recent Documents." Publication no. AL-3. Philadelphia, Pa.: Research for Better Schools.

———. 1972. Peoplemaking. Palo Alto, Calif.: Science and Behavior Books.

Satir, V. 1967. Conjoint Family Therapy. Palo Alto, Calif.: Science and Behavior Books.

Scharf, P. 1978. Moral Education. Davis, Calif.: Dialogue Books.

———. 1977. "School Democracy: Promise and Paradox." In Readings in Moral Education, edited by Peter Scharf. Minneapolis, Minn.: Winston Press.

Scheffler, I. 1965. Conditions of Knowledge. Chicago: Scott, Foresman.

Schleifer, M. 1977. "How to Avoid Indoctrination." Unpublished manuscript. Université du Québec à Montreal, Départment de Sciences de l'éducation.

Schur, E. E. 1973. Radical Nonintervention. Englewood Cliffs, N.J.: Prentice-Hall.

Schwitzgabel, R. 1973. "Use of Electronic Devices to Monitor Juvenile Delinquent Behaviors." Paper presented at the colloquium on May 10, 1973. University of California at Irvine.

Sears, R. R., E. E. Maccoby, and H. Levin. 1957. Patterns of Child Rearing. Evanston, Ill.: Rowe, Peterson.

Sedlacek, W. E., and G. C. Brooks, Jr. 1976. Racism in American Education: A Model for Change. Chicago: Nelson-Hall.

Selman, R. L. 1971. "The Relation of Role Taking to the Development of Moral Judgment in Children." Child Development 42:79-91.

Seshadri, C. 1978. "Moral Education in India." Journal of Moral Education 8:7-13.

SFU Week (Simon Fraser University). 1978. January 5, 1978, p.
1, and January 26, 1978, p. 1.

Shaw, R. V. 1979. "New Zealand's Recent Concern with Moral
Education." Journal of Moral Education 9:23-35.

Shoffeitt, P. G. 1971. "The Moral Development of Children as a
Function of Parental Moral Judgments and Child Rearing." Ph.D.
dissertation, George Peabody College of Teachers, Nashville,
Tenn.

Shorter, E. 1975. The Making of the Modern Family. New York:
Basic Books.

Sex Information and Education Council of the United States. SIECUS
News Letter. 1969.

Silberman, C. 1978. Criminal Justice, Criminal Violence. New
York: Random House.

———. 1970. Crisis in the Classroom. New York: Random
House.

Singer, M. 1963. Generalization in Ethics. London: Eyre and
Spottiswoode.

Stanley, S. 1979. "The Family and Moral Education." In Adolescent Development and Education, edited by R. Mosher, pp. 447-63.
Berkeley, Calif. McCutchan.

———. 1976. "A Curriculum to Affect the Moral Atmosphere of
the Family and the Moral Development of Adolescents." Ph.D.
dissertation, Boston University.

Staub, E. 1978. Positive Social Behavior and Morality. Vols. 1
and 2. New York: Academic Press.

———. 1976. The Development of Prosocial Behavior in Children.
Morristown, N.J.: General Learning Press.

———. 1970. "A Child in Distress: The Influence of Age and Number of Witnesses of Children's Attempts to Help." Journal of
Personality and Social Psychology 14:130-40.

Staub, E., R. Leavy, and J. Shortsleeves. 1974. "Teaching
Others as a Means of Learning to be Helpful." Unpublished
manuscript. University of Massachusetts.

Superka, D., et al. 1976. Values Education Sourcebook: Conceptual Approaches, Methods, Analyses and an Annotated Bibliography.
Boulder, Colo.: Social Sciences Consortium.

Sutherland, E. 1948. Principles of Criminology. New York:
Lippincott.

Suttles, G. 1968. The Social Order of the Slum. Chicago: University of Chicago Press.

Szasz, T. 1963. Law, Liberty and Psychiatry. New York:
Macmillan.

Szwed, H. 1969. "An American Anthropological Dilemma: The
Politics of Afro-American Culture." In Reinventing Anthropology,
edited by D. Hymes. New York: Random House.

Tapp, J. 1971. "Socialization, the Law and Society." Journal of
Social Issues 27.

Taylor, D. L. 1970. "Dimensions of Sex Education." In Human
Sexual Development: Perspectives in Sex Education, edited by
D. L. Taylor, pp. 270-86. Philadelphia, Pa.: F. A. Davis.

Termon, L. M., and L. E. Tyler. 1954. "Psychological Sex Differences." In Manual of Child Psychology, edited by L. Carmichael, pp. 1064-1114. 2d ed. New York: John Wiley & Sons.

Triandis, H. C. 1972. The Analysis of Subjective Culture. New
York: John Wiley & Sons.

Turiel, E. 1975. "Conflict and Transactions in Adolescent Moral
Development." Child Development 45:14-29.

————. 1966. "An Experimental Test of the Sequentiality of Developmental Stages in the Child's Moral Judgment." Journal of
Personality and Social Psychology 3:611-18.

Tyler, L. E. 1965. The Psychology of Human Differences. New
York: Appleton-Century-Crofts.

Valentine, C. C. 1971. "Deficit, Difference, and Bicultural Models of Afro-American Behavior." Harvard Educational Review 41: 137-57.

Vancouver Sun. 1978. October 23, 1978, pp. A1-A2.

Vandervale, L. 1970. "Efforts to Measure Moral Development at the Educational Testing Service." Speech given at Harvard University.

Van Pragg, J. 1979. "Moral Education in the Netherlands." Journal of Moral Education 8:202-5.

Waller, W. 1967. The Sociology of Teaching. New York: John Wiley & Sons.

Warren, J., and B. J. Kelly. 1979. "Ford Felt Pinto Changes More Costly Than Claims." Fargo Forum, October 17, 1979, pp. 20-21.

Warren, M. 1974. "I" Level Treatment among Delinquent Youth. Sacramento, California Youth Authority.

Wasserman, E. 1978. "Implementing Kohlberg's Just Community Approach to Education in an Alternative High School." In Readings in Moral Education, edited by P. Scharf. Minneapolis, Minn.: Winston Press.

———. 1977. "The Development of an Alternative High School Based on Kohlberg's Just Community Approach to Education." Ph.D. dissertation, Boston University.

White, R. 1959. "Motivation Reconsidered: The Concept of Competence." Psychological Review 66(September):297-333.

Williams, N., and S. Williams. 1970. The Moral Development of Children. London: Macmillan.

Wilson, J. 1979. A Preface to the Philosophy of Education. London: Routledge and Kegan Paul.

———. 1977. Philosophy and Practical Education. London: Routledge and Kegan Paul.

330

————. 1975. "Moral Education and the Curriculum." In Problems and Progress in Moral Education, edited by M. Taylor. Slough, U.K.: National Foundation of Educational Research.

————. 1973. The Assessment of Morality. Slough, U.K.: National Foundation of Educational Research.

————. 1971. Practical Methods of Moral Education. London: Heinemann.

————. 1970. Moral Thinking: A Guide for Students. London: Heinemann.

Witherell, C., and V. L. Erickson. 1978. "Teacher Education as Adult Development." Theory into Practice 17(June):229-38.

Wojtyła, K. (Pope John Paul II). 1965. Amour et résponsabilité. Etude de moral sexuelle. Translated by Thérèse Sas. Paris: Societé d'Editions Internationales.

Wolfgang, M. 1972. Delinquency in a Birth Cohort. Chicago: University of Chicago Press.

INDEX

ABOUT THE EDITORS AND CONTRIBUTORS

DONALD B. COCHRANE is Head of the Department of Educational Foundations, College of Education, University of Saskatchewan. He has had visiting appointments in philosophy of education and moral education at Queen's University, McGill University, the University of British Columbia, Simon Fraser University, and the University of Calgary. He has written many articles on moral education, compiled several extensive bibliographies, and edited several books and journals including, with C. M. Hamm and A. C. Kazepides, The Domain of Moral Education. Since 1976 he has been Associate Editor of Moral Education Forum.

MICHAEL MANLEY-CASIMIR is Associate Professor in the Faculty of Education at Simon Fraser University. He has written articles on children and social justice, equal educational opportunity, and student rights, which have been published in Administrator's Notebook, the Alberta Journal of Educational Research, School Review, and Canadian Welfare. In addition, he has worked as an editor for Administrator's Notebook, School Review, and the Canadian Journal of Education.

JERROLD R. COOMBS is a Professor of Education at the University of British Columbia. His writing in the area of moral education includes several reports for the Association for Values Education and Research and articles for Values Education and The Teaching of Values in Canadian Education.

V. LOIS ERICKSON is Associate Professor of Educational Psychology at the University of Minnesota. Her work has been published extensively in the fields of counseling, guidance, and moral education in such journals as Counseling Psychologist, Counseling and Values, Counselor Education and Supervision, and Journal of Moral Education.

YVONNE V. HARDAWAY is Assistant Professor of Psychology at Baylor University. In 1979 she was a participant in a summer institute at Stanford University entitled "The Nature of Morality and Moral Development," and she is currently preparing a book on abnormal behavior for publication in 1981.

RICHARD HEY is Professor of Family Social Science at the University of Minnesota and was Head of the Department of Family Social Science from 1970 through 1978. His article (with G. B. Peterson and L. R. Peterson) on family development and moral stage frameworks was published in the Journal of Marriage and the Family in 1979.

JOHN T. HOWER is Staff Psychologist at Philhaven Hospital in Pennsylvania. He has done considerable research on the effect of parent-child relationships on moral character. He work has been published in Journal of Genetic Psychology and Journal of Psychology and Theology.

THOMAS LICKONA is Associate Professor in the Department of Education, State University of New York at Cortland. He edited Moral Development and Behavior in 1976 and has two additional books in preparation on moral development in children. His articles have been published in the Journal of Moral Education, Young Children, Learning, Social Education, and Moral Education Forum.

DON C. LOCKE is Associate Professor of Counselor Education at North Carolina State University. He has worked in counseling in high schools, prisons, and universities and has had articles published in Guidance Clinic, Measurement and Evaluation in Guidance, Journal of Counseling Services, Journal of Instructional Psychology, and Counselor Education and Supervision.

RALPH L. MOSHER is Professor of Education and Director of the Program in Human Development and Education at Boston University. His books include Value Development as an Aim of Education (with N. A. Sprinthall), Adolescents' Development and Education: A Janus Knot, and Moral Education: A First Generation of Research and Development (New York: Praeger, in press).

GAIL B. PETERSON is Assistant Professor in Child Development and Family Relations at North Dakota State University. Her articles have been published in Counseling and Values and Journal of Marriage and the Family.

LARRY PETERSON is Assistant Professor of History at North Dakota State University. His doctoral dissertation for the University of Minnesota was in the area of moral development psychology, and he has written articles for Family Co-ordinator and Journal of Marriage and the Family.

337

JEAN-MARC SAMSON is Head of the Department of Sexology at the University of Quebec at Montreal where he has assumed responsibility for the sex education aspects of sexology. He has published extensively in both English and French, including contributions to the Journal of Moral Education and his book L'éducation sexuelle a l'école?

PETER SCHARF is an Assistant Professor in the Department of Social Ecology at the University of California, Irvine, where he has been working to facilitate moral reasoning among police officers. In addition to publishing numerous articles, he has edited Readings in Moral Education, written Moral Education: Theory and Praxis, and has been commissioned to write Democracy and Prisons.

BARRY WALKER is a teacher associated with the Coquitlam School District in British Columbia. He participated in the Summer Institute on Moral Education at Simon Fraser University in 1978 and is particularly interested in the moral education of high school athletes.

JOHN WILSON is Lecturer and Tutor in the Oxford University Department of Educational Studies and Director of the Warborough Trust, an interdisciplinary unit concerned with research in moral education. He has written more than eight books in the areas of educational philosophy and moral and religious education, including The Assessment of Morality, Practical Methods of Moral Education, and Moral Thinking: A Guide for Students. He has had articles published in such journals as Bulletin of Psychology, Mind, Analysis, Classical Quarterly, and the Oxford Review of Education.